BON COURAGE

B·O·N
COURAGE

Rediscovering the Art of Living

IN THE HEART *of* FRANCE

KEN McADAMS

•

illustrations by

MARIAN "BING" BINGHAM

Moyer Bell • *New York*

FIRST EDITION

This book is based on real events, involving real people, but the names of those people and the places the events occurred have been changed to protect their privacy. Many conversations replicated in English actually occurred in the French language and the translations presented in this work are only approximations, though their content is appropriately representative.

Library of Congress Cataloging-in-Publication Data

McAdams, Ken.
 Bon courage : rediscovering the art of living in the heart of France / Ken McAdams ; with illustrations by Marian "Bing" Bingham.
    p. cm.
 ISBN 978-1-55921-398-1 (alk. paper)
  1. Toulouse Region (France—Social life and customs. 2. Toulouse Region (France)—Description and travel. 3. City and town life—France—Toulouse Region. 4. McAdams, Ken—Homes and haunts—France—Toulouse Region. I. Title.
 DC611.T718M35 2010
 944'.739—dc22
                          2010002310

For inquiries about volume orders, please contact:

Beaufort Books
27 West 20th Street, Suite 1102
New York, NY 10011
sales@beaufortbooks.com

Published in the United States by Moyer Bell
www.beaufortbooks.com

Distributed by Midpoint Trade Books
www.midpointtrade.com

Printed in the United States of America

10 9 8 7 6 5 4 3 2

First, to Bobbye who believed from the beginning, but didn't live to see the dream come true. And to our kids, Lexi and Brit, who endlessly had to hear the promise, "Yes, we will do that after the book sells," which never sold. Despite those unfulfilled promises, they still loved their dad. And finally to Bing, who picked up my broken pieces, so ably helped pull them back together, then pitched in with her brush and pen to add the pictorials my words were not enough to fully convey, becoming such a strong part of BON COURAGE.

ACKNOWLEDGMENTS

Dr. Judith Briles who found me Eric Kampmann who gave me Margot Atwell (Associate Publisher), Erin Smith (Director of Marketing), and Trish Hoard (Editor), along with Gordon McAdams of Radio Boston, who never stopped saying, "Yes you can!" And, of course, the late Vernon Scott and Cecil Scott, both masters of the edited word.

CONTENTS

NEVER AGAIN

Much of this story began one Sunday after a church luncheon. I was helping clean the kitchen with Clare, a beautiful, very tall blonde married to Bill, a friend of mine. I have a terrible time with tall blondes. When I was twelve years old, the girl next door was four or five inches taller than me and blonde. I could run faster and out-wrestle her; still, she could hit a baseball farther. She was my first love. To kiss her I had to stand at least one step up on her front porch. It was painfully demeaning. I never got over it. So, talking to the charming, yet towering Clare, I blurted out, "Don't you have a *regular-sized* sister around somewhere?" She stopped drying the plate in her hand, looked slightly down for a moment as a smile played around the corners of her mouth. Then, turning and unfortunately looking still further down at me, she said, "Actually, Ken, I do."

A week later, at Clare and Bill's Halloween party, I met Regular-Sized Bing. My costume was that of a man run over by the tractor-trailer of life, while *hers* was a smart suit and the guarded face of a survivor. I learned that though she'd lost a marriage, after getting her kids off on their own, she'd gritted her teeth, saying to herself, "Okay, that's that, now I'm moving on." She went back to college, finishing her long-delayed BA, then added a Masters in Art, graduating both magna cum laude! Today she is a talented and successful artist who graciously agreed to illustrate this book.

M Y Q U E S T I O N to Clare had come about three years after leukemia made me a widower and the bankruptcies of Pan Am and Kiwi International Airlines ended my flying and executive careers for good. Then my brother died. Not long after that my literary agent dumped me on the basis that, though he thought I wrote well, without more blood and guts in my stuff, he didn't see me selling beyond paperbacks, and he couldn't feed his wife and kids on the royalties they bring in. My new life as a writer, after forty or so years as an aviator, also seemed dead in the water.

So here I was, having been a husband for thirty-five years, still deeply in love with the wife departed; my brother gone; a pilot without an airline; an executive without a company; and a totally rejected writer. I was on a roll of sorts . . . but one that left me empty. The needle of my emotional gauge was near zero, my spirits running on fumes. I began to wonder what the hell life was all about. I prayed a lot. I went to church a lot, even became active in its leadership, but I was still alone . . . until my question to Clare in the kitchen.

From our first meeting, it was clear to me that Bing was not one to suffer whiners. I kept my mouth shut about my troubles for a couple of weeks. Then I broke that silence, not to whine, but to ask her to marry me. She accepted! At our ages, with new careers to pursue, neither of us felt time was on our side. Why wait?

I sold my house, moving out of Chappaqua, in New York's Westchester County, about the time the Clintons moved in. Bing put her farm in eastern Connecticut up for sale. We needed to start fresh with a nest of our own. We bid on a rundown place in Greenwich, Connecticut, one we thought would be a cinch to rehab. The house was Bing's find. I didn't like it for its closed-in 1950s interior and its yard resembling a mini landfill, but it was within walking distance to town. Bing and the realtor said, "Forget how the house looks right now; in real estate it's all about location."

We found an architect and a contractor. Gutting and reconstructing the house was predicted to take six months. It took nearly two years. One fiasco after another led us to feel like we'd hired Laurel and Hardy. For that matter, the sub-contractors could have been out of the Three Stooges' shop. The various town inspectors weren't much better.

For starters, no one thought to file for a building permit! So we lost all the subcontractors, costing us months. Then, when we had inspectors out to evaluate the existing underground oil tank, they said it was okay. A week later the same crew returned for the final approval but declared the tank faulty. With some agitation I asked how one week it was okay and the next it was not? With a straight face, the lead guy said, "That was then. This is now. Hey, shit happens." We switched to town gas.

When the electrical inspector came by he failed our new wiring. I asked him to show me what was wrong with it. In the basement he pointed to a cluster of cut-off bare wires. I admitted they looked scary, but following them back a few feet, I showed him they were cut at that end too and simply had not been pulled out and thrown away. Since he was embarrassed, we had to wait weeks for his sensitivities to sort themselves out and his final sign-off to be recorded.

Before the master bathroom's marble floor was laid, I tore up a section of old subfloor that looked suspicious. Laurel and Hardy had told me not to bother. When it was out of the way, however, we found a major support joist wasn't even attached at the end where the new floor would be laid. If the marble had gone down without that joist attached, the whole bathroom could have ended up in the dining room.

Next we wanted to turn the empty attic into a guest suite. We were told it couldn't be done because a stairway could not be constructed for it that would meet code. But we weren't convinced. That night Bing got out her sketchpad and started to work. An hour or two later she'd solved all the problems. A couple of days after that the guest suite was okayed by the Building Department, this time to our architect and contractor's major embarrassment.

Week after week, month after month, Bing and I plodded on, doing much of the work ourselves, struggling with one absurdity after another, until finally, about a year and a half behind schedule, the job was done. The awful house had become a beautiful house, but we were exhausted. We'd been married close to two years and hadn't even had time for a honeymoon. So, as our housewarming party drew to a close and the tail lights of our friends' cars faded into the dusk, Bing and I looked at each other and said, in unison, NEVER AGAIN!

What follows is what came of that *NEVER AGAIN*. Everything it describes actually happened, though in some cases the events have been adjusted in time and place to help the flow. We also decided to call the village we found ourselves in *La Montagne Noire*, or the Black Mountain, in order to shield the dear people we came to know and love there from panting hordes of tourists, like those who pushed and shoved their way around Peter Mayle's village in his most entertaining *A Year in Provence*. And finally, names were changed to protect the innocent, of which I was not one.

Our story has its ups and downs, but basically it is fun. Most importantly, though, it is the real-life response of two people who have been through a lot in life, who find each other late in life, and who do carry on, together. Bing and I hope you'll enjoy reading *Bon Courage* as much as we have enjoyed living it.

Ken McAdams
Haute-Garonne, France
September 9, 2009

ONE

SITE UNSEEN

T HROUGHOUT THAT first year together, we lived all over
the place, but mainly on Bing's farm across the state, in Salem,
while she was trying to sell it. I wasn't particularly happy with
the arrangement. I don't do well in someone else's house. I need
to be at least semi in charge. And too, being so far from Greenwich meant most days we had to drive from one end of Connecticut to the other to keep the renovation moving. In the process I
rebuilt an old trailer Bing had behind her barn, using it to haul
rocks from the fields and wooded trails. A *twofer*. We were clearing the way for horseback riders on the farm as well as supplying
rocks for the façades of the new garage and retaining walls going
up in Greenwich.

Six months of this grew to twelve, making our marriage pretty much an in-transit affair. No stability, just endless back and forth. We were tearing down a house to better build it back up, but what were we doing to our marriage? We felt like a pair of long-haul truckers trying to build a life together in the cab of a Kenworth. When the house was finally finished, we solemnly agreed we would *never never ever again* get involved in another renovation. Life was too short and we were too old for any more of this nonsense. From now on our marriage had to be primary. We had to focus on our serious pursuits—my writing and Bing's painting.

In an effort to renew our sanity, Bing mentioned she'd heard of an artist who ran summer workshops in a small southwestern French village. "Not far from Toulouse," she added. "Being January, the off season, maybe it would be available for a couple of months. We could go, hide, paint, write, recreate. Really get our new lives moving. Finally have our honeymoon. What do you think, Kenny?"

Wow! Toulouse sure rang my bell. I had gone through Airbus A-300 flight school there with Pan Am, and years earlier had been part of another flight program in not too distant Bordeaux, where I'd been an acceptance test pilot. It had been my job to evaluate the Dassault executive jets being offered to Pan Am for sale worldwide. I loved the area and still had an acquaintance or two living nearby. One was Adrian, who had been with the French Air Force in a program similar to mine, and had also been in Bordeaux. He was retired now and operating the largest barge, or *péniche,* on the Canal du Midi. We'd renew old times. Catch up. And, most importantly, Bing and I would have that honeymoon we'd missed.

I gave the whole project an enthusiastic two thumbs up, which put Bing, the to-do-list queen of America, on the phone to the artsy lady, Brie, booking the house for two months; airline tickets next;

then another call to friends living near Paris who even offered to pick us up at Charles de Gaulle Airport. An Internet-booked Avis car was set for pick up near their house so, *bang, bang,* everything was in gear to go.

Finally, I exchanged e-mails with Adrian, lining up five days and four nights on his barge. We would motor on it from Port Lauragais southeastward to the great medieval fortress city of Carcassonne. Ah yes, re-creation (and recreation) to the max lay ahead.

SITTING IN the airline's departure lounge at JFK, a terminal which had once belonged to my beloved Pan Am, our carry-on stuff snuggled by our feet, I was staring off into space, struck first by how quickly the journey's nuts and bolts had come together and by how quickly my life had previously been pulled apart. First wife Bobbye's death. Corporate bankruptcies. Selling my Westchester house, which had given me and the kids thirty years of stability. Now, only two years into a new life with Bing, our kids gone, along with Bing's marriage, it wasn't easy for either of us.

Rebuilding the Connecticut house was our metaphor: First everything had to be ripped apart. Our lives were on the same track now, we were finally getting started with what we had envisioned. This trip would be the first time we would be free together. For that matter, we'd be in another country without externals to distract us. Even the different language might act as a shield from the outside world's intrusion. Then we'd have only ourselves to blame if things started unraveling. No architects. No contractors. No building inspectors to point fingers at.

Bing, probably trying for a cultural head start, was reading *France Magazine.* I wasn't so creative. For the moment I was just exchanging air—in with the good, out with the bad—letting all those conflicted thoughts tumble as they would through my brain.

"You know, Bing," I finally said, trying to shake myself out of it, "after maybe forty years in cockpits, everything from fighters to 747s, it feels a little strange, maybe even unsettling, sitting around an airport waiting to board a plane someone else will fly. I'd always been the four-striper at the controls. Now I'm just another seat warmer. I don't miss the flying, but there's a feeling I get sometimes in airports that's kind of tickling me now. Maybe it's memories of the uniform, special IDs, door combinations, and all that access and authority stuff. Look at those pilots at the coffee bar," I added with a nod in their direction. "That used to be me looking at who I'd be flying—nice folks, problem children, terrorists? I never knew which for sure."

Bing glanced at the three then back to her magazine. "Two of them are fat, and the skinny one's jacket sleeves are too short. I'll bet you looked right out of central casting in *your* uniform," she said. Her eyes came off the page to give me a cool once-over, then scooted back. I don't think my thoughts were capturing her imagination. I went back to my basic breathing.

M O S T   P E O P L E expect a pilot's retirement to leave a huge void in his or her life, but as I sat watching the take-offs and landings through the big windows, I knew for me it had been the other way around. My years punching holes in the sky had been the void in my life. I'd always wanted to be a writer, but I wasn't good enough. Well, in my own defense, my first novel, written while I was still in the Marine Corps, was well received by John Farrar, one of America's leading publishers. He'd written a wonderful letter praising my work and welcoming me into the Farrar & Straus fraternity.

At the time it had seemed so easy. Too easy. Prior to his letter I'd expected to endure years of coldwater walk-ups. Hacking coughs from lack of heat. Gloves with those cut-off fingertips so I could still tap the keys of my trusty Remington while fighting hypothermia. Privation, deprivation, and frustration to be expected, yet all sprinkled with the dandruff of youthful self-confidence.

God must have been listening. Not wanting to disappoint, He had Straus cancel the contract. I'd suddenly been de-pledged from their fraternity. Out on my ass.

For two years I'd lived off first wife Bobbye's labors as a teacher. Then, with the news my promising writing career had tanked, the time had come for me to stand on my own two feet. Bobbye deserved better than a coldwater walk-up and cut-finger gloves. I had to get a real job, if flying airliners even qualified as such.

Glancing at Bing out of the corner of my eye, another fragmented thought popped into my head—she was no stranger to travel either. Barely into her twenties, she'd driven a Land Rover from Paris to Calcutta and back. For her, zipping off on this French adventure would be, as the fly guys liked to say, *a piece of cake.*

Our Atlantic crossing was uneventful, except for the purser learning of my Pan Am past and bumping us up from "bag lunch" to first class. Then, before disembarking at Charles de Gaulle, she slipped us a bottle of champagne for old time's sake.

My friends from Paris, Pierre and Marie-Claude, were waiting for us outside customs. They had lived in America when Pierre was Dassault's senior U.S. representative, working with me in the Falcon Jet program at Pan Am. They had a pile of kids—even an adopted girl who, as an infant, had been tortured and thrown off Pont Neuf into the Seine, but was saved by them—and grandkids; extraordinary people, and fortunately for us, fluent in English. They would be our bridge to the linguistic challenges of *la belle France* we knew lay ahead.

Day one, despite the usual sleep deprivation, Marie-Claude and Bing went searching for art supplies while Pierre and I set off to pick up our rental car. Rather than go for anything exciting, I'd Interneted for the practical and economic. An Opel, as I recall.

Actually a tiny Opel with an engine about the size of a Harley-Davidson. "8V" was jauntily displayed on the rear hatch. Smiling, Pierre assured me we couldn't go wrong with something packing as much as *eight volts* of power. I shrugged and signed the stack of papers.

The first insight gained from the process was a fuller understanding of my linguistic inadequacies. We had gone to a local Avis office, not one of those sophisticated international airport jobs, so everything was in French. Pierre seemed to feel this was important. When in Rome (or Paris) and all that. He and Marie-Claude had faced the same thing when they first came to America. (Sauce for the goose, yada yada.)

Even if I'd remembered every word of my high school French, along with the technical stuff from testing airplanes years later, I'd still have been wiped out. These locals spoke so fast, idiomatically, and with non-school accents, I followed very little of what was said, especially of what was said to me. The agent was enthusiastic, however, and expounded on contract items he somehow assumed I understood. I guess having Pierre by my side lent me a degree of *savoir faire*. Who knows, but when he asked me questions about insurance, and did I want a gas contract or would I bring the thing back *plein* (full), I had hardly a clue. With lifted brows he stared hopefully at me. I stared back with an expression along the lines of a cow watching someone relieve himself by the side of the road.

Pierre, operating well within Gaullist norms, let me sweat a minute or two before jumping in. He later explained he was prepping me for the two months of village living ahead. Good medicine, actually, considering the art lady we were renting from had mentioned no one spoke English there. Over the phone in Connecticut that sounded rather *charming*, but on site, like at the Avis counter, it became something else for sure. I sensed trouble ahead.

The next day we hugged Pierre and Marie-Claude goodbye and set off toward Black Mountain. With the new *autoroute* not yet finished, it would be about an eight-hour ride. We decided to break it up into two days of sight seeing. No problems arose for the first hundred kilometers. Then we had a collision . . . with reality.

No Pierre and Marie-Claude by our side. When we picked up the car, Avis had not had a chance to fill the tank, which was indicated on our contract, and meant we had to stop along our way. At a gas station (*une station-service*) we were confronted by a blaring voice emanating from who knew where? And directed at whom or what? We had no idea what the officious racket was about, though its volume and intensity implied that if we *were* involved, it must be pretty damn serious. After a lot of deer-in-the-headlights looking around (no other cars were there so we assuredly were *it;* whatever "it" was), a man burst from the station office, theatrically shaking his head from side to side, with cavernous nostrils in a stallion's flare as he strode toward me. This blue-coveralled agent of Esso breezed past where I stood rooted by the pumps. Arching his eyebrows to cathedral proportions, he pointed (I thought over-dramatically) to each fuel type sequentially, verbalizing (as if to the village idiot)—"*Gasohol*" (diesel); "*Essence*" (gas); "*Super*" (high-test with lead); "*Quatre-vingt-quinze sans plumb*" (95-octane without lead); "*Quatre-vingt-dix-sept sans plumb*" (97-octane without lead); "*ou quatre-vingt-dix-neuf sans plumb*" (or 99-octane lead-free). Good grief. Those French numbers were like Roman numerals—99 being four twenties plus ten plus nine.

"*Monsieur, quel est-ce votre choix?*" Understanding any of this came weeks later. For the moment I just stared at the man, stupidly.

He gave me *95 sans plumb.*

Brave-heart Bing tried to lift my spirits with a shrug and a smile. Of course, she'd been hiding behind the map inside the car the whole time and had not been about to come out to join me in the line of fire.

Happily full of gas, our little 8-Volt (eight valves, actually) got back onto the highway and held its own, handily. Within its class, the little devil stormed, nudging the equivalent of 110 mph! Nevertheless, there were bigger dogs in the hunt—Mercedes, Peugeots, Saab turbos, BMWs, the usual list of suspects—all flashing their lights for us to get back to the right lane where we belonged. Since the speed limit is 130 kilometers per hour, or the equivalent of a little over 80 mph, our 190 kms were not shabby. Nobody seemed to be sweating the police. As a matter of fact, wherever a radar unit was in place, a kilometer or so earlier had a gentlemanly positioned sign advising of the same. Which made it all the more bizarre to be a part of gaggle going like hell, then all slowing together with each appearance of the sign.

I've got to give the French drivers credit for *élan*: considering being caught 40 km/hr over the limit would cost them their licenses, they still let it roll. Seasoned high-speed travelers had advised us to get international permits. If caught going *really* fast, those could be surrendered, while the regular U.S. license remained valid.

Already we were discovering how a lot of French brainpower seems to go into living life free of government complications, despite the huge government they always vote to keep. A kind of a have-your-cake-and-eat-it-too caper as they dodged police on the highways and tax collectors on business byways, all in a tradition of good sportsmanship. In time we learned that life, to the confident and generally smiling Frenchmen, is a game, an art form to be enjoyed but not taken too seriously.

That evening we stopped at a wonderful little hotel in a village north of Poitiers. Our plan had been to roar almost due south to the Loire, drop off onto the small roads along it to meander a while, then find a snug *auberge* for the night. Typically the snuggly-inn-for-the-night part didn't come until after I'd managed a significant riverside screw up. Always trying for another Boy Scout badge, I found a road not even on the map. My gut told me this would be a test of my path-finding skills.

"Kenny," Bing offered uncritically (our delayed honeymoon still in effect), "we're awfully close to the river."

"Exciting, isn't it?" I said, my eyes glued to the diminishing road ahead.

"I can almost put my fingertips into it."

"Exactly," I offered, as if I'd planned this all along. Trying to turn around just then would have been dicey. The pavement was narrowing and turning to gravel. Then dirt. With ruts. Make those *puddles*. Short grass. Long grass. A faint track to no track at all . . . and finally, just plain water.

"The river Loire," I announced with authority.

"Kenny," Bing observed, "I think our ride beside the Loire has become a ride *into* the Loire. Now what?"

"Time for some exercise," was all I could think of.

Trying to turn around a slightly submerged 8-Volt in any river is a chore, but in the Loire? *Dieu.*

Bing gave me a quizzical look. One I was seeing more of each day.

"Why don't I get behind the wheel," she offered, "while you push?"

Good plan. Actually, no other plan was available. And the sun was setting. Hell of a way to end a day, or a honeymoon, or a marriage for that matter. So, up to my ankles in mud, I shoved from the front. I shoved from the rear. Bing raced the engine, skillfully working the clutch to rock the sucker, but also managing to blow a lot of mud all over me.

By the time we got to the hotel, the car and I were mud cakes. It seemed best for Bing to negotiate our *pension* since I looked more like Sasquatch than anything human, much less continental.

Only French was spoken, she reported, but she got the room without problem. I was impressed and a bit discouraged. I had flunked at the Avis counter and yet Bing had starred at the check-in desk. My personal hygiene problem didn't raise my spirits much either. If cleanliness was next to Godliness, I was halfway to hell.

THE NEXT morning we ran the little car through a wash, then charged back onto the *autoroute*'s last finished segment.

"You know," I offered, "when a car has just been washed it seems to run better."

"Husbands too." Bing smiled with a knowing nod.

After a few hours of serious km's, getting off onto the "D," or departmental, roads, I noticed something of more than just passing interest. Time after time, as a car would appear in our rearview mirror, it would quickly close to where it seemed about to kiss our rear bumper. No matter what the road ahead looked like.

Now, French road signs are great. One that shows an "S" means just that. The road ahead would be like a slalom course. And speed reductions were not to be ignored either. You have to be careful. Unless, of course, you are French.

As we motored southeast on the departmental road from Toulouse to Black Mountain, coming out of the second wiggle of an "S," I looked at the approaching traffic on what was now a relatively straight stretch. Then I checked the rearview mirror again.

"Holy shit," I said.

"What?" Bing asked, disappointment in her eyes for my slip of the tongue. She is a very well-bred lady.

I made a thumb gesture to look behind.

Bing turned, and then let out her own version of an exclamation.

"*Pest!*" she said. "Kenny, he's practically in our back seat. His bumper must be touching ours."

It was true. Through my rearview mirror I could see the guy had missed a spot or two shaving this morning. All of which reminded me of a Far Side cartoon I'd seen showing a driver glancing at his side mirror that was filled with one huge eyeball, and written on the bottom of the mirror was: *Objects in mirror are closer than they appear.*

"Tap the brake," Bing suggested.

"That'll put him in the *front* seat," I countered.

"Then he can teach us French," she quipped.

"I've learned enough for today," I said. "Next chance I get, I'm letting him by. There's not enough room for the two of us on these two lanes."

Which worked for that car, but within a few kilometers another Frenchman blew up to our backside. As a matter of fact, that was the way they all handled it.

Having driven a lot in Italy, sometimes touted as *la derrière* of the world's driving scene, I still found myself more comfortable there than how I was feeling in France. The Italians are crazy drivers, granted, but their madness makes sense and can be anticipated. Once I understood they considered themselves eternally in a *grand prix*, I had no problem. By figuring out what Giacomo Agostini or Juan Fangio would have done in a given situation, I adjusted. Everything was a *Mille de Miglia*. Dangerous? Sure, but each wild stunt, every insane swerve, dive, or dice could be counted on to be executed with skill. And *that* seemed to be lacking here. *Skill.*

Above all, the basic Frenchman appeared deeply affected by a sense of self-esteem, especially *regionally based* self-esteem. As we would learn, cars from other *départements* suffered appropriate disdain, but those of supposedly rustic regions were treated most shabbily. A car's number plate told where it was from and implied what might be expected of the driver's competence. That, in itself, led to animosities. The Parisian plate had little respect for those of, say, Narbonne. And in turn, those of Narbonne hardly considered Paris a part of France.

"Hey, Napoleon, you're putting our lives on the line," I muttered to a wandering car approaching from ahead while another hotshot was jamming up from behind us.

"Where is he now, Bing?" I asked, as that hotshot slid into my blind spot.

"He's wide left, even with our backdoor. And he's got a cell phone to his ear!" Bing reported.

For the moment I couldn't see him, but I could see the wobbly oncoming car which, oh no, was an *auto-école*, a driver's ed number. This was going to be close. I touched the brake, but I had to be careful of still another idiot rolling up behind. All of a sudden, counting the car next to us, which I assumed would swerve in front of us, and the slow auto-schooler approaching, the four cars were locking onto a collision course.

The cell phone guy was up to our front fender now, as the face of the approaching driving student registered stark terror. Next to her, the teacher looked confident and unconcerned as he lit a cigarette. Then *WHOOSH!* Monsieur Cellphone did make it in line ahead of us, only an instant before the *auto-ècole* car wobbled by.

"Are we dead?" Bing asked, eyes closed.

"My heart's stopped, but other than that I'm still here," I replied, shaken, but still curious over what M. Cellphone figured he'd accomplished by being only one car length ahead of where he had been. He'd nearly had a head-on collision.

"Kenny, did you see the driving teacher lighting a cigarette while all that was going on?" Bing asked in amazement.

"Maybe he figured it would be his last, like before a firing squad," I said.

"That's when I closed my eyes. It had to be our end the way the student was wiggling her wheel." Bing sighed. "I've never seen anything like it."

"I'll bet we haven't seen the last of it though," I said, shaking my head and watching the clown ahead make another move. "Oh boy, there he goes again. And here comes a guy from behind." My hands were sweaty on the wheel as that next car thrashed past.

T H E "D" of these routes could also stand for *delightful*. Though generally two lanes, their surfaces are nearly as smooth as the elaborately built *autoroutes*. The Ds wind from town to town, village to village, and, in rural southern France, are often lined by massive sycamore trees (*platanes*) trimmed to form cathedral-like arches, shading those under them. Hundreds of years earlier, under Louis XIV, Bing's research told us, the concept of protecting travelers from sun, wind, and rain had led to the trees' planting. There also was mention that they served defensively, first against arrows, then musket fire, as a carriage or rider moved rapidly along them. Which all made sense, and had left a wonderful legacy for modern travelers to enjoy as well.

Unfortunately, in much of France, they are being cut down, victims of road expansion or for *safety* reasons as drunken drivers plow into them late at night. Of course environmentalists will argue, I think with irrefutable logic, that the velocity of a tree rarely exceeds zero, and that the collision is more likely a product of a driver's speed, inattention, or alcohol consumption, not by any action of the tree.

"I don't understand why the trees should be punished," Bing said as we started to see rows of *platanes* with large red Xs on them designating each for cutting. Under the Xs the word *NON* was written emphatically in bright blue, the color of protest here. It would be interesting to see how this small war resolved itself during our stay in France.

The further from Toulouse we drove, the deeper into farm country we found ourselves. Every turn in the road opened another stunning panorama of rolling hills which folded into gentle valleys all just starting to lift from their winter beds, anxious for spring's color blasts of mustard, lavender, and sunflower orange to take hold as the seas of green winter wheat awaits harvest.

Bing, ever the artist, had her sketchpad out and was recording it all, blocking out the studies she would later turn into oils on canvas. But for me, I was more caught by how the countryside of this part of France was a reverse of what we are used to in America. Our villages tend to nestle in valleys, along rivers with roads and railroad tracks running by, connecting them for commerce, one to the next. What we were seeing here were hilltop towns of walled *châteaux* or churches surrounded by tile-roofed stone houses. The hillsides and valleys around them were populated by fields and pastures with only an occasional barn or shed standing lonely vigil.

Finally it all struck me: Thousands of years of invasions, brigandage, wars large and small, had forced the people to cluster defensively on the high ground. Walls for *bodily* security surrounded them, with churches inside those walls for protection of the *soul*. For centuries the land outside had not been safe for man nor beast. A sad fact then, but rewarding for us today with the beauty left behind.

America is so different. A new country, free from ancient conflicts, with the wilderness and attackers subdued, the settlers freed to build next to streams, erect barns and farmhouses where their crops where, not having to depend on a hilltop lord or priest to guard over them.

FROM THE last hillock along our way, across a broad valley pressed against what we later learned was called La Montagne Noire, and the Massif Central's high plateau beyond, I could make out the ancient abbey tower we'd been told about. We pulled off the road onto a graveled overlook. I was all breathy, fixated on the tower and village at its feet.

"Bing, look over here. There's the tower that Brie said to look for. And there's the village," I babbled while I sensed her ignoring me. "Bing, come on, check this out," I pressed.

"Kenny," she whispered, "look over here. This way," she indicated pointing generally to the south. "What do you see?"

I did look . . . and oh my goodness. What a sight! The Pyrenees! A snowcapped wall of mountains marching across the whole southwestern horizon. They appeared so close. Like a bigger-than-life movie set. Incredible. And a breathtaking prelude to our entry into what would soon be our hideaway village of La Montagne Noire, Black Mountain.

TWO

BLACK MOUNTAIN

BEFORE TURNING from our view of the grand white wall of mountains, Bing's all-seeing artist's eyes caught a distant dark ribbon winding like a caterpillar between us and the Pyrenees.

"Look at that grayish line . . . of trees. On the far side of the *autoroute*," she said, her index finger moving across the landscape like she was pushing the carriage of an old typewriter.

"Ah, um," I mumbled, seeing only the vast hillock-dotted valley marching toward the mountains. "Oh, wait a minute . . . I see the highway," I recovered. "So you mean the streak, kind of broken here and there?"

"More *platanes*, probably bordering the Canal du Midi," she nodded up at me as she leaned her head against my shoulder. There

were times Bing could be the teenage girl next door. I thanked God
I wasn't still alone, then felt a nibble of guilt for the thought.

"And on the canal, on his boat, is where you'll meet Adrian.
Dinner, four nights, five days cruising down to Carcassonne. It'll
be terrific. And he is terrific too," I assured her. "A real gentleman,
who loves his Lauragais."

"Lauragais? Is that a wine or cheese?" Bing asked, raising a
needling eyebrow as she turned back toward the car.

"It's the department, or region, whatever," I informed her, feeling a bit full of myself.

"Do tell," Bing said, giving me a bounce of her hip, which put
me off balance as I was reaching to lay my arm across her shoulders. My stumble must have made us look like a pair of drunks to
the passing Peugeot that honked its horn, the young couple inside
smiling and waving.

In our car, pulling the seatbelt over my shoulder and turning
on the ignition, I said, "So, off we go toward yonder tower and the
house before we set sail for Carcassonne. Is what's-her-name, I
just *said* her name, the art school lady, is she going to be there
with the key or what?"

"Brie. She'd better be," Bing murmured, snapping her belt in
place and reaching for her sketchbook. "I wouldn't have the faint-
est idea who to ask for one if she isn't around."

"I wonder what the village looks like," I said, pulling back onto
the road. "As old as the place is, it's got to be crawling with history.
Maybe a guillotine in the town square. Should we have chocolate
bars for the kids? Cigarettes for dad, nylons for mom?"

"You're dating yourself," Bing quipped, deciding to close the
sketchbook. "Right out of Pathé Newsreels, between the double
features," she concluded, flipping the eyeshade down on her side
to check her hair in the mirror.

"Don't forget Fleer's Dubble Bubble gum," I threw in.

"Nor Pud and his Pals' comics on the backside of the wrappers," she countered.

I was impressed. She'd been born about the time bombs were raining down on Pearl Harbor, but still absorbed so much at such a tender age. I'd have to be careful with my usual BS-ing. It's like I'd married Miss Snopes, the Internet authority, or the Spell Check Lady.

I started paying more attention to the road, prepping for the next idiot committed to bumping against our backside. But Bing's mention of my having dated myself started me thinking about how our drive from Toulouse toward Black Mountain had been a turning back through the pages of a history book. From the airport we left the twentieth century. The city itself took us into the eighteen and seventeen hundreds, while speeding down these roads really set the pages flipping. Under Louis XIV's *platanes*, those wonderful trees lining the canal and shading our way along the road, we were deep into the seventeenth century. The closer to the Abbey Tower we got, the nearer we were to the Cathars, Charlemagne, then Visigoth and Roman times. As a matter of fact, I later read, the first construction of the tower had been in the sixth Century, 560 or so AD. The Visigoths smashed everything down including the tower, but later Charlemagne's father, Pepin le Bref, a little guy I guess, built it back up. And we'd thought Bing's 1790 farmhouse was old.

Twenty minutes later we passed a HISTORIC MEDIEVAL VILLAGE sign announcing our arrival in Black Mountain. We turned off in front of a large church. Though there was an arrow pointing to the *Centre Ville*, it was more of a walking street and one way against us for cars. We parked in one of the spaces under a large canopy of *platanes* lining the promenade from the church, past the town hall and around the corner toward a market and *café*.

Brie had faxed a map that showed rue Basque starting from a central fountain in the middle of the village. Number 10 would be

down from there, where we would meet her, get the key, come
back for our stuff in the car, then settle most of it in the house for
our return after the barge ride.

Only two steps down that street, we were *ooh*ing and *ahh*ing
like total tourists.

"Oh Bing, look at that," I whispered as if anything louder
would make it all disappear. "The street is so narrow. The second
and third stories hang over and practically touch each other. It's
like a movie set. Pinocchio or something."

She didn't say anything for a moment until, "Oh, Kenny, look
all the way down . . . to the end and how the tower is centered. I'll
bet that's the standard postcard shot of the village. It's perfect. I've
got to paint it."

We stood taking it all in like kids licking the edges of new ice
cream cones, not wanting to disturb their symmetry too soon and
filled with the special joy of delicious anticipation.

Continuing down what proved to be rue de la Victoire, I knew
I'd write something about this scene someday, like Bing would put
it on canvas. Many of the façades of the private homes we passed
were faced in stone, while others were in the style we think of as
Tudor, known here as *colombage*. Its exposed wood framing was
separated by mortared stone, Toulousian brick, or the stucco-like
material we later learned was called *crépi*. Shutters on the upper
floors were generally open to the sunlight, while many at street
level were closed for privacy. As people passed, we were charmed
by their nodding and offering, *Bonjour Monsieur et Madame.*

The first shop we passed was a *boulangerie* where the breads
were baked in a wood-fired oven. A little further down, a huge
pair of scissors hanging over the road from a second-story bracket
announced a haircutting salon. Next to that, a meter-long replica
of a snail crawling up the side of the building somehow indicated
the local bar or *cave* was below, ready for all day or long-into-the-
night sipping. Appropriately, across from it was a lawyer's office,

as well as that of the *notaire,* similar to a town clerk in our world.

We passed a lovely stone-fronted restaurant named Le Tournesol, the sunflower, next to two small art galleries and a *librairie* or bookshop. These faced, of all things, a tiny pizza shop, medieval of course, as indicated by the young proprietor in front juggling as many as five wooden balls at a time. As our eyes went up and down and all around following their flight, we hardly dared smile for fear we'd break his concentration. He kept juggling with an ease and authority I found a bit intimidating.

La dépêche, or newspaper store, finished the street's shops and connected to a cobbled, heart-shaped plaza, or *place,* where rue Basque began. A road going off to our left led to the gates of the old Abbey Hotel while straight ahead, across the *place,* was a tiny mews or *ruelle* overshadowed by the Abbey Tower itself. And to the right, the cobbles took us to the little square with its fountain.

As if the tower's belfry arches hid huge suspicious eyes, our stepping into the plaza seemed to set off one very loud *clang!* I jumped. What was that all about?

"Eleven-thirty," Bing announced, as if reading my mind. "We're right on schedule. Brie should be at the house." Then, checking her map, she added, "Which looks to be down here to that fountain, with a slight right. Rue Basque, yes, and . . . number 10, again on the right."

Bing is terrific navigationally. She's not only Miss Snopes, the Spell Check Lady, but Ms. Garmin too. She always "orients" her map, as the term goes in Marine Platoon Leader School, and quickly gets us off on the right foot, or path, or direction. Dear wife Bobbye had been much the same. I guess it's a female thing. Whatever.

Walking around the fountain we passed a tiny mom-and-pop grocery, Le Petit Casino, and a second *boulangerie/patisserie* across from that. A butcher shop was off on a side street. Later, when we walked the full length of rue Basque, past number 10

down to the *café* at the end, we found we were back at the same
main road we'd arrived on where there was another cluster of
shops, a post office and bank, bus stop, telephone and *pissotière,* or
public toilet. And yes, still a third *patisserie* across the way too!
All of which impressed me with the logic and social engineering
going into French village planning—food, communications, trans-
portation, and especially for my age group, *relief.*

As we approached number 10, we saw a marginally California
hippyish-looking woman backing out of the doorway with a large
valise in tow. Brie for sure, I thought, and Bing confirmed by calling, "Brie. Is that you, Brie?"

The attractive middle-aged brunette with very white teeth
smiled and replied, "Yes, indeed it is. And you two are Bing and
Ken, of course. Well, welcome to Black Mountain. I must say,
your timing couldn't be better. My husband will be here with the
car in a moment, then we will be off for Paris and home. But,
while we wait, let me walk you through the place."

"Fair enough," I said, and fell in behind Bing, who was already
in step with Brie.

"First, here are the keys," she said, handing Bing the ring. She
cautioned, "Be careful when you open or close the front door. It's
ancient. I think the latch was designed to smash invaders' fingers
or something. Hurts like hell. I've done it a million times."

We entered the front sitting room with its slightly bayed window, fireplace, sofa, two easy chairs, and very old reddish tile floor.
Walking across the room and starting down a small hallway leading from the foot of the stairs to the kitchen, Brie swished back a
curtain covering a half-shelved cubby, pointed to a large red propane tank, and started her rapid-fire monologue.

"That tank is your backup. The one feeding the stove and
kitchen water heater is in the courtyard." Letting the curtain fall
back, she breezed into the kitchen, announcing, "The wrench is in
the knife draw under the counter."

My eyes followed her outstretched index finger, but missed seeing any drawer.

"There's another tank under the counter in the bathroom upstairs. That takes care of the shower. The grocery has replacement bottles. The house has no heat but Anton has wood. Just give him a call. But only use the fireplace in the kitchen. The others are no good. The phone only does local. For long distance, the pay phone at the bus stop takes cards you can get most anywhere. The main water shutoff is out front under the cover, but there is one under the sink too, for downstairs. If you have problems with any of this, Anton is your man. Be sure to close the upstairs shutters Mondays, Wednesdays, and Thursdays, or is it Fridays, I'm not sure. The big truck has to get up to the Petit Casino to unload. So, that's about it. I hear Don out front. Love those Volvo diesels. We certainly should have more of them in the States. I love electrics too. We are Sierra Club and vote Nader. Got to run. Peace . . . and *ENJOY!*"

She was to the front door in a bound, opened then pulled it shut with a *bang!* Followed by a loud "Oh shit!" confirming what she'd just warned us about: jamming fingers in the latch. A car door slammed, then the gravelly rev of their diesel engine sounded as it crackled off down the road in the general direction of . . . Haight-Ashbury.

Bing stood mute, eyes wide, a chain of keys dangling from her hand. My head was spinning. I hadn't a clue what Brie had said, about anything. I should have thought to tape her. I remembered something about Anton. But who was Anton? Where was Anton? How were we supposed to find this guy?

I WENT to bring the car around while Bing explored the house. It was quarter to twelve. That whole exercise with Brie had only lasted two and half minutes.

I took a different street back to the church. No shops on it, though there was a *maison de la retraite,* or retirement home, and more wonderful façades. I felt like one of the Three Musketeers, or someone time-warped into the long ago. But it wasn't scary. It was warm, *embracing,* as if the old houses along the way had arms reaching out to pull me close.

Oh man, how I love old houses. I've been that way all my life. As early as I can remember, my mother would take me for drives around town just to look at houses, to dream out loud about how it would be living in this one or that one, or fixing another up, discovering their secret gardens or learning the dark mysteries of the families who owned them. We spent hours at this. My father thought we were crazy. He'd shake his head and wonder aloud, why would anybody want to "go off looking at curtains all the time like you two do?"

Noon still hadn't struck when I pulled the car up on the sidewalk at number 10 and unloaded our stuff into the front room. We had four big bags, plus two overnighters I left in the car for our canal trip. The four big suckers were heavy, but had wheels. I had rolled them in one by one and to the foot of the stairs when I heard Bing call down from the second floor.

"Ken, you've got to see this. It's everywhere. It's like what's on your Harley-Davidson belt buckle," she laughed.

"Huh?" was my less than brilliant reply as I started humping the first big suitcase up to where she was. After stashing it in what Bing designated our bedroom, she led me from one room to the next, pointing to the painted inscriptions on every wall. They were done large, in pink, blue, and violet. *LIVE TO PAINT! PAINT TO LIVE! MAKE ART NOT WAR! LOVE ART AND ART WILL LOVE YOU!*

"Who's Art?" I asked as I headed down for another bag. Then from the bottom of the stairs I found my own notables. "Bing," I called back up, "I've got some beauties down here for you too."

"Artsy sayings?" she asked, starting down.

"Artsy *morphings* are more like it. Check these out," I said as Bing came down, stopping beside me.

Halves of plates and dishes, cups and saucers were *growing* out of the walls.

"I don't know if they had holes in the plaster and shoved this stuff into them as shelves or whatever, then gooped around the mess, or if they made the holes first to stuff the junk in, all for art's sake. Whichever, but I *really* would like to know who Art is."

"Interesting," Bing offered, professionally ignoring me. "I'd give them a ten for execution, and another ten for *ugliness*."

"Careful," I cautioned, smiling, "they may hear you."

"They're halfway to Toulouse by now," Bing shrugged.

As we trouped through the house, mentally placing Bing's stuff here, my computer there, books on the shelves, that sort of thing, we both became aware that *something* had happened, just after the church bells and the tower bell had done their twelve noon toll.

"What's up?" I asked, not really expecting an answer.

"I think we're hearing *the sound of silence*," Bing offered, moving her widened eyes up, down, and around like a silent movie queen would have done.

"Huh?" I grunted, before fully realizing what she was saying. *Silence.* All of a sudden no more car sounds or people on the sidewalk chatting as they passed by. I went to the front window and looked through the curtains. Nothing. Not the whisper of movement. It was eerie. No cats. No dogs. No people. Nothing.

"Ah hah," Bing smiled, having figured what was up.

Oh boy, I thought. Just like grammar school all over again. The girl with the answer had her hand up, waving it.

"Midday," she nodded. "Remember what the guidebook said? How everything in southern France stops, totally stops, at noon? So . . . it's noon."

Simple as that. But what had really caught our attention was that there had been no *slowing* down. It was more a *click*. Like a flipped light switch. Probably the only things up and running at the moment were the restaurants.

"So what do we do now?" I asked, finding the quiet vaguely unnerving.

"How about some lunch? At the *café* on the corner?" Bing suggested, marching the four or five steps up to me for a big hug and a small kiss.

I moved the car out of rue Basque while Bing walked the thirty paces to *Le Café des Fleurs*. I caught up and we started through the front door. As we entered, every head in the place turned up, over, or around to stare at us. We just stood there not knowing what to do. They stared. We stared. Silence prevailed. Then the *propriétaire* came around the bar offering a hearty *"Bonjour."* We mumbled the same in return and everyone in the *café* boomed their own *bonjours,* and then went back to their meals.

The proprietor's name turned out to be Claude, but with my void of linguistic skills it took quite a while for me to figure that out. He had what we later learned was a Tarnese accent, which really did a number on the sound of the simplest French. *Demain,* meaning tomorrow, came out something like *derminggah.* Bing and I both felt adrift.

Claude guided us to a table for two, then stood over us, nostrils flaring, as he blasted away with what, we assumed, was a summary of the *plat du jour* and whatever else was of culinary interest that day.

When he paused, his dark brown eyes bounced from me, to Bing, to the bar, back to several other tables, then to us again.

With a sweet smile Bing said, *"Oui."*

Then he looked to me, so I said, *"Oui."*

"Merci," he replied with a nod and headed toward the kitchen.

"What did he say?" I asked, feeling a bit silly.

"I have no idea," she smiled, "but being in a restaurant I knew it had to be related to food and I'm hungry. So, *yes* struck me a lot better than *no*."

"You are brilliant," I offered, raising my water glass, which she clicked with hers and we both sipped.

Bing's *oui* brought us two huge salads. I don't mean just the wimpy leafy stuff. These were major kick-butt salads with slabs of meat, cheese, tomatoes, endive, veggies galore. And bread. My goodness! Crisp on the outside and billowy soft on the inside. Heaven. With a half liter of red wine. Then came the main course, which we were practically too stuffed to tackle, but eat it all we did. It was some kind of brisket, with onions and carrots and olives and leeks, all garlicked to the max. Along with mashed potatoes on one side, zucchini on the other; paradise in between. Then cheeses. And desert. Finally espresso, or whatever the French call it. By the end of all that I felt like a tree stump. Across the table Bing looked ready to plop her forehead down for a good snooze

After handing Claude a two-hundred-franc note (then about twenty-five dollars; euros weren't in yet) and getting a mess of change in return, we stumbled back to the house to put things in some kind of order before we left for our barge trip. Which I really was looking forward to. Seeing Adrian again and joining him on his boat was going to be a blast. All the lies we would tell, which is basic fighter-pilot talk, American or French anyway. And like my friend Pierre, thankfully, Adrian was fluent in English.

After throwing cold water on our faces, "freshening up," and all that business to keep from dozing off on our drive south to the Canal du Midi, we both experienced the thrill of anticipation.

"Kenny, I haven't been on a canal barge since I was a little girl, in the Netherlands with my folks. The barge owner and his wife had a schipperke. Such a sweet little dog. I wonder if Adrian has one," she said, turning toward me, her ever-present road map slipping to the floor.

"I think he has a cat," I said. "Adrian told me in an e-mail that it wanders. When he is in port it sticks around, but when he starts down the canal, it goes off on its own, but somehow figures out where he will dock for the night. Then, *voilà*, it jumps onboard for dinner. Cats can be amazing animals."

"I miss Georgia. If we ever come back here, we'll have to bring her. Maybe introduce her to Adrian's. Male or female?"

"I haven't the foggiest," I answered, trying to sound as much like Alex Guinness in *Bridge on the River Kwai* as I could.

"This is so exciting," she said, ignoring my effort without so much as a mention.

I just nodded, leaving it at that, and focused on the road ahead.

THREE

ISATIS

T HE REST of our drive to Port Lauragais was a delight. As afternoon shadows lengthened, ahead on our right, the sun's slanting rays shimmered hues of copper off a lone tower nestled among fir trees atop a small *colline*, or hill.

"Bing, over there, at our two o'clock. Isn't that some kind of little castle?" I asked, nodding in the direction of the sun's reflections.

She looked where I'd indicated. "I think so. Here comes a sign. Maybe that'll tell us something."

I slowed so we could try to decipher the rather elegant script announcing—Hostellerie du Château de la Pomarède, with a blue arrow pointing in that direction.

"Little castles deserve as much a look as big ones," Bing smiled, opening our Michelin guide. After a short flip through the pages she added, "It got a mention as newly opened. No stars, but I guess they think it's a place to keep an eye on."

"So let's do it," I said, taking the right turn a couple of hundred meters further down the road.

We wound across fields, through a small forest stand, and finally came to an intersecting road leading up and over the bridged dry moat and through a narrow archway cut into the ancient circular wall. And what a delightful surprise lay on the other side. A full cobbled courtyard with a restaurant and *auberge* snuggled under the tower to our right; the wall continuing in front and around to the left shielding a private residence, also built from massive stones, along with a school, the *mairie*, or town hall, and a post office. Directly ahead, beyond the wall, the peaks of the tallest village roofs were visible. Getting out of the car, looking down twenty or thirty feet to the tight little road snaking from the battlement's base into the village, I spied a *patisserie*'s sign. My heart skipped a beat—a castle tall standing guard over *baguettes* and *pain au chocolat!* In a heartbeat I was transported back to my childhood with its stories of noblemen and knights errant. Could this *château* have been the reward some brave heart received for riding off to a Crusade or for battling Moors on behalf of Aquitaine's grand duke? I looked over at Bing, whose head was tipped way back sighting the top of the tower. She was probably time-traveling too, seeing herself in a long gown waving to me from way up there as I rode off in defense of *croissants*, decent *fromage*, and fine wine at cheap prices.

The picture-book charm of the place captured our hearts. Mine especially. I could feel my long-suffering addiction to such things growing unrestrainedly. "Looking at curtains," as my dad had called such childhood dreaming back home in Boston. Now, here in southwestern France, it was beyond anything I'd expected. And it was infectious. Bing's eyes were all dreamy too. Like the Mad

Cow Disease cropping up in England, we could be France's first victims of a similar affliction . . . Mad House Disease! The more sweet little castles like this we came across, the more threatened we would be.

Back in the car, we continued our circle over the cobbles, back through the arch and off on the road again toward Port Lauragais.

To better get our minds off castles, Bing had found an alternate route that went by several windmills. The first of these was in Saint-Félix-Lauragais. It was on a hilltop slightly lower than the village's and was bracketed by two ruins, one on each side. We later learned the three original windmills had been built in the twelfth century by the Cathars, as a declaration of their break with the Roman church. They'd dedicated the three structures to their conception of—*the Father, the Son, and the Holy Spirit.*

Farther down the road we found another hill with an all white windmill (*moulin*) topping it. This one still had its huge blades. At first glance my heart lusted for that beauty, but then I realized it stood alone. No *patisserie* nearby. Though we'd been in France just a matter of days, we'd already concluded that a *château*, a windmill, even a village, without a *boulangerie/patisserie*, was off our list. Though man was said not to live by bread alone, in France life sure as hell was easier having the stuff close at hand. So, though the windmill was magnificent, it would just have to wait to win the hearts of another Don Quixote and his wife.

Twenty minutes later, at the Canal du Midi, we found a slip of a road paralleling the waterway, which we took in an eastward direction. A mile or two down it put us at Port Lauragais, where we got our first look at Adrian's boat dominating the others at the quay. It was by far the largest and most tastefully appointed. The hull was a glistening black, set off by green trim and white hatch covers. A cluster of wicker chairs and low tables graced the canopied foredeck. The tricolor of France caught the occasional breeze at the stern while the departmental banner, its gold Toulousian

cross on a field of red, fluttered at the bow. The *Isatis*. Our honeymoon hotel. What a splendid sight.

I HADN'T seen Adrian for years. I was a bit taken aback by the
fact that he looked so fit. I try to keep in shape, but clearly my old
friend was doing a better job of it. Super slim. I hoped Bing didn't
notice. I wasn't running marathons anymore so I'd put on a pound
or two or three or . . . whatever.

As we walked the quay toward the boat, watching Adrian jump
from the deck to the dock, the advice of a college classmate popped
into my head. He'd explained that in choosing whom to room
with, he looked for at least one fellow shorter than he was; one
fatter; and the last, less bright. As Adrian approached, I realized I
personally had covered all three slots for him. He was taller than
me. Much slimmer. Fluent in English, along with Spanish, Farsi,
his native French, and I don't know how many other languages.
He had been a fighter pilot, as had I, but he'd reached higher rank
while on active duty. Then, on top of all that, I found out he drove
a vintage Corvette and rode a Harley-Davidson! Good heavens.
My friend had become France's answer to *Top Gun* Tom Cruise.
Not to mention his glorious canal boat, and his skills as a chef, his
knowledge of the region's history, wines, and foods, to all of which
we would soon be treated. And then there was that sexy French
accent. Ah man, Adrian could be the death of me.

Bing adored him. Of course.

WE HAD the bow stateroom. No one else was booked. Adrian
showed us the way and helped with our bags. While we got
unpacked he went to the galley to prepare the *aperitifs* he would
serve in the salon, above deck being too chilly with the sun just
setting. This gave Bing and me a few moments to get the feel of
what our world would be like for the next few days.

Quiet at night, for sure, because most of our room was below the waterline. Of course the portholes giving light were above it, but we found we were in a capsule of silence, sound blocked by the surrounding walls of water. It was so quiet it was almost scary. On deck, I didn't imagine cruising would be much different. The speed of the sturdy steel barge through the calm canal waters wouldn't be much more than at a walking pace, so there would hardly be much noise of water slapping against the bow, nor the rumble of a rolling wake from the stern. In fact I was beginning to see the whole experience as something like floating on a post-card, seeing and being a part of its picture, moving at an almost imperceptible pace from one port to another.

Dinner was what gourmets write articles about. Our wines, *pâtés*, lamb, and *légumes* a blur of excellence I have no record of, only the remembrance of delicious things past. Adrian prepared and served everything. He was ship's master, captain, cook and regional guide all rolled into one. So, as we ate, we encouraged him to tell us the history of *his* canal. Taking his seat across from Bing he began *l'histoire*.

"Since Roman times," he said, "there had been dreams of building a canal to link the Mediterranean Sea and the Atlantic Ocean. Not only would it reduce the distance for boats to travel, but there would be less chance of attack by pirates around Gibraltar. But no one who proposed it could figure how to build it. Not the Romans, François I, Henri IV, nor Richelieu. The major problem was how to deal with the Seuil de Naurouze pass, a six-hundred-forty-foot high point near Béziers. Finally, in 1662 the Baron of Bonrepos, Pierre-Paul Riquet, committing his entire fortune, even his daughters' dowries, *everything* . . . convinced the powers-that-be he had a plan that would work. Over the next four years he detailed how locks would be installed along the approaches to that highest point, from both the east and the west. Water to feed it all would be channeled down from the highland lakes of La Montagne Noire.

"They started work in 1666. It took over ten thousand men and fourteen years to build. But, six months before it was opened, Riquet, poor fellow, died. They said it was from sheer exhaustion."

"Sounds about like my writing career," I threw in, reaching for more bread.

"Probably more like trying to get this boat venture up and running," Adrian countered, with a smile and nod toward Bing.

"Anyway," Adrian said, returning to his narrative, "the canal part of the water route is one-hundred-fifty miles long. Boats pass from the Atlantic Ocean, into Gironde Estuary to the Garonne River at Bordeaux, then cross all of southern France to the Thau lagoon on the Mediterranean, at Port des Onglous. There are ninety-one locks, but one stretch, between Argens-Minervois and Béziers, fifty-four kilometers long, is lock-free. Near Béziers, Riquet even cut a quarter mile tunnel through the ridge there, which he reached with a stairway of locks, up and down either side."

Getting to his feet to clear our dessert plates Adrian added, "The longest a boat can be and still mange those steps, allowing it to sail the entire canal, is thirty meters, about ninety-eight feet. *Le Péniche-Hôtel Isatis*, which you are on right now, is one of them," he said, and nodded with gentle pride. "She is steel hulled, originally ten meters longer, which I had sliced out, then welded the two halves back together, making a proper floating hotel . . . for your Lauragais honeymoon," he concluded with a wave of his hand.

THE CHAMPAGNE by our bed, with a dozen roses beside it, was such a thoughtful touch. We had no idea when he'd done it. What a kind, dear man. How fortunate to have thought of him and his boat for this late beginning of our lives together.

We'd had a long couple of days. Sleep was calling. The plane ride, meeting Pierre and Marie-Claude, and the car events by the Loire the day before, getting to rue Basque, and then on to the Canal du Midi all lined up to keep the cork in our champagne bottle. A sign of our maturity?

As the bathroom Jacuzzi's deep rumble ended and the drain opened, Bing came through the door in clinging silk. So beautiful! My heart was in my throat but, alas, my eyelids were heavy. She walked around the foot of the bed to lift the covers and slip under, sliding warmly, lovingly close. Hugging against me, her golden head lying gently on my shoulder, she whispered, "We have the rest of our lives to love each other. Now we will sleep and dream of all the wonderful things that lie ahead then start fresh in the morning."

FOUR

DOWN TO THE SEA
AND SHIPS

WHETHER ABOARD a Hagerty Sea Shell or the aircraft carrier USS *Constellation*, there's still a common protocol for putting to sea. Well, in this case, moving away from a dock. Lines must be cast off, in many cases knots untied, technical stuff like that. So, having had a career in state-of-the-art aviation, I felt qualified to man the bowlines as Adrian revved the mighty diesel from the wheelhouse, and Bing did the honors with the lines at the stern.

Adrian slipped the prop into reverse and the *Isatis* shuddered momentarily as it groaned into motion. Another sort of rumble followed as the blades dug deeper into the water, kicking up a few wads of sunken sycamore leaves from the shallow bottom, floating them the length of the barge as we pulled from the quay.

I found all this rather exciting. Hardly a catapult shot from a carrier deck, as in the old days, but it was still satisfying to feel the great steel beast churning into life beneath my feet.

Making a smart curl of my line, trying to coil it on the deck like I figured a real sailor would, I straightened up to see Bing waving to me from the stern, smiling like a teenager. What a great smile. Shining blue eyes, flashing white teeth, a delightful girlishness about her that made my heart crinkle.

"We're on our way!" I shouted to the two of them . . . only to feel totally out of place as heads on the quay turned to see who the foreigner was making all the noise.

Adrian continued powering us rearward the fifty yards to the end of the quay where the harbor bulged into a small lagoon. Once there, he swung the stern further starboard, adding throttle for better headway to the harbor mouth and entry into the canal itself.

"Slick as a water snake between the stumps," a Cajun might have said as he centered the bow to point straight down the canal's centerline in the direction of Castelnaudary, bean capitol of Europe no less, and home of *cassoulet*. Though all this was done in heavy-boat slow-motion, it was a demanding and well-executed feat. Maybe, I speculated, these French Air Force types were qualified for more than just modeling reflective sunglasses, white silk scarves, and smart leather jackets.

"Bravo Adrian," I called out, this time without embarrassment, even adding a continental salute for good measure.

The weather was good, crisp but unusually mild for late January. The canal was clear. The vacation season still lay ahead so we expected little traffic along the way, at least from Port Lauragais through the nine locks to Castelnaudary and the score beyond to Carcassonne. Though this first leg to Castelnaudary was just eighteen and a half kilometers, about eleven miles, we would be rumbling down the canal for more than four hours. As

I said, the barge only made three nautical miles per hour, and having the locks to contend with, slow motion was the mode of the day.

In the off-season the locks were only open from 9 AM to 7 PM and closed at midday for an hour. Generally there was a lockmaster's house, an *auberge*, by each cluster of these gateways. In the seventeenth century, the barges were dependant on mules pulling them along paths or they used sails where possible for the Mediterranean to Atlantic run, totaling about five hundred miles and weeks of travel. Places to stay and to eat along the way had been important. Adrian explained that in modern times, since the traffic is only for pleasure, the places open now are more *cafés*, bars, and small restaurants. The old mule paths are used for bicycling, jogging, and hiking.

Over dinner the night before, Adrian had made clear how proud he was of his *Isatis*. Not only its size, but its steel hull too. As a definite traditionalist and historian of the Lauragais, he respected the wood barges, though his heart was with steel. He had only distain for boats made from anything but wood or steel.

"Tupperware," he said, "that's what I call the things with fiberglass hulls. Plastic. Tupperware."

The rule of the road approaching locks is to line up first come, first serve. Small vessels can jam into a lock together, but a boat as large as the *Isatis* has to be the sole occupant as the gates close behind it and the water pours in or out as the case may be. So there can be some dashing and dicing when a lock appears around a bend and a big boat like the *Isatis* is ahead of the pack. Since each transit takes up to twenty minutes, the little boats can get frustrated trailing behind one so big.

As our first lock loomed ahead, a Tupperware, a cabin cruiser of about thirty-five feet, sleeping maybe six, appeared some distance behind and started to accelerate, hoping to wedge in ahead of us at the last minute. To me the move was just the water version of the

French driver on macadam. This little guy roared up to our butt (stern), just as he would on the road, then zigged to his left, following with a zag to his right, trying to scoot ahead between us and the bank. Though the lock was only a few boat lengths ahead, the captain thought he could squeeze past and slip in front.

Mais au contraire, mon ami. Little did M. Tupperware know we had a fighter pilot at the helm. Adrian deftly added left rudder, closing us toward the bank and threatening to jam the smaller boat against it. At the last second the captain of the plastic boat accepted that his hull was no match for the *Isatis'* steel, to say nothing of the boats' relative sizes, and cut power. Then he threw his prop into reverse, all the while shouting and rude-gesturing, a nasty black cigar bobbing precariously in his mouth and holding a glass of something dark in his tiller hand.

Adrian, always the gentleman, nodded gracefully, smiled, and waved a friendly hand to the puffing red-faced fellow while he threw his own engine into reverse to stop us short of the lock's gate. Perhaps he overdid the revs a bit. The bubble and boil our prop kicked up was enough to set the little boat bobbing, causing the captain's drink to spill all over his red-and-white tunic. A delightful sight. How I'd love to put wheels on the *Isatis* and roll it onto the roads of *la belle France* to deal with the idiots we encountered the last few days. Bravo Adrian!

As we continued down the canal, I was stunned by the cathedral arches of the stately sycamore branches reaching from each side of the waterway, like fingertips touching over our heads.

"Bing, it's our drive from Toulouse all over again," I said, my hands spreading apart like a conductor in front of his orchestra.

"*So* beautiful! Oh Kenny, look over there," she said pointing to our left. "A pottery. It looks ancient. We've got to come back. Years ago I worked in clay. I'd love to see how these people do it. I'll bet their techniques go way back, before the canal was built."

As we slipped past the rustic old factory, Adrian's waving from the wheelhouse caught my eye. I took Bing's hand and we joined him there.

"Up ahead, I'll pull to the bank for a stop. Not very long," he said. "We are approaching the *obélisque* de Riquet built by his descendents in 1825. It is near the place he had wanted a town— where the canal waters divide, west to the Atlantic, east to the Mediterranean Sea. There is a pumping station there and what originally had been a lagoon, filled in now, but with a magnificent promenade through the *platanes*, the sycamores as you call them. I want you to see it. I go there to . . ." he paused an instant, his eyes seemed to mist, "I go there to . . . re-create. When times are difficult. You will see what I mean. There is peace there. Perhaps it will be your place for peacefulness too."

After we left the boat the three of us walked together, Adrian pointing out what had once been a checkerboard lagoon, divided into parts by dikes, but was now all filled in for picnicking and pleasure. We saw the pumping station and the obelisk, but when we turned to walk the long tree-lined promenade, Adrian asked to walk ahead, alone.

Bing and I followed at a distance, hand in hand, drinking it all in—the sunlight shimmering through the barely budding branches, the growing whispers of wind telling us of changes in the weather ahead. So peaceful. We understood Adrian's wish for a private moment. For whatever might be bothering him, this was the place to sort it out.

O U R   N E X T stop, Bram, is the midpoint between Port Lauragais and Carcassonne. We hoped to make it by dark. The four and a half hours of our morning cruise had put us in the lovely lake-like Grand Basin at Castelnaudary.

Since the five locks on the far side of the basin were closed for the noon hour, we took the lead position in the queue, and then hove to at a piling. Adrian scooted to the galley, returning with hot *cassoulet*, a column of steam curling from its traditional huge beige pottery bowl. Bing lent a hand with the dishes, fresh bread, and salad. I was entrusted with opening what turned out to be a delightful Gaillac red (Château Vignalles), which Adrian assured us was required to properly tamp down all the beans and things.

If you haven't experienced *cassoulet*, it is a must. It's a stew of large pinto beans in a thick sauce wrapped around sausage and ducks' legs. Absolutely perfect for crisp days when traveling at a snail's pace down canals like the Midi.

Waiting for the lock to open, Bing stationed herself in the galley to do the clean-up. She and I were both helping with whatever jobs we could to free Adrian for piloting.

With Bing below, the two of us took a few moments on the forward deck to catch up. It had been a long time since Adrian and I had seen each other. I was interested to know what was going on with his family—his wife Emilie, daughter Aimee, and his son Paul. He was already up to speed with my circumstances. I had written shortly after Bobbye died and then later told him of Bing. That letter had asked about a honeymoon on the *Isatis*.

"Will Emilie be meeting us in Carcassonne?" I asked, plopping down onto one of the deck chairs.

Adrian didn't respond immediately, taking the chair opposite. Then, after a long pause, time enough for me to realize my old friend was carrying some extra baggage, he rubbed the heel of his right hand against his forehead before looking back at me, his hand falling into his lap and forming a fist.

"Emilie and I are divorced . . ."

"Oh, Adrian, I . . ." I started to offer condolences but hesitated when I saw there was more he wanted to say.

". . . And she is in hospital."

Looking away for a moment, past the bow and toward the waiting lock, his eyes came back to mine and he added, "She tried to commit suicide. She used a knife on her wrists. Aimee found her.

I don't know what affect that has had on my girl. Paul is away at school. We haven't told him of it. Any of it . . ." he trailed off.

"Adrian, I am so sorry. If there is anything I can do . . . Oh man, we shouldn't be taking you away on this cruise. Let's turn around. You should be with your family."

"No, no," he said, shaking his head, the fist he'd formed opening and closing almost spasmodically. "She did this last year and the year before too. She used pills then. The second time she even packed an overnight bag before she tried."

"She packed a bag first?" I exclaimed, eyes wide. "What the hell?"

"I don't think she is trying as hard as she might. I think . . ." he paused looking for the right words, "I think she's doing this to kill me."

I could only watch while he searched for the best way to go on.

"After the suitcase attempt, I felt it was time for me to get out of her life. Things had been going terribly since I left the air force. While I was in the military she had the benefits of my rank as a colonel. We had a maid. I was the air attaché at several embassies. It was an exciting life with all the comforts. Then I retired, for my dream, this boat. It was as if life evaporated for her. Everything changed. No more servants. No more embassy parties. No more limousines. While we were in Germany overseeing the modification of the *Isatis,* she was truly miserable. She didn't adapt very well to my being a boat worker, nor did she have any interest in being one herself.

"The more I think about our lives together, the more I think she married my career, not me. When I elected not to go for general, there was no longer a career to love. Just me. Apparently I am not enough. So now her focus is to make me pay for taking away her exciting life. She knows I love her and always will; so she hurts herself to hurt me. I had to get out. Remove myself. For her sake. And for the kids. It is all so crazy. But I have no choice. Maybe the hospital will help. I cannot."

I didn't know what to say. I felt terribly awkward.

"The last time I was called to the hospital, Aimee was with me," he continued. "I'd had a difficult day. The bank had been a problem. The canal authority was another. And then I got word Emilie had tried to kill herself again. When I got there and was assured she was stabilized for the night, I was shaking with exhaustion . . . anger, perhaps. I don't know. Aimee seemed to understand and got me out to the car. She said she would drive, which was okay with me. After a half hour I dozed off. I don't know how long I was asleep, but something . . . God Himself maybe, told me to wake up. When I opened my eyes, I saw a sharp turn ahead, a row of trees, and Aimee's hands locked on the wheel with the accelerator to the floor. She was going to kill us both.

"My hand shot out for the key, but everything was in slow motion, shutting down the ignition . . . and grabbing the wheel. But I made it. A second more and we'd never have made the turn.

"After we stopped, she broke down. Totally. I got out of the car, keeping the keys, opened her door, lifted her out, and held her tight as she cried . . . cried her heart out. I have no idea how long it was before I was able to load her into the back seat, cover her with a blanket, and then drive back to the psychiatric hospital. Where she still is . . . with her mother.

"So, Ken, my two girls are looking after each other and Paul is away. This, *here*, is the only place for me to be right now. With you and with your new wife. To help you and Bing find the happiness you and Bobbye shared. You are one of the lucky ones. You find women to love who love you in return. I envy you that. I am left to love . . . well, I guess my *Isatis*. I help her. She helps me. We have a very simple relationship. Something I have never had with a woman. So, for now, the two of us, *Isatis* and me, we are at your service. Let that be. Let yourself and your Bing enjoy it. For me . . ."

Oh God, I could have cried. In the midst of such deep pain, he was thinking of nothing but what was best for me and Bing. I

didn't know if Adrian was a religious man, but his instincts surely
were what true faith is all about. And, in a way, the *Isatis* was his
floating church and he its pastor.

Up ahead the lockmaster was coming out to the gates. Adrian
saw him and got to his feet, squeezing my shoulder as he started
back to the wheelhouse.

"Time to be on our way, *mon camarade*. I'll start the engine."

WE TIED up for the night at Bram. As if our discussion had
never taken place, Adrian prepared another of his famous dinners.
Five courses! *Foie gras.* Then slender slices of salmon sautéed in
sunflower oil with garlic and *herbes de Provence*, quickly seared
and served deliciously hot. Rack of lamb next, with red potatoes
and creamed spinach, followed by an endive and tomato salad. A
selection of cheeses brought us to a dessert of chocolate mousse
with a sprinkling of chopped nuts. And finally coffee with
Armagnac. A cigar would have been nice too, but what the hell,
we weren't fighter pilots anymore.

While Adrian put the galley in order, Bing and I bundled up
against the night chill, and climbed the stairs to the deck to watch
the stars. More memories for me, of course. Bittersweet, confusing. Settling onto the deck's one rattan love seat, I put my arm
around Bing and we both hiked our feet onto the low table. I
wasn't feeling much like talking after all Adrian had told me. I
hadn't shared any of it with Bing yet. Another time. Besides, she
seemed in a wandering mood ready to let the stars be her guide.

"Sitting out under the night sky like this makes me think
about Connecticut as a young girl, with my father" she said. "As
a professor he was always formal, scholarly, but we had a wonderful relationship. I was the last of *his little girls*. I guess that made
me special. He'd probably softened a lot from when my sisters
were that age. Which I'm sure didn't make them very happy. His
love radiated in a special way whenever we'd be alone, reading,

listening to music, or just staring up at these same stars," she said, nodding skyward.

These same stars. Bobbye and I had shared them in Boston when we were first married. And they had been overhead the night she died, when I'd searched them for a sign. Something, anything . . . It would have been easy to start crying.

"Tell me more about you and your dad," I encouraged, trying to get some distance from the stars and the tears they seemed to be commanding.

"He didn't want me *corrupted* by the world," she said with a little chuckle.

"I guess it's good he never met me then," I threw in.

"He would have liked you. You have spirit. Strength," Bing said, squeezing my hand. "He was strong too, but not so much physically. He just stood up to things. Doing battle at the university for his department. Making sure his daughters studied hard and had the best advantages. Which was a problem for me. I was the youngest and a tomboy. I think he secretly liked that. My sisters were always *such ladies.* He'd catch me doing things he'd forbid them from doing, and didn't really punish me. Mainly because by the time my transgressions came along, he realized they weren't very important. Too late for the others though.

"Comic books, for instance. No comic books allowed. They were too shallow. But I was seven years old, knew my own mind, and I loved *Felix the Cat.* Simple as that. One of my friends had a subscription. Since I wasn't allowed to have such rubbish in our house, I'd have to go to hers for my reading. So, one day I cut out the subscription page from my friend's Felix comic, filled in my address and all, scotch taped nickels and dimes from my allowance to it, and mailed it in."

"How did you figure you wouldn't be caught?" I asked.

"Daddy would go off to his office at the university, and I would get home from school before the mailman got to our house. So

the one day a month Felix would come, I would be at the box
ready and waiting. My parents never knew about it. And I grew
up okay. No huge character defects."

"I hope."

"Careful," she said smiling, digging an elbow into my ribs.
"Then there was the radio I found in somebody's trash. Daddy
wouldn't let us listen to radios either, other than the Texaco Saturday afternoon opera at the Met. Not even *One Man's Family*
Sunday nights.

"So, on the way home from school one day, as fate would have
it, I found this old radio in a trash can and brought it home. By
then I was eleven, vastly smarter and more resourceful than I had
been at seven. After looking for obvious damage, which I didn't
find, I started checking wires. With a screwdriver I took the back
panel off and actually found the main black wire had one of its
connections broken off. I didn't know if that was all that was
wrong, but I knew it wouldn't work with that wire broken, so I
found the handyman's soldering stuff in the basement and, when
no one was around, I soldered the wire myself. Then everything
worked! I hid it under my bed and when no one was around, I got
to hear *One Man's Family* and *The Shadow* and *Captain Midnight* and *Hop Harrigan*, even *Amos 'n' Andy* . . . all kinds of
forbidden fruit my goodie-two-shoes sisters never tasted. Maybe
that's why I wasn't always so popular with them."

"Maybe it was a PC issue. You know, *Amos 'n' Andy*."

"Maybe," she said thoughtfully. "Actually Daddy finally did
catch me and was angry. He was most upset over how much I
must have spent for the radio. I told him I paid nothing for it, that
I found it in somebody's trash can and that I figured out what was
wrong with it and fixed it. Well, his eyes went wide and a little
smile tweaked at the corners of his mouth. I could tell I'd made
him proud. He let me keep it too. When my sisters came back
from college and saw me listening to such a forbidden thing, you

can imagine what ran through their minds about their spoiled
baby sister. But hey, it wasn't my fault my sisters weren't into
fixing broken junk."

I hugged Bing real tight. Then we both fell silent, letting the
stars, and the hugeness they filled, do the talking.

The second night in our sweet submerged cabin was more lov-
ing. I was finally getting to know Bing much better. Her moods,
her need for quiet time—something difficult to adapt to for a very
noisy guy. But at least we were out of the house-repair rat race.
Out of the hustle of house selling, moving, and renovating. We
weren't just spinning our wheels anymore. We were finally focusing on our love, our marriage, writing, painting, the remainder of
our lives together. Already we could feel the canal was giving us a
soft landing.

FIVE

BEDSIDE ROSES

T HAT NIGHT Bing slept as soundly as she always and miraculously did. Instantly asleep: unwakeable until dawn's early light. An amazing ability I have never been so lucky to have. The night for me was nothing but a wrestle with my concern for Adrian. How could such a sweet and gentle man be so brutalized by the hand of fate? What the hell could he do about it? The divorce hadn't ended his love for Emilie, Aimee, and Paul. Though he wasn't bound to anything legally, his heart and soul were locked in this terrible struggle, perhaps for their very lives. Were he a different man, one without such a sense of honor, he would have just walked away.

THE NEXT morning it rained. The good news was there were few other boats on the canal. However, and only God knew why, Adrian decided it was time for me to take the helm. Of course a lesser man would have begged off, but I had been a Marine. And a fighter pilot! All of which meant I couldn't let my Frog friend show me up. So I cinched my belt, ground my sneakers into the deck, took throttle and wheel in hand while pointing the big steel son-of-a-bitch down the canal's center line, and zeroed in on the lock ahead.

Perhaps because we moved through the water at a dog-paddle pace, I found tracking the center line difficult. We had a crosswind that nudged us starboard. I corrected port. Having been used to fine-tuning jet aircraft on final approach with my fingertips, having to spin a huge wheel round and round to get the slightest rudder correction out of this huge heavy boat was something else for me. And, just as one adjustment started to take hold, most of it had to be taken out with a lot more wheel-spinning in the other direction. It was like the stone age of piloting. I was amazed how much easier a 747 was to control than a flat-bottomed canal barge.

Unfortunately, from my point of view, Adrian decided I was doing well enough to enter a lock on my own. So, about a hundred yards out, he had me cut power, explaining I could depend on the barge's momentum for rudder control. He also showed me how to get into reverse and accelerate the prop for an emergency stop if I really messed up.

Despite heavy sweating through most of the exercise, I actually slipped that big beauty between the gates without so much as a kiss to either side and barely a touch of the forward gate as we came gently to a stop! The *matelot* (sailor) had become *sous capitaine* (first officer). From that moment till our arrival in Carcassonne the next day, I shared the helm. Adrian even put a white barge cap on my head and a striped sailing sweater over my shoulders. I had arrived. *Bien sûr.*

We made Carcassonne in excellent time. And what a sight that great walled city was! Once a center of the heretical Cathars of the twelfth century, and the bloody Crusade they attracted, the patina of its great high lichen-kissed walls had softened into something with a magic kingdom touch. Towers, turrets, battlements, dry moats, drawbridges, ancient stone, cobbled street, lyres, flutes, and fluttering banners were all there, and of the real stuff.

As we made harbor near the Aude River, which was bracketed by bridges dating back hundreds of years, the skies cleared and the setting sun treated us to a golden sandstone dreamscape. The canal and castle loomed above the layers of lingering fog. What a thrilling treasure to behold. Breathtaking in every way.

Adrian was showing signs of fatigue. He was wearing all the hats on the *Isatis*—captain, *maître d'hôtel*, chef, and chief bottle washer—not to mention the added weight of his personal problems. He needed some down time and was receptive when I proposed Bing and I walk up to the old city, sightsee, and have dinner there on our own.

Bing wore the red jacket she'd worn the first day I was at her farm, when we loaded firewood together. I loved the way it set off her blonde hair and brought out the blue of her eyes, kind of Marlene Dietrich style. She was wearing black wool slacks that showed off her great legs. As she walked ahead of me from our mooring, I was taken by her slim waist that emphasized the curves of her very feminine *derrière*. Often today, women think little boy bottoms are the thing, but that's not so for most men. As far as I was concerned, Bing's figure was just right. A real woman. And my black leather jacket and matching jeans added more Deutschland to Bing's touch of Dietrich. I hoped we looked European enough not to offend our French hosts. I'd pulled it off years before living in Berlin and working hard on a good Deutsche accent. Maybe we'd decide to spend more time in France than just these two months and get a better leg up on their language.

We walked again hand-in-hand across the bridge, from the lower town to the castle on the hill, where we spent two hours discovering *la cité's* cobbled streets, map in hand. We started from the main entrance at Porte Narbonnaise, went across the *lices* (the open area between the outer and inner walls), and on through the entire fortress. Rue Cros led us to rue Viollet le Duc and on to the Place St. Jean, the Château Comtal, and the museum. We walked the ramparts, on through the cathedral, and into the amphitheater. It was especially charming the way each tiny street led us to another still smaller one, all winding up and down steep misting hills. By the time we'd made a complete circuit of it all we were ready to fall into one of the restaurants on the Place St. Jean. Being the off-season, it was easy to get a table close to a warm fire.

We were comfortable. The flickering blaze made Bing's face glow, her eyes sparkle, and those teeth flash when she smiled. I'll admit to having had more of the wine than she, and with our coffee I added a snifter of *Armagnac*.

"I'm sorry I'm not a great success, Bing," I threw out from nowhere. "No best-sellers. No movies. It's sad if not bizarre that my only accomplishments are in things I've never given a damn about," I said. "But now, together, finally focusing on the writing, maybe I'll be able to turn it around."

She looked across the candlelight then reached and put her hand over mine.

"Kenny," she said softly. "I understand what you're saying, but you aren't being fair to yourself. You have done amazing things. World's records. Created an airline from scratch. Ran another. Built a family. And loved your wife with all your heart. Which is not a problem for me. You have honored Bobbye. I am touched, honestly, deeply touched. And I hope you will feel the same way about me as time goes by," she added with a chuck of her chin. Then she paused, looking down at our hands on the table. Her eyes misted as she looked back up to me and said, "I had been deceived and deeply hurt . . . in ways I won't even go into. All the trust built up over the years was killed. I was left empty, desperately empty. Losing Bobbye made you empty too. So, we both share an understanding of the worst kind of pain."

Tears dampened Bing's cheeks as she continued, "Even though Bobbye is gone, I know she still lives in your heart. I accept that, without sadness or reservations . . . because it tells me how true you are, how true you will be to me . . . until again . . . death comes."

She slid her hand back, took her napkin, and dried her eyes.

Everything she'd said was so gentle, poignant . . . like she'd lifted a burden from my heart.

I T   M U S T have been close to midnight by the time we got back to the boat. Though Adrian's aft cabin's light was out, the salon was dimly light, as was our stateroom. Bing started down the narrow way forward while I locked the door to the deck and turned off the salon light. Then I followed her to our room. At the door she reached back for my hand.

"Look what he did," she said, pointing to the rose on each of our pillows and the split of champagne chilling on the bedside table.

Picking up a note on the bed she read, "*We shall find peace. We shall hear the angels and we shall see the sky sparkling with diamonds —Anton Chekhov.*"

Bing walked to the table, lifted the little bottle from the cooler, and handed it and a glass to me.

"Go back to the salon. Read a book until I call," she said, her head slightly down as she looked up in that Princess Di way she had.

"Yes, ma'am," I said, turning and feeling undeniably . . . *good*.

When Bing called, I took what was left of the champagne and walked to the stateroom door. She was standing by the bed. She was just barely wearing a slight dark silk thing . . .

"You are absolutely gorgeous," I whispered.

"I thought you'd never notice," she said with a smile. "Come over here . . ."

I did as I was told. Then, standing there in the dim light from the moon and stars peeking in through the portholes, I watched her slide out of the silk . . . felt her touch . . . I pulled her close . . . and we were one.

S I X

ON A HILL FAR AWAY

T HUMP! THUMP! *Thump!*

"Wha . . ?" I mumbled.

"Ummm," Bing returned, even less awake than I was.

More *thumps*, followed by an urgent male voice rasping from the other side of our door. "Ken, Bing, I have to talk with you. Right now."

Of course it was Adrian, and by the sound of his voice something was terribly wrong.

"Come in, Adrian. We're still in bed, but come on in," I called as we untangled and sat up, backs against the headboard.

Adrian opened the door and embarrassedly poked his head in. He looked distraught.

"Forgive my barging in this way, but I just got a call. My son has run away from his school. His bed was empty this morning. His roommate admitted he'd seen him leave the room in the middle of the night. Earlier he'd received a phone call. Probably from his sister at the hospital. I expect he is headed there. I am going to town to rent a car to find him."

I jumped out of bed, grabbing my trousers. "I'll go with you. Bing can watch the boat," I said, trying to find a missing shoe under the drape of covers.

"No, no Ken. The rental car office is nearby. I will walk there. After that . . . I don't know. I have to find him. He can do crazy things sometimes when he is angry. With his mother and sister as they are, I don't know what he might do. I—"

"I'm coming with you. We'll need a car to get back to Port Lauragais ourselves. If the boat can stay here, Bing and I'll lock it up . . . leave the keys with the harbormaster, if that's all right. We'll exchange rentals, then go back to Black Mountain to settle in. You won't have to worry about us sitting around here. And Adrian," I added, knowing he was not flush with cash, "you keep the contract money. It's important to us that you do. No argument."

Bing nodded her agreement as I tied my shoes.

He didn't say anything. It looked like he couldn't. His eyes were brimming with tears as he turned back to the passageway. Pulling on a sweater, I followed. Bing, a nude sleeper, was out of bed behind me. I hoped Adrian didn't turn around. For that matter, I hoped Bing didn't follow us all the way to the deck.

Considering the pressure Adrian was under, things went smoothly. We got our cars and I followed him back to the wharf where he spoke to the harbormaster. Then, back at the boat, Adrian showed us what to do about locking up after we had our stuff together. He tossed a few clumps of his own clothes into a knapsack, hugged me, kissed Bing, and was on his way.

We waved our goodbyes, silently praying things would be all

right with his son. How much more must this good man be put through?

Once the barge doors were locked, hatches bolted and our rental car loaded, we put Adrian's keys in an envelope and left them with the harbormaster. Returning to Black Mountain three days early was not a big deal for us, but our hearts went out to Adrian. The poor man was being torn in all directions. Hopefully we'd be able to help when the time came, whenever that might be.

BACK AT number 10 rue Basque we started settling in for the long-delayed working honeymoon we'd envisioned this adventure would be. On our first drive-through of Black Mountain, I'd hauled our monster suitcases up one flight to the rear bedroom. Bing's painting materials had gone to the high ceiling floor above. The openness there, with a good fifteen feet to the rafters, looked to have studio potential. There was also a large skylight making the area open and airy, with good light. We slid two long tables end to end for workspace that could handle murals, then assembled her portable easel, and added a tall stool from the kitchen. *Presto,* Bing had her studio.

I cracked the skylight, letting some brisk afternoon breezes waft down, freshening the interior air. Bing hopped onto the stool and happily surveyed her new domain. Wisps of blonde hair tickled her smiling cheeks. Knowing she would soon have her palette and brushes in hand, she looked happy. I felt the same.

DAYS OF focus and accomplishment passed into warm snuggly nights. We were totally in synch, finally pursuing what we had first imagined our lives together would be. The single negative nipping around the edges of our bliss was Adrian and his struggles. I'd told Bing what he'd described on the boat—Emilie and their daughter's troubles. Bing was touched by how kind he had been with us despite all he'd been struggling with. The whole situation was further frustrating because no one returned the messages we left on the barge phone and I didn't have his cell number.

Our telephone experiences were complicated in other ways. Since settling in at 10 rue Basque we hadn't met anyone who spoke English, or received calls from any who spoke anything but French. Beyond *bonjour* and *au revoir*, *oui* and *non*, I was pretty much speechless. Bing was a bit better, but overall our lack of language skills gave us a kind of enforced seclusion. The telephone was downstairs, in the kitchen where I worked with my laptop. Initially I'd had a terrible time trying to answer, until I learned the phrase *ne quittez pas*, which roughly means "don't hang up." Using that, with as convincing a French accent as I could muster, *I* would then hang up! Why not? I hadn't a clue what anybody said anyway. Accordingly our call count diminished.

The village was small. Only a few minutes walk in any direction put us beyond its once-walled boundaries and off into a lot of interesting places. To the east was La Montagne Noire itself: A 4,000-foot foothill to the Massif Central's 6,000-foot-high plateau. It offered great mountain bike trails with awesome views. There were also Roman ruins up there along with poisonous vipers lying in wait. What more could you want? (Actually we learned to bang hiking sticks against rocks and trees to scare the vipers off as we approached.)

A three-kilometer hike to the south (less than two miles) would take us to the next village, a precious but dark place tucked into a rocky vale leading to an ancient copper mine. Though the ancients were gone, several copper shops whispered of their time there. Moving west of town, as Bing started doing with regular daily walks, there were paths through fields pillared with huge sycamores, cows clustering beneath them, goats and sheep foraging nearby. To the north, ribbon-like country lanes wound into miles of what would be summer sunflower fields where Vincent Van Gogh probably once walked. Northwestward and beyond, fortified hillocks stood guard over it all, their steeples or *château* roofs shimmering in the crisp afternoon sun.

From our earliest walks on these roads we felt a living earth, and all that grew from it, reaching to embrace us, pulling us into the very heart of La Montage Noire. Never in the U.S. had I experienced such a powerful presence around me as here. Bing felt it too. Every day, my runs and her walks became a time of meditation, a bonding with another world we were discovering for the first time . . . together.

THERE WERE, of course, a few problems. Our first morning back from the boat, while I was in mid-shower (*douche*), the gas ran out (*eeeyow!*). Instant freeze. Throwing on some clothes but still goose-bumped and shivering, I trooped to the small grocery around the corner to swap our empty tank of propane for a full one.

"*Bonjour*," I opened confidently, eyes bright with anticipation though mouth dry and nearly empty of words beyond, "*Gaz, s'il vous plaît.*"

"*Bonjour, Monsieur. Je vois votre bouteille est orange mais notre service est bleu. Il faut aller à l'autre magasin par la fontaine. Leur gaz est rouge.*"

Hello.

I hadn't understood a word. What to do now? Then I thought of what Bing pulled off at the *café* our first day.

"*Oui*," I said.

All well and good, except for the dumb look on my face. Though my *oui* had made sense, my standing, shifting, and staring canceled that out. The clerk rolled her eyes, puffed one cheek and blew the air out that side as she got to her feet. She came around the counter, curling a finger for me to follow. We went through the front door, turned left, and walked the fifteen yards past the little bank to the corner, across from Claude's Café des Fleurs. I had the empty tank on my shoulder. From the corner, Sylvie, as I later learned was her name, pointed a long index finger up rue Basque toward the fountain. Clearly I was to walk up there to the smaller market to exchange my tank.

"*Merci beaucoup,*" I mumbled.

"*De rien, Monsieur. Et bon courage,*" she said with the slightest smile. (I sensed she wasn't totally writing me off.)

I started up the street, slowly, goose-bumps down, embarrassment up. I wasn't looking forward to my next language hassle. As I recall, it was Kermit the Frog who said it wasn't easy being green. He should have tried being a linguistically challenged American in France.

The mini-grocery man said, "*Bonjour Monsieur.*"

"*Bonjour,*" I said, taking the tank off my shoulder.

He smiled and said, "*Mais Monsieur, le réservoir manque le morceau du transport qui est aussi le garde de la valve.*"

Ummmm. Right.

He looked at me. I looked at him. Then he looked down at the tank standing between us. I did the same. The pressure was mounting for me to say something. Anything. But what?

"*Oui,*" I muttered thoughtfully.

"*Peut-être vous ne me comprenez pas. En tout cas, je vous donnerai un plein qui a aussi un garde.*"

After another painful pause I threw out another "*Oui.*"

"*Bien,*" he concluded and took my tank through a door in the back, returning with another. This one was different in two ways. It had a guard around the valve, which also doubled as the carrying handle. (*Eureka,* now I at least had a clue of what he had said.) And the thing weighed a ton, which told me more.

Fumbling through paying him, I lugged the tank out to the door, but was blocked by a little old lady pushing a wheelbarrow carrying another propane tank.

"*Bonjour messieurs,*" she said, nodding to both of us. We returned her greeting as she easily lifted her empty from the wheelbarrow, putting it on the floor in front of the proprietor and, without the slightest hesitation or strain, lifted mine into her barrow.

"*Allons,*" she said with an almost coquettish smile, and started back down rue Basque toward our house.

I looked at the mini-grocer. He smiled, shrugged, puffed a cheek, and did the familiar blow. I turned and hurried after her.

Everything was backward. I was supposed to help little old ladies, not the other way around. I'd been a Marine! (At the height of peace perhaps, but, damn it, a U.S. Marine nevertheless.) I had to jog to catch up. When I got beside her, all I could say was "*Oui. Merci, merci. Oui.*" (I really needed language work.)

At our door, I lifted the tank out of the wheelbarrow, smiled, and thanked her again. She tossed me a shrug with kind of a girl-ish grin (*sourire*), then headed back to the mini-market, a definite sashay to her walk. What a gal. Surprisingly enough, the next day Bing and I had to dodge the same octogenarian as she barreled down rue Basque on her 125cc Honda motorcycle! She was decked out in all the gear—helmet (*casque*), goggles (*lunettes*), another flapping blue skirt (*jupe*), and a big Evil Knievel grin!

IT WASN'T long before things fell into a rhythm. With few evening distractions we would read by the kitchen fire or go upstairs to snuggle under goose-down blankets. Early to bed led to the proverbial early to rise, the abbey tower bell announcing each hour and half hour. By 5:30 AM we were in motion. I'd go downstairs to check the Internet for how the world had fared while we slept, and Bing would stay upstairs to meditate. (Visiting Yoda, as I called it.) After my news fix, I'd start some tea water for Bing, get my coffee going, then walk to one of the three *patisseries*.

Early on, we discovered the crispiest bread and flakiest crois-sants were baked by a stolid, almost grumpy pair at their *bou-langerie/patisserie* across from Claude's *café* and whose names we never got. On the other hand, the least tasty bread and less flaky croissants were produced by a delightful young couple whose shop was just up by the fountain who immediately volunteered their names, Caroline and François. What to do? Nice bread or nice people? So we split the difference, one day here, the next there. And from time to time we'd finesse the whole issue by walking to the third *boulangerie* near the church that specialized in wood-fired *pain de campagne*, Bing's favorite.

One day I went up there, to the wood-fired place, and discovered the young *propriétaire* had decided to tie-dye his hair. His choice of colors was the real attention-getter. Platinum blonde on a field of blue with smudges of red here and there. My French being as undependable as it was, I tried to congratulate him on his new look, but I later learned it had come out *"Pretty colored horses on your head, my friend."*

As time went on, my performance with the fellow did not improve at all. Another morning, for example, the weather was especially rainy and cold. The cloud cover off La Montagne Noire pressed down on the village like an anvil, severely concentrating the glorious smell of his wood-fired croissants. My nose took over from my brain. I was led like a zombie directly to the shop of Pretty-Horses-on-Head.

I entered, but for the moment, found the place empty. *"Bonjour,"* I called. Then I heard some shuffling in the back room where the oven was.

"Bonjour Monsieur." The multicolored young man returned, carrying a load of bread and croissants on a tray. Unfortunately, as he swung around the counter, a small baguette dropped to the floor.

"Merde," he said. Which he repeated when I bent to help, bumping his colorful head with my gray one, and causing more of everything to fall to the floor.

My original problem—calling his hair *horses*—had been a

confusion of the word *chevaux* (horses) with *cheveux* (hair). I had been close, but this time he was doing the talking, and as usual I was not catching it all. As we were together on the floor picking up the dropped goods, he muttered, *"Merci bien, trou de balle."*

Naturally I understood the *merci bien* part, but I missed the significance of *trou de balle*. I did know *trou* meant hole and that *balle* was a ball, but I didn't know what they meant put together.

In keeping with my functional ignorance of his language, and trying to be an ambassador of American goodwill, I replied, *"Je vous en prie. Merci beaucoup. Vous êtes très aimable."* (You're welcome. Thank you very much. You are very kind.) To which he shook his head, puffed a cheek, and blew air out of the side of his mouth, like everyone seemed to do, and rolled his eyes. He then popped four fresh croissants into a bag and prodded me out the door.

The croissants were delicious. Then, as always, I settled down at the kitchen's back window with my laptop while Bing marched up two floors to her studio loft. From eight o'clock to noon we would work with amazing concentration. No interruptions, no telephone calls anymore. For lunch we'd have something simple, a salad or soup, then go back to work. About three, three-thirty, sometimes four o'clock, I'd lace up the Adidas for a 10K run. Bing would strap on her backpack filled with pad, pencils, and pastels for a hike to whatever venue she needed to sketch as a study for her latest canvas.

My daily runs would end at either Claude and Sophie's Café des Fleurs, or La Brasserie, owned and run by Michel, a French-man, with an English last name, Bond. A cool beer adjusted my depleted electrolytes on the one hand, while an effort to speak French hammered my ego on the other.

The afternoon of the day I knocked Pretty Horse's croissants onto the floor I'd had a decent jog and felt a little cocky about how I'd handled myself with the baker. I ordered my beer at Claude's, then stumbled through a recount of my adventure, making sure to mention I'd been referred to as a *trou de balle*. Claude gave me a knowing smile and then carefully explained, with the help of a book of vernacular translation, that I had been called an asshole. Which I found disappointing. However, Claude also pointed out, after another shuffle through the pages of his book, that even a little kid might be referred to as *un trou de balle*, so it didn't have the full negative force of the American expression. Then, he went on to show me that the American *asshole* in French was better expressed using the word for cunt! Oh my. What could I say? I left it with Claude that being called any level of asshole in any language was not the end of the world. All considered, he thought I'd taken it rather well and gave me a free refill for keeping my cool.

Generally we ate in. After dinner I would read to Bing what I'd written that day. I knew if I stumbled at all that the writing wasn't crisp. A basic proof-test. Bing, on the other hand, wouldn't show me her work until it was complete. Sometimes she would sneak me a preliminary sketch to look at, but little more. One time she put a series of still lifes she'd done on the mantle over the kitchen fireplace. They were extraordinary. Though only studies for other work, I honestly felt Cezanne would have traded his best brushes to have painted them. Bing is a hell of a talent.

SATURDAY MORNINGS the nearby town of Revel has its farmers' market. For that matter, most every town of size has a market day sometime during the week. Regionally they are staggered so not to interfere with each other.

Revel's is outstanding. The central market, roofed but otherwise open, is year round. We found it charming and practical, as such a market had to have been to run for a thousand years or more. The area under its great sloping tile roof had prime space reserved for the local farmers showing off their ducks, geese, rabbits, chickens, eggs, produce, and cheeses. Watching a cluster of these rustics was a sideshow in itself.

"Bing, check those old guys with the geese," I said, nodding to a cluster of five farmers. Each had something hanging from his mouth—a hand-rolled cigarette, a wet drooping cigar, or a gnarly old pipe. They wore either high brown rubber boots or rundown clodhoppers. Bib overalls with heavy, nondescript jackets covered their good-sized farm bellies.

"Watch what happens when the customer looking at the ducks gets near them."

As the man approached, the gent with the pipe tapped the nearest goose on its butt with his foot. A barrage of *squawk, squawk, squawk*s filled the air as the others joined in, the whole lot flopping around as best they could, tied as they were, but certainly all looking very healthy.

Then Bing let out one of those long *aaawww*s. "Kenny," she said, "look at the bunnies in the boxes, and the children around them."

A whole crowd of little kids squatted down on their heels, hunched over, tickling and petting the rabbits. So cute. Precious. Though I had difficulty not thinking that most of those bunnies would be someone's dinner by nightfall.

Staying under the *marché*'s big roof, Bing and I would buy our cheeses, small veggies, and baked goods from the mom & pops there. Our hearts ached for the elderly couples in their worn clothes who set up shaky card tables, spread cloths or newspaper over them, and carefully laid out their meager collections for sale. One couple we always looked for had as few as six plump tomatoes, a few garlic bulbs, some leeks, a cabbage, and maybe two dozen eggs on their table. They'd sit on their rickety chairs, eyes wide and hopeful, looking for someone who knew quality and the worth of their labor. So few francs changed hands, but each that did would be handled thankfully, almost reverently, as it was put into a battered cigar box by the wife while her husband slipped the purchases into a sack their croissants had been carried in the day before. As the few things laid out became fewer still, their eyes twinkled and their smiles broadened. When all was gone, they were satisfied. They'd had a good day. For Bing and me, it had been an even better day buying from them and being a part of their small success.

Out from under the roof were the lorries (*camion*) and vans of the itinerant professionals who spent their lives driving market to market, shopping fish (*poisson*), meat (*viande*), oysters (*huitres*), olives (*olives*), cheeses (*fromages*), herbs (*herbes*), flowers (*fleurs*), chicken (*poulet*), duck (*canard*), as well as fruits (*fruits*) and vegetables (*legumes*) so fresh the scents alone made our mouths water.

In time we came to have our favorite vendors. There was one olive seller who never failed to unload on us twice what we needed or wanted. He had such flair and a boyish, devilish smile, we couldn't resist. He introduced us to regional tastes we'd otherwise never have known, so what the heck. I also got along with a butcher, a large brisk character who'd wink at my feigned military salute as I'd bark my order in mock response to his soldierly parading up and down behind his counter. His protruding chin, mustache, and grand-elegant Gallic nose was raised high as if to distance the wondrous device from possible damage caused by the odor of plebeian shoppers pressing against his cases.

BING COULD never get past an herb lady's caravan of spices, potions, and potpourris of scents *extraordinaire.* The woman could have been off the set of *Les Miserables.* Once beautiful, now at least attractive, with a harried, almost wolfish elegance, she moved restlessly back and forth behind her trays. Eyes darting, long fingers flashing to snatch and bag the items indicated before a customer could change her mind. The lady was a pro in a hard line of work. Yet when Bing stood at her counter, she slowed to help with a sisterly air. Her day was short, its profit window small, but she'd slow her pace for *l'Americaine,* gently smiling as she used simpler words to explain a product's value. I'd watch the process, creating stories in my mind of her secret past—*carrying contraband through Basque mountain passes; a long-ago lover with his yacht anchored near Monaco; the pilot who had left her; the daughter who'd died in her arms* . . . My gut told me her life had been filled with wrenching tragedy. Had I a sword I'd have drawn it on her behalf.

The market plaza was ringed with regular shops whose only part in Saturday morning's events was to put tables of sale items in front of their windows. But outside that central square, a few blocks beyond where the old walls had once been, larger caravans, flatbeds, and side-opening lorries aligned themselves end to end, displaying their shoes, clothing, tools, glassware, bedding, books, curtains, tablecloths, everything for house, body, or mind. Extraordinary offerings. Great walks. Fun shopping.

Our first market day had been warm and led to a Montagne Noire hike, complete with a knapsack of cheese, fresh bread, olives, apples, 750cc's of Tarn Valley wine, and a couple of chunks of awesome nut-filled chocolate—*au lait* for me, *noire* for Bing.

From the village, La Montagne Noire itself looked a bit wimpy, considering our Appalachian and Rocky Mountain roots. Once we started up the old cart tracks, however, our respect grew. Steeper and steeper the double ruts pitched till they whispered off to little more than a grassy path of slippery switchbacks. About halfway to the top we passed some ruins, what looked to have been a cluster of houses, perhaps a tiny village, centuries old. Sadly, now the only remains were a cluster of roofless walls, empty doorways, haunting window openings choked with vines, tree limbs growing through them.

The high reaches of the ridge had several peaks. The first was edged with a cliff that plunged to the neighboring village of copper and brass shops below. Over the next crest was a cave, reputed to have been a hiding place for Partisans fighting the Nazis in World War II. We later saw confirmation of their resistance etched on the town hall walls of several nearby villages— weathered lists of names, each with its specific fate—incarceration, torture, execution by firing squad, or deportation to death camps. Nazis' lists meant to intimidate and terrify. History's lists to identify and glorify.

Further along our path were traces of Roman and Visigoth hamlets. We later learned that much of Black Mountain's building stone came from these ruins, rolled down to the village from above and used again to rebuild the abbey tower, town walls, and bridges.

Despite the calendar saying it was winter, the bright sun was calling for spring. Taking advantage of the sudden warmeth, Bing and I spread a cloth on the highest outcropping, settling down for a bite, to relax, perhaps even snooze. The views were marvelous. The vast expanse of fields to the north with their sprinkling of châteaux-topped hillocks made our eyes dance. Another ridge to the west offered a sun-sparkled lake, man-made we later learned, built in the late 1600s to feed water to the Canal du Midi. Southwest of that, the Pyrenees rose like a wall of white, while to the east, vast forests swept to the high Massif Central. From our small perch, the view eastward with its forested ridges was wilder than we had expected, surprisingly like that of my beloved Vermont.

The food, wine, and warmth brought on a drowsiness relieved only by the surprising event taking shape below, down the ridge, starkly visible over Bing's shoulder. *Eh bien,* before my inquiring eyes I was witnessing explicit confirmation of America's idea of France's sexual liberation. Two other hikers, a man and a woman, had topped the lower crest. They were athletic, with tanned legs and arms, each wearing khaki shorts, despite the chill, and white tee shirts . . . but only briefly. Before I could say "French kiss" the two stripped to the buff, fell into each other's arms, and started getting it on!

What to do? For the sake of propriety, Bing and I elected to wait a bit before we started down. Neither of us felt we had the language skills to deal with two people so aggressively naked. Even in English we'd have been challenged. What would be appropriate?

"Nice day, nipples too." Or, "Got a name for the big fella?" Maybe, "Which way to the monastery?" Then again, just a Rocky Mountain "Hi!" probably would have been enough.

SEVEN

THE KNOCK ON THE DOOR

As CONCERNED as we'd first been with telephone calls, the threat of someone knocking on our door took on an even more frightening life of its own. I was the one working downstairs, at the table in the kitchen with its view of the tiny courtyard. That meant if we did get a knock, I would have to deal with it. Each day my paranoia grew. What would I do when it happened? *Ne quitter pas* had worked with the phone. How about the line I recalled from an old love song, *allez vous-en* (go away), would that work? It seemed to make sense, but again, slamming the door in someone's face could be interpreted as a bit harsh. I had to think of something. The knock would come.

I prepared like modern athletes do. I tried mentally walking myself through the event, step by step. I *conceptualized*. First—

the knock. Okay, open the door. Do I peek around it or pull the sucker open wide like a man? Do I say *bonjour*, or stand silent? But, and a big *but* at that, no matter how or what I did, there would be someone standing there waiting to say something to me, something I probably would not understand at all.

And the day did come, on a Thursday morning.

KNOCK! KNOCK!

Panic! I was in front of my computer, frozen, cursor flashing, jaw slammed shut. I had to get a grip. Okay, I'd run this through my mind a million times. Now it was just a matter of doing it.

I got to my feet. *KNOCK*. I stood straight and took a step. *KNOCK*. Several more steps . . . to the door; where I paused to collect myself. Yes. I reached for the doorknob. What next? Things were moving too fast. But I was a man of action, damn it. Firmly I swung the door fully open (no wimpy half-shit), to see two people, a man and a woman, standing, a bit wide-eyed, staring at me. Now what?

I tried *"Bonjour,"* keeping *oui* in reserve.

"Bonjour, Monsieur. Je m'appelle Jean-Jacques Kurtz. Ma femme Laila et moi souhaitons vous accueillir à la Montagne Noire."

Not to be intimidated by whatever the hell had been said, I . . . ah, stood my ground. In silence. Mouth slightly agape.

Then, from the mouth of an angel, came "Would English be better?"

Thank you God.

"Oui," I offered, a hair out of sync.

"Have you been here long, in the village I mean?" the man asked with a smile and a rather charmingly elevated left eyebrow.

"Ah, yes. Perhaps, no," I stumbled. What was the matter with me? "I mean, my wife Bing, who is an artist and is upstairs working in her studio right now, and I . . . I am a writer . . . we arrived a couple of weeks ago." Why did I have to give so damned much information? Why do we Americans tell too much about our-selves to anyone who will listen?

"If you have a moment," he said with a smile, "Laila and I would like to speak with you about the Bible."

Though Bing and I were active in our church at home, my first reaction to Jean-Jacques' announcement was a non-Biblical, "Oh shit." I admit that seemed somewhat judgmental, but religious door-knockers make me nervous. And now, here in our little French hideaway, a pair of them had sniffed us out. Even worse, other than Pierre and Marie-Claude, and Adrian on the barge, they were the only people we'd met who spoke English and didn't just point at pages in a book. I felt trapped, but stepped aside any-way. Fumbling a bit, I got them to the sofa and called up to Bing to come meet our visitors.

English eased the way for us all. Bing and I explained that we had reasonable scriptural backgrounds and came from traditions of tolerance. Interestingly, not long after that, Jean-Jacques and Laila moved the conversation from their door-to-door ministry to how we felt about the village.

"It's wonderful," Bing said. "The people are so open and help-ful. We get all tangled up with our French, but they only chuckle as they try to untie the knots."

"I've never had too much trouble in France, even in Paris," I added, fibbing horribly. "I work hard on pronunciation. There's an old wives' tail that says you folks don't care what somebody says or does, just how they pronounce it. The brutal American accent is a problem for Parisian ears. Avoiding it seems to make a difference."

Jean-Jacques nodded and Laila smiled. His accent said he was French, while Laila looked vaguely Middle Eastern. When she spoke French, however, she sounded rather American. Great.

We were delighted the Kurtzes had found us. Once comfort-able in our living room, they were chatty and fun. By the time

Jean-Jacques and Laila got up to leave, we knew quite a bit about them too. He was from northeastern France, on the German boarder. Laila was originally from Iraq, of all places. She was born a Muslim but was introduced to Christianity by a Bible she found on an airplane. She'd read it several times. When her family learned of this her father was so upset he demanded she repent publicly or face a religious trial that could have led to her death. She ran away. First to America, where she was hunted down and given a warning by her brother, then to England, and finally to France, where she met and married Jean-Jacques. Jean-Jacques told us he'd spent a year in prison as a conscientious objector. They were both committed Jehovah's Witnesses.

Their stories were gripping stuff. Bing and I were fascinated. We were eager to know Jean-Jacques and Laila Kurtz better. They promised they'd have us to their home for dinner. We were delighted and looked forward to it.

EIGHT

FROM FLOWERS TO FIRES

T HE NEXT Saturday we were surprised to bump into Jean-Jacques and Laila at the farmers' market. Taking advantage of their English, we told them about Adrian and his situation. We hadn't gotten callbacks from the messages we left on Adrian's machine, so we assumed he hadn't found his son. We were worried. Jean-Jacques and Laila understood but explained that even if we traced his wife and daughter to a hospital, not being family, they wouldn't give us any information or let us talk to them. It was frustrating, but as Jean-Jacques said, "You can only do what you can do."

After saying goodbye and having them take their English away with them, I fell back into my discouraging struggle with French.

"Kenny, the main thing is we are *trying*. People here appreciate that."

"Easy for you to say," I said. "You're a lot better at understanding what's going on than I am."

"That never stops you from speaking your mind," she said. "Sometimes though you come up with answers that have nothing to do with the questions. You're like politicians on TV. To heck with the question, here's what I'm going to say. But you *sound* good. Your accent, and sometimes even the grammar. Your only problem is . . . content."

"Thank you for your support," I said with an edge of irritation.

"Oh come on," Bing chided, bumping me with her hip. "I get so nervous trying to speak, sometimes I just give up. Maybe we're the perfect team. I receive, you transmit."

"Whatever," I said, leaving it at that.

Everyday we did improve a little. At home we had tapes and wherever we went we carried our trusty dictionaries. I had a Hugo pocket job. Michel at La Brasserie wondered if it was one of Chairman Mao's little red books because it was quite small and red. Claude at the Café des Fleurs, a confirmed Trotskyite, assumed it was and thought better of me for it.

The next Monday, more English speakers entered our lives. Hallelujah! We'd come out our front door just before noon and found two people standing on the sidewalk as if they'd been waiting for us to appear. The first to speak, and happily in English, was a woman who introduced herself as Trakya. We later learned she was Turkish, but with her blue eyes and streaky brown hair, we were surprised. With her super complexion and petit but very feminine figure, she was an unusually pretty young lady. We noted that her English was pretty good as she introduced Anton, her stiff-appearing husband.

"Ah hah, *Anton*," Bing nodded, her eyes rolling in my direction to see if I'd picked up on the name.

At first I looked back at her quizzically, then I said, smiling, "Anton, you are the man who knows everything and can do everything."

"I *am* Austrian," he replied.

Bing had to turn away to hide her amusement.

"Of course," I said, causing Bing's shoulders to shake even harder.

"Trakya," Bing recovered, "Brie told us about you and Anton when we first arrived. I think we have things pretty well sorted out so far. Ken replaced one of the gas tanks. Otherwise we've had no problems."

"You will," Anton said without elaboration. Odd duck, I thought.

"If you don't mind," Bing said, going to her purse and pulling out her notepad and tiny black pen, "could we have your telephone number in case something does come up?"

"05 73 63 16 21," Anton replied, efficiently but without much poetry.

"We came to invite you to our house for dinner," Trakya said, head down but looking up into our faces. She was very charming in a schoolgirl way.

"Tomorrow," Anton chimed in.

"Seven o'clock, if you can," Trakya added.

"That would be wonderful," Bing said. "What can we bring and where is your house?"

"Past the abbey. Small bridge. End of road," Anton explained.

Wow, I thought, tomorrow night should be chock-a-block full of scintillating conversation with this guy.

"What can we bring?" Bing repeated.

"We have everything we need," Trakya said. "Just having you visit will be wonderful."

"You are very kind," Bing said. "We look forward to tomorrow night."

The next evening we set out for their place at six-thirty. We
didn't know how long the walk would take and we didn't want to
be late, not yet attuned to the general French propensity for being
late. Then, as we passed the Abbey and crossed the small bridge
Anton had mentioned, Bing put her hand on my arm and pulled
me to a stop.

"We don't have a gift," she said. "I forgot to get something."

"Trakya said we didn't need to bring anything."

"That's not the issue. We *have* to bring something. It's disrespectful not to."

"Bing, please, Trakya was very specific about it. Maybe here it
would be disrespectful ignoring what she said. Besides, it's quarter to seven. What could we find now? And even if we did find
something somewhere, we'd probably be late getting to their
house," I said, wrapping myself in reasonableness.

"I am walking back to Sylvie's grocery for some flowers. You
go on."

"Oh come on, Bing, that would be ridiculous. You go on and *I'll*
go for the flowers."

"I know flowers," she said, turning and striding back across the
bridge.

Damn. Bing could be tough. Sweet too. But still, tough.

I fell in behind, irritated. As we trudged along, retracing our
steps back past La Brasserie and on down rue Basque, it occurred
to me that Bing had come into my life little more than two years
earlier. Now we were married and still coping with leftovers—
Bobbye's death and Bing's divorce, all the company bankruptcies
I'd weathered, long-term failure as a writer, selling our respective
homes. While our "new" lives move on, we still feel and deal with
our pasts, even as new pressures are added. And on top of all that,
we had Adrian's problems and this whole language exercise. On
anybody's stress meter, we were probably topping out. But we
were doing well. Only a few rubs here and there, like forgetting

something at the last minute and reversing course. Oh how I hated having to turn around. It was probably a pilot thing. After take-off, you fly to your destination. Period.

I paid for the flowers, but that didn't qualify me to carry them. I was getting more irritated. I tried to think about something else as we re-retraced our steps past La Brasserie, over the bridge for *the third time*, and finally up the dirt lane to Trakya and Anton's stone farmhouse.

"Now we are late," I said, knowing I should have let it go.

"Kenny, you're getting paranoid. Relax," she said. "We aren't in New York City."

I hate to hear "relax," but I managed to keep my mouth shut.

When we got to the door it was clear nobody was worrying about the clock. Several guests were already there, but a couple of cars were coming up the lane as we rang the bell. Only *then* did Bing hand me the flowers.

"It's the man's job," she half whispered as Trakya appeared smiling and presented both her cheeks for the French hello.

"Two touches," she bubbled. "In Mazamet they double that. Four for each hello. I went to a wedding there last year and I thought it would take all night to get through the reception line."

Nodding, I held out the flowers.

"No, no, no, Bing. I said no gifts . . . but they *are* very pretty. Thank you. I will put them in a vase on the dining room table," she said, her eyes wandering to the other guests coming down the path from their cars. She left me holding the bouquet.

"I'll do that for you," Bing said to Trakya, taking the flowers back from me. I felt vaguely robotic.

Ducking into the living room behind Bing, the first thing that struck me was the rush of different languages coming at us. First German, from their daughter and Anton. Then she spoke French to some other kids, followed by English to us. By then, Anton was chatting in Polish to a newly arrived young man from Warsaw, then switching to Turkish with his mother-in-law, and back to German with his daughter. Another couple chatted in what sounded like German but we learned was Dutch. I felt like the village idiot gazing up in wonder at the Tower of Babel. But this tower worked. Despite all the languages, I found that laughs, gestures, even hand signals helped bridge the gaps. It turned out to be an extraordinary evening, especially for Bing and me. Great food, delicious wines, open hearts. Even though everything around us was so different, we actually felt warm and at home.

SOON AFTER that party, Pierre and Marie-Claude called from Paris to say they were driving down to visit their son and his family in Toulouse. They wanted to spend a few days in Black Mountain with us, if possible, to see how we were holding up. We were delighted. But their stay would have its dark side too. They announced they would speak as much French with us as we could handle. "Tough love," they explained. The idea was to get us up to speed with the language as quickly as possible for whatever plans we might have for the future.

Then the weather turned really cold. Before leaving Connecticut we'd been told Black Mountain had dependably mild winters. Hah.

The morning of their arrival we woke up to frost on our windows, inside and out. And snow on the high ridges behind the village. With no central heating or, for that matter, nothing but the one kitchen fireplace, we could be in for trouble. In the bedrooms, blankets and heavy-duty snuggling would be the rule. The kitchen fireplace could handle part of the downstairs, but what about the third floor and the rest of the house? I figured we'd have to give all the fireplaces a shot if the cold snap didn't let up. There was no way we could have guests in a meat locker like this.

Throughout the morning the temperature continued to drop. The snow worked its way from the hills down to rue Basque.

What little wood we had had was now gone. Who ever thought spring would be winter? We'd have to get hold of Anton. After an icy breakfast, Bing and I hustled back to his house to buy a load.

In Yogi Berra French, the whole process became *déjà vu all over again.* We hadn't noticed it the night before, but near their small barn was a long stack of moss-covered gnarly wood. As I started to park the car clear of Anton's trailer, Bing hopped out to open negotiations without me. I was a little surprised. By the time I was out of the car, Bing was already handing Anton a bunch of francs.

"We're all set, Kenny. Anton will hook up his trailer, then we can load a cord," she said, taking charge, giving my feathers a ruffle. I didn't say anything, just stood watching while she guided Anton as he backed up to the wood. Then, before I could get myself into gear, she was throwing wood into the trailer, without gloves. All I could do was roll my eyes and pitch in by her side.

With the three of us working, the job was finished in minutes. We drove the two cars back to rue Basque. Bing rode with Anton. Hmm.

While they carried the wood through our house at number 10 and stacked it in the back courtyard, I started building a fire in the kitchen fireplace. Then Bing walked Anton to the door and waved goodbye.

"I've had it," I announced, putting more into the statement than Bing probably understood. "We've got to get heat into the rest of the house. Pierre and Marie-Claude are on their way. Icicles on the bed boards are unacceptable. They can't sleep in the kitchen. I'm firing up all the fireplaces."

"Kenny, please. You know what Brie said about not using the other fireplaces," Bing answered.

"Screw it," I said, "we need heat."

I piled a stack of wood on the living room hearth, built a Boy Scout's teepee of faggots over old newspaper directly under the flu. There was a good draft. We would have a good fire. Setting a trusty *allumette* to the teepee, I smiled as it caught. Fingers of flame ran up the kindling. I added handfuls of twigs to help the fire grow. In short order we had a real blaze. American ingenuity at work.

Rising, chest puffing a bit, I smiled condescendingly to Bing on the sofa.

"How's that?" Ripples of warmth were already spreading across the chilly tile floor toward her slippered feet.

"So far so good," she said as I piled a few medium sized logs on my rising inferno. The heat was great. Straightening out a nasty situation was great. I felt great. Yes, I was back in familiar territory, getting the job done. Man stuff.

"Don't use the other fireplaces, hah," I chortled, brushing the wood fragments off my shirt. "The whole house is going to be warm as toast by the time Pierre and Marie-Claude get here."

"Let's hope."

"Hey, give me a break. I *know* what I'm doing," I said, taking more wood to the stairway to fire up the bedrooms.

IT TOOK about an hour for the excitement to begin. We heard loud *whee whaa, whee whaa*s, first in the distance, then closer and closer yet. Finally there was a lot of diesel clatter on the street outside. I thought it might be the delivery truck for the minimarket up by the fountain. Damn, what day was it? Had we left the top shutters open? Peeking through the front curtains, all I could see was a wall of red. What the hell?

"Bing, something big is going on out here. Come take a look," I said, curious and a touch excited.

She slip-slopped in her fuzzy slippers to my side at the window, but couldn't make out much more than what I had. I reached over and opened the door. We both stepped out.

The wall of red was actually the side of a huge *voiture des pompiers* (a fire engine) filling the street with a team of firemen busying themselves opening panels, pulling on hoses, blowing whistles, and peering up through the thick layer of smoke hanging over rue Basque. Bing and I looked up. Wow. Smoke was rolling out of our neighbor's second-floor windows . . . and from the spaces between *our* shutters too. I'd been ready to say something smart like, "That turkey sure didn't know how to manage *his* fire," but seeing the smoke coming from our windows too, I amended it to "Oh shit."

We rushed back inside and up the stairs. The fire in the bedroom fireplace was just getting underway, its smoke going up the flue (like good smoke should); but there was also some seeping from below through the hearth (bad smoke). The flu from the living room must have breaks that let smoke crawl under the bedroom floor, up through this hearth, and into the neighbor's apartment. The bedroom fireplace was probably doing much the same to the floor above. Oh man, why hadn't I paid attention to what Brie had said? Or even heard the questioning in Bing's voice when I spouted off about warming the house?

Wet towels from the bathroom stopped the flow into our bedroom. We each threw windows open, then rushed downstairs to the kitchen. Bing grabbed two metal spatulas and a huge roasting pan. I snatched up the dustpan and a pail from the closet where the propane tanks lived. She charged back upstairs while I ran to the living room fireplace and started shoveling the smaller burning stuff into the pail. I assumed Bing was doing the same above. I sped back to the kitchen and threw my pail of embers into the one good fireplace there.

To the living room again for the partially burned logs. I nearly knocked Bing over as she came flying down the stairs with the roasting pan full of smoldering embers also bound for the kitchen. What a drill. We were both sweaty and puffing. The only difference in our demeanors was the expression on her face that shouted, "*J'accuse*," while mine muttered, "Guilty as charged."

Now that the source of the problem (by that I mean the *combustible* source, not the human source) had been identified, removed, and allowed our breathing to return to normal, we walked into the street to see where things stood with the fire department and the neighbor's house—which was still giving out the odd wisp of smoke, though not *belching* like before. The firemen, apparently used to these situations in ancient houses, were dealing with things comfortably and systematically. They'd gone into our place as we came out, and into next door too. Fortunately they didn't have to use hoses in either, and once they'd made a run through, checking that nothing more was burning in our offending fireplaces, word seemed to pass in the street that *les Americans* were no longer a threat to Black Mountain—nor, for that matter, to themselves.

The next bit of good news was that we got to meet our neighbor. You might say we'd smoked him out. His looks gave me a scare. As things calmed down and the firemen were exiting his place, he was being assisted by the last two. He was an old fellow, hunched over and unsteady on his feet. His face was covered with soot; one rheumy eye looking questioningly about while the other was closed tight. His jaw was scrunched against his left shoulder like he expected a punch was coming his way. Which made me feel even worse for what I'd done. And, being an American, I prayed the old gentleman was not a lawyer.

Surprisingly, nobody else seemed to pay his appearance any attention. Nor did he act particularly troubled by the events when I walked over to him and offered my hand and my apology. He didn't resist the handshake, nodded to my "*Je suis très désolé,*" then eased himself free of me and the firemen, gave a perfunctory wave of the hand, and set off down the street to the Claude's *café*.

As the prime perpetrator of these events, I felt obligated to thank the firemen for their help, the village for not lynching me, Bing for not leaving me, and our neighbor for not having the police haul me off to the Bastille. Of course, trying to deal with so much guilt in a foreign language made it all the more daunting. As best I could, I explained to the *pompiers* that our son-in-law is a fireman in Vermont, one of our states, with French roots. They warmed to this, but declined my offered of *pastis*, the hard drinker's choice, in honor of our common bond. They had to get their equipment back to the firehouse.

The chief smiled with a *"peut-être la prochaine fois"* (maybe next time), as he climbed up into the cab of the huge red truck.

Anton, having followed the sirens, was now by my side. He'd already been briefed about the situation by the firemen and passed their directives on to me. He asked me if I understood everything.

"Oui," I answered firmly.

Was I sure?

"Oui."

Any questions?

"Oui, I mean no. Honest, trust me. I got it all, Anton," I said adamantly. "Tell the nice man I understand everything and will never do such a stupid thing again."

"Yes, I will tell him of your regret, but I will not use the word for stupid. Frenchmen never admit to such things. Trust me."

"Good idea. Thank you. *Oui."*

When all was said and done, we'd dodged one bullet, but another was still headed our way. How to keep Pierre and Marie-Claude from freezing to death during their stay? What to do? Then Trakya showed up with the answer. She dropped off blankets, gloves and scarves, and two electric space heaters! God bless friends who really did know how cold it could get in Black Mountain, even in the winter.

IN LINGUISTIC self-defense, we'd invited Jean-Jacques and Laila to join with us and Pierre and Marie-Claude for dinner. Laila spoke even less French than we did, it turned out, so the evening would have to be in English. Yeah! We had been running into them occasionally, having good chats and laughs over coffee at Café des Fleurs or a glass of wine at our place or theirs. Oddly enough, we never seemed to get back to discussing the Bible.

Over *aperitifs* and a scrumptious dinner served in the toasty kitchen, Pierre went on at length about France's archaic prison system and how, in retirement, he was involved with trying to reform it. He told us of the men, the prisoners, he'd worked with who had come out of the most destitute slums as street kids; no parents, no schooling beyond that of those streets, and the horrendous crimes such upbringing often led to. He told how he'd helped start in-prison schooling, counseling, religious studies, any number of programs designed to turn things around.

Then Jean-Jacques told them of his experience in prison as a conscientious objector, over France's Algerian war. He affirmed all Pierre said.

As Bing and I cleared the table and the last of the *digestif* was sipped, our conversation moved to the issue of Jean-Jacques and Laila's church being one of those designated a cult by the French government. Huge taxes could be levied against them. And for those who already had prison records, like Jean-Jacques, more jail time could be in the offing if he couldn't pay what was designated as his share of the new taxes on the entire church. It was like something out of the Middle Ages or the Inquisition.

What Bing and I found most interesting in all this was how such a free-ranging discussion of religion could be so open and ecumenical. Interestingly, Jean-Jacques, a man who had already been subject to religious oppression, concluded his part in the discussion with, "If ever I am wrong in my understanding of man's relationship with God and how I should pursue my faith . . . I want to know it. All I ask is for Scripture to be laid before me showing that to be the case." A statement that months later would play a large part in the disintegration of our friendship.

Pierre, one of the two Catholics in the room, concluded gently with, "There are many roads leading to God's kingdom. It is not important which we take; it is only that the road we do choose is one that actually leads there . . . and we walk it with grace."

Bing, with her Quaker roots, added, "We hold thee in the light."

All things considered, it could have been a very cold evening indeed. Not just from the night's chill, but from the divergence of backgrounds each of us brought to the table. Yet it didn't work out that way. I thought some profound things had been said. Jean-Jacques and Pierre both seemed directly engaged in life's challenges, not just observers on the sidelines. And their wives were with them all the way.

Thinking back on it, with Bing's food, that one warm hearth, and good cheer in all our hearts, the evening couldn't have gone better . . . despite how it had begun.

As the candles burned down, Bing concluded the evening with a smiling "*Bonne nuit.*"

I reached across the table for her hand. I was so grateful she was in my life.

NINE

⚜

BREBIS AND *FRAMBOISE*

T HE NEXT day, Pierre, Marie-Claude, Bing, and I drove up and across La Montagne Noire to the southwestern toe of the six-thousand-foot craggy plateau known as the Massif Central. We'd had in mind to explore a bit, as well as try to locate the farm supplying a special *brebis* (sheep cheese) we'd found at the *marché* the previous Saturday.

Over breakfast we told our friends about a particular farmer selling the cheese. Quite the fellow. Tall, mustached, hazel-eyed, he looked straight out of a Hollywood studio. Seriously. He'd worn a black woolen cape and a matching *chapeau gaucho laine*, a floppy-brimmed cowboy hat made of wool. He looked very fit, *très chic*. Which didn't hurt his business any. The few kilos of *brebis* he'd stacked on his wobbly card table had gone quickly as a steady stream of younger women stopped to add his product to their baskets.

"This guy could have been d'Artagnan with the Three Muske-teers," I mumbled, "and he paid a lot of attention to Bing. I didn't understand much of what came out of his mouth, but he said a lot with his eyes. He was really checking her out."

"Oh Kenny," Bing said, pouring Marie-Claude and Pierre more tea and rolling her beautiful blue eyes.

"He couldn't get his business card into your hand fast enough," I added. "And he made darn sure you turned it over to see the map to his place on the back. He wanted *you* to visit him . . . and *me* to visit the sheep and goats."

"You're probably right," Bing said, fluffing her hair. "He *was* cute, Marie-Claude. I think he's worth a ride up onto the mountain."

Our drive was eye-opening. We'd had no idea the mountain was so high, or the Massif Central so much higher still. It was heavily wooded. Two hundred years earlier, Pierre told us, the region had been far more populated, but in the last century it lost hundreds of thousands of people to the cities and to war. Seeing so much of nature springing up where people and farms had once been gave me an eerie sense of an inexorable return of the wild. Steven King stuff—the forest beaten down by man was coming back to encircle and entrap those who had tried to kill it.

Bing's map showed the farm in the center of a triangle formed by the towns of Mazamet, Angles, and a place named La Bastide. *Bastides*, by the way, were the product of two hundred years of war between England and France throughout the region. Towns would be created, mostly laid out in block form with defensive walls around them, and then friendly populations would be trans-ported in to farm and form a base of support for the English or French army dominating the area. That explains why many totally French families bore English names. Michel Bond, owner of La Brasserie in Black Mountain was a case in point. At midday, still bumping along, we saw a sign for La Cuisine de Ferme, The Farm Kitchen, not our destination but a place open for lunch and dinner. It seemed a good idea to stop for a bite. Why risk an encounter with the handsome cheese fellow and his nanny goats or black sheep on empty stomachs?

We turned off our little road onto one even less traveled. Jostling over its grassy traces, we wondered how anyone could run a business so far into nowhere. Finally we caught sight of some smoke curling above the next rise. Topping that, we were relieved to see a stone-sided, slate-roofed gem of a house nestled next to a pond. La Cuisine de Ferme.

Pierre did the talking. *Merci Dieu.* But even he had trouble penetrating the local accent with its Spanish roots and metallic twang of the Tarn. We were shown into the dining room, probably a living room originally. There was only one person seated there at the moment, a straight-laced fellow sitting bolt upright wearing a gray three-piece suit with white shirt and soiled tie. His downcast eyes were busy guiding his knife and fork noisily around his plate. The clatter and the focus told me he was British. (My years as a pilot, dining throughout the world, gave me a feel for national types at table.) Cutlery in English hands is noisy. American mouths the same. The French, on the other hand, treat restaurants with the hushed respect due libraries and cathedrals everywhere else.

Taking a chair next to the wall at the fireplace end of the room, I found another guest we'd first missed. Wearing a smartly appointed white (unstained) bib (supplied by Mother Nature), busy with a bread crust, was a self-possessed mouse (*une souris*). I knew Marie-Claude was not a mouse person, so I was circumspect about the little fellow. He seemed content and not particularly interested in joining our table anyway.

After ordering, Marie-Claude went to the WC. About five minutes later she returned with a breathless bit of news. "There was a mouse in the toilette. Not in the water, in the room," she clarified. "While I was . . . occupied," she said, her violet eyes popping embarrassedly up and away. "I noticed him sitting looking at me. He sat and I sat. He wasn't frightened in the least, just interested. Even when I went to the sink he continued to watch."

I glanced down at his friend by the baseboard. He looked up with what seemed a nod, then returned to his munching.

Everyone's meal was wonderful. Everyone's but mine. Though the *foie gras* was superb, bread magnificent, local rosé light and delightful, my main course was like leather. Marie-Claude and Pierre had excellent roast duck. Bing and I had wild hare. She enjoyed her leg and haunch very much. I got the back or butt. I couldn't say for sure what part it was—unchewable and loaded with, of all things, buckshot.

The *propriétaire*, a very informal fellow, invited himself to sit with us for a glass of wine. He said his summer campsite rentals did very well since his was the only eating place for kilometers around.

"As a matter of fact," he added, nodding toward the other diner, "some summer people just stay on. That fellow came here from Sussexshire two years ago. He told me he was so charmed by the area he couldn't leave. Think of that."

WE FOUND the cheese farm, but we didn't find d'Artagnan, only his lady. And a lot of lady she was. Solid and strong, pretty much like a Maginot Line cannon. No wonder d'Artagnan found Bing interesting.

Pierre's Parisian French seemed a mystery to her and of little interest. She turned her back on us and strode into the barn. She was the first and perhaps only person throughout our time in the Lauragais who blew us off, but remember, the person doing our talking was from Paris.

Back at Black Mountain there was a note slipped under our

door from Jean-Jacques and Laila. There had been horrendous mudslides at Carcassonne and they'd put together a team of their church people to go help. We later learned they had been the first relief workers into the area, well ahead of any from the government. Jean-Jacques set up a tent kitchen to feed the workers along with the people impacted by the slides. The others of their team, about ninety strong, went door to door shoveling out mud, cleaning up and repairing whatever had to be repaired.

The locals in Carcassonne were doubly amazed. First, that anyone got to them so quickly, and also that the team refused any payment. They'd explained they were Christians. Their reward would come later and elsewhere. All of which was ironic: A group singled out to be hit by the government was first to help the government.

It had been a long day. We were tired, so rather than rustle up a dinner in the cold house, we opted to walk to La Brasserie for dinner. A jazz group was playing. Good food and good music seemed the easy way to end our busy day. As we walked past the fountain and across town, the sun was tucking down for the night. Long shadows were folding over the buildings, the fading light set off the raspberry-colored exterior of a lovely house on the village's second and quietest square. We hadn't noticed it before. LA MAISON FRAMBOISE read the small plaque over the doorbell. And just above that was a white card announcing—*A VENDRE*. For sale! That set our minds wandering.

"Oh my goodness," Bing said, stopping. She reached to take my hand. We'd both been hit. Together we backed into the street, looking up at the tall raspberry façade smiling down at us. Pierre and Marie-Claude cocked their heads questioningly.

"Three stories," Bing muttered, looking up to the left, right, and back again. "Kenny, it even has a small garage in the front. And there's shop space on the corner. Perfect for a studio/gallery? And ooh, look, a garden in the rear. Oh heavens, Kenny, the house looks in perfect condition. For long stays or renting when we weren't here. I mean it's got . . . got . . ."

"Everything."

"Exactly," she said, her eyes going dreamy.

I felt it too. Could La Maison Framboise be our next crazy challenge? Greenwich was finished. We really enjoyed Black Mountain and we were productive here. Did a medieval French village make sense, even part-time? What would the kids say? What would our friends say? What would everyone say? But, and here was the bottom line, whose lives were we talking about anyway?

For the rest of the night, actually for several days, we hardly dared discuss it—discuss that whatever had been, was no longer an issue. Things would never be the same. We could only look ahead.

TEN

A HOT HOUSE?

T HE NEXT day, Pierre and Marie-Claude left for Paris. The Kurtzes came back from Carcassonne and wanted to get together. They really had gone the extra mile, which made us feel vaguely inadequate. We hadn't helped Adrian, much less even located him. All we'd done was worry about him, and in broken French at that.

At least the work we'd committed to here was going well. Bing was on her way to completing twenty-five ink sketches and oil canvases by the end of our two months in Black Mountain. And I was close to finishing *When Eagles Fall*, the novel I'd started writing half a dozen years earlier, based on terrorist-related events in my career with Pan Am.

Before our departure to France, early that year of 2001, I had had the final chapters outlined. The book opened with a fictional airline's Boeing 747 being blown from the sky over Scotland (sound familiar?), and my terrorist mastermind bringing the company to its knees, as he hopes to do to America and Israel as well. His last act on U.S. soil, before returning to the Middle East, is his *Day of Jihad*, in which an attack is launched against New York City, its landmarks, most prominent among these . . . the Empire State Building and the Twin Towers!

I hoped to finish the manuscript by the time we left Black Mountain, to get it to an interested contact high up at Dream-Works through Vernon Scott of UPI, who was now representing me. Vernon and I both thought that America was being far too complacent regarding terrorism. Having been with America's leading flag carrier, and having had dozens of my colleagues murdered by these bastards, we saw no reason they wouldn't come after us on our own soil. We thought the book could be a wake-up call to the new Bush administration. But, of course, I had to finish writing it. That was the rub, the rub that was nibbling away at me to one degree or another day and night.

THE MORNING after seeing the *A VENDRE* sign on La Maison Framboise, Bing peeked over the top of her lavender teacup and said, "Kenny, I've been thinking . . ."

"And I've been thinking too," I threw in before she could get started. "Could we be thinking the same thing?"

"*La Maison Framboise,*" she concluded.

"Exactly," I affirmed.

"If we owned it, we could come here every year," she said. "Maybe for six months and six back home. We do get a lot done here, and we could rent it when we are away."

"To say nothing of the good therapy it is against aging," I said. "Think of the workout our brains get with the language. And that house really looks to be a turn-key deal."

Ah yes, with La Maison Framboise, Black Mountain was working its way into our hearts: the house, the location—two hours to the Mediterranean, two to the Atlantic, the same to ski stations in the Pyrenees. Big cites like Toulouse and Albi close by, to say nothing of castles large and small around every corner. The possibility of actually buying a place, hopefully in good shape, was getting exciting. No question.

"Yesterday afternoon, after I got my hair cut . . . you know the little place up past the *tabac* . . . I stopped by the *notaire*'s office," Bing confessed a little sheepishly.

"Really," I said, raising an eyebrow. "What about?"

Putting her teacup back on its saucer she said, "I asked about the condition of *Framboise* and the asking price." She paused, kind of puffing her cheeks, "Kenny, there's nothing left to do. It's all been done."

"How much are they asking?"

"It has central heat. New wiring. New double-pane windows . . ."

"How much?"

"The third floor's been refitted as an office. Up under the eaves. It would be just right for you—"

"How—"

"The corner shop had been a sports therapist's office. Perfect for a studio. I'm not sure what the garden situation is, but—"

"—much?"

"And the price is the best part, Kenny. Everything, taxes, fees, all of it is about the same as a used car at home. Tops, twenty-thousand dollars. I'm not kidding. Three stories, renovated, on a quiet square, with a garage, studio, office, garden. Oh Kenny . . ."

"Umm," I mumbled, feeling my own excitement growing.

THOUGH BING had been to the *notaire,* and because no one in the office spoke English, she confessed she'd only been handed documents on the house. The talk had been like most of our discussions at that stage, rudimentary, primitive. It was clear we needed somebody who could really talk to them and translate for us. Jean-Jacques agreed to help

We found real estate worked differently in French villages than what we are accustomed to at home. Rather than a high-powered realty firm ginning up brochures describing places like *Framboise,* or listing them in magazines and newspapers, it was standard for the owner of a property just to tack a 3 × 5 card to the door announcing *A Vendre,* with a telephone number, as we'd seen. So, Jean-Jacques had a follow-up conversation with the *notaire,* who spoke to the owner, and together they arranged for us to walk through the place the following Saturday. Unfortunately, he and Laila would be out of town, so we were on our own.

"No problem," I announced, convincing no one.

Friday night we prepped for the inspection. We wrote down the words for *room, wall, floor, ceiling, pipes, wires, windows, bathroom, heating, furnace, water heater,* all that good stuff. If that failed us, we always had gestures, grimaces, and winks to fall back on.

The owner was M. Riquet, but not of Canal du Midi fame. On our knock, he opened the door and offered a warm *bonjour.* Stepping back into the small foyer, he indicated for us to mount the stairs to the *premiere étage,* first floor in France, second in America.

The Riquets' work had been beautifully executed. On every level the massive ceiling beams (*poutres*) were exposed, stained, and treated against wee beasties. The top floor was exquisitely redone in Shakespearian Tudor, *colombage* as I've mentioned it's known in France, all dark structural wood pulled together with white plaster. I could see myself there, snug and warm, with a lovely view of La Montagne Noire out the wide windows peeking from under the tile roof's classic overhang. The same or similar views for the two bedrooms up there, along with a full bath.

The main floor, one flight above the street, had a well-appointed modern kitchen with dining area. The living room was large and airy with another bath next to the third bedroom. Two full bathrooms in a French village house was, by the way, top of the mark.

The rear of the house looked onto a neglected garden. We asked about that, but didn't have enough French to understand what exactly the situation was. All we picked up was something about a lady, an old lady next door. (We'd have to get Jean-Jacques to clarify that situation.)

The house's street level (*le rez de chaussée*), facing the square, was also a find: a small garage with workshop space behind, which added a lot of value. And it had a laundry room and WC too, along with the gem of the shop on the corner, which could be Bing's studio and gallery. We were really excited. All the work had been done. It was turn-key. And cheap. We didn't make any promises but, in serviceable pidgin, explained we'd be back that next week with our French friend to discuss things further. Everyone was smiling.

A s s o often happens with dreams, reality has a way of messing them up. Right off the bat we found this deal had its share of catch-22s. Jean-Jacques learned from the *notaire* that decades earlier the block-sized building had been one house. Then the owner died. His wife inherited it. She had little to live on, so she sliced the place up, creating a one-quarter sliver for herself. The Riquets bought the remaining three quarters of the house, but she retained what had been the rabbit and chicken shed attached the length of the rear, just above ground level. She also hung on to the garden. Though it now was nothing more than a neglected tangle, and the coop on the back a weathered shamble, the lady would not part with any of it.

Jean-Jacques made several proposals on our behalf. First he offered to buy both the garden and shed from her. She said *non*. Next we'd rent the garden, return it to its original condition, and give her unlimited access. She said *non*. Then we proposed buying just the shed . . . *non*! Or renting the shed to refurbish it into a covered deck overlooking the garden. *Non*!

All of which led us sadly back to M. Riquet with the news that we could not make an offer on his lovely home. He gave one of the usual puffed-cheek air pops, throwing in a shrug for good measure. *C'est la vie* for him. Crushing news for us.

For the rest of the morning Bing and I took a hike up "our" mountain. We were the only climbers. Which was fine. We needed quiet time to think. About the future. Where we would spend it, and whether or not we'd fallen in love with a kind of Brigadoon. Something there but not there. Possible but impossible.

Unfortunately, we didn't get very far in the process because on our return to rue Basque we could hear the phone ringing as we wrestled with the door. It was my son Brit. I was surprised. After awkward hellos he broke the news. Bad news. Granddaddy, Bobbye's father, was gravely ill. We were going to have to get back as soon as possible to be able to see him before he passed away.

It was too late to make Paris before the last flight to New York. We decided to get all our stuff together, box Bing's paintings and sketches for Anton or Jean-Jacques to ship to us later. The rental car could be turned in at Charles de Gaulle. In a huge hurry we loaded all our other stuff in it, figuring to hit the *autoroute* around three in the morning. The Delta fight left at noon. From JFK we would connect to Nashville, praying we would not be too late.

Our need to get to Paris was sudden, abrupt, and unexpected. So far to go with so little time to do it, all in the dark of night. As I drove, I'd glance across at Bing, who, at first, was wide awake, also focused on the road ahead. I could tell her mind was probably moving as fast as the car. All this rush, this sudden uprooting of the slight shoots just sprouting in Black Mountain had to be a shock for her. And it all involved Bobbye's father, her brother, her children with me. I sensed all this was making Bing feel alone, peripheral to me and my past life.

The fact that we had each been married before gave us a common bond, but a fragile one at that. Bing's first husband still lived, as did a level of pain between them. My Bobbye was gone, leaving me with only memories . . . of love and joy. I knew these realities were difficult for her. In one discussion she'd made a simple but very real point when she said, "Ken, I can't compete with a memory."

What lay ahead for Bing in all this amounted to a wrenching test. She would be the outsider, alone (though with me) in another family's emotional struggle of goodbye. Then, as her head gentled against the side window and her eyes slowly closed, I said a small prayer that I could be her lifeline of love, keeping her and our union afloat and safe.

WE GOT to Nashville in time. The last Sunday of his life, three generations of family were gathered around Warren's, Granddaddy's, bed. It was Bing's first time meeting him. She was terrific. Despite the sad reality of what hung over that hospital room, the two hit it off very well. For me and especially for my kids, Lexi and Brit, that had been an important blessing.

Warren was a gentle person, a genuinely sweet man who loved people and life so much that his positive warmth and ironic humor attracted all generations. Gathered there that morning, everyone joined in singing the hymns he had loved so much. Even as he was slipping away, he managed to smile and moved his right hand, index finger high like a baton, the conductor leading his choir of teary-eyed singers. He seemed to appreciate Bing's perfect pitch. He smiled at her and nodded to us, his own voice unavailable, so close to leaving as he was.

It was a difficult day, but one of love. A soft time of quiet as each of us dealt with the reality of this passing. Long after midnight, Brit was with his grandfather for the final goodbye.

Days later, the last tears shed, we returned to Connecticut to get on with our lives.

ELEVEN

HOME, LOOSE ENDS, AND
A MIDNIGHT CALL

W E ' D B E E N back in the States ten days when we decided not to return to France for the few days left of our two-month rental. Actually, we started to doubt if there would even be room for France in our future. Dreams have a way of ending. We'd left our Brigadoon and now found ourselves again walking down the main streets of reality.

Bing had been splendid in Tennessee. The kids picked up on how supportive she was of all of us during Warren's farewell to life. She had blended seamlessly into a family not hers. It could not have been easy for her with so many memories of Bobbye everywhere around.

BACK IN Greenwich, we both dove into our work. My novel, *When Eagles Fall,* was coming together, only the last few chapters to go, while Bing already had completed the collection of canvases she'd started in Black Mountain. Originally entitled *Night Mares,* her agent thought that could have had negative connotations, so they settled on *Dream Horses.*

The focus of each canvas is an almost mystical relationship between horses and humans. Remember, in our dreams we can do anything. There's no problem riding a great stallion through the air, over the tops of mountains, or close to the reach of a medieval steeple. Bing set some of these fantasies in the lush fields she'd walked in around Black Mountain, which became the equestrian parade grounds where her dream horses pranced. And, like Marc Chagall had tucked small remembrances of his native Russia into his work, Bing did much the same. A familiar house here, trees there, a hint of the village itself. Her backgrounds embraced bits and pieces of the Black Mountain that had so lovingly embraced us.

And in *When Eagles Fall,* I toyed with introducing a character from the Tarn valley, more precisely, La Montagne Noire. There was no question our French experience had become part of our very beings, which now begged the question: could we simply turn our backs on it all? We were not yet even a month away, but the separation was beginning to weigh heavy on us both.

We had discovered Peter Mayle. His English couple's stumbling into new lives in Provence set off bells. We'd started pursuing any novel telling of distant places where artistic people found happiness. *The Magic of Provence* by Yvone Lenard, for example, was about a couple from California following suit, but with the twist that they actually buy and restore a village house in the Luberon, site unseen! A realty agent described a tumbled-down ruin over the phone, and less than a year later, while they were still in California, the place was restored exactly as they'd prescribed. Maybe amazing things could happen in France. Like dream horses, dream houses.

About two o'clock one early March morning, our phone rang. I was in a total fog, fumbling around in the dark to find the damn thing, sending my bedside lamp crashing to the floor. Give me a break. Who would call at such an hour?

"Hello," I mumbled, ready to be furious.

"Hello Ken, this is Jean-Jacques. From France. Am I disturbing you?"

"No, no problem. I had to get up to answer the phone anyway." I'd once heard that line in a movie and thought I'd see how it'd play in real life.

"Oh good," Jean-Jacques said, accepting it without question. "Say Ken, I'm calling this early because I believe Laila and I have something very exciting for you and Bing."

By now Bing had her light on. "Waah?" she offered fuzzily.

"It's two in the morning, Jean-Jacques. Can't this wait?"

"Time could be important. Ever since you and Bing did not take La Maison Framboise, we've kept our eyes out for something else. I think we have found it."

I started to reply, but Jean-Jacques seemed too wound up to listen. I pushed the speaker button so Bing could hear this too.

"You recall the place diagonally across from where you were on rue Basque? It was on the market briefly. One side of the front had been a *tabac* years ago."

"Yes, I remember you pointing it out. Bing and I looked in the windows once when the shutters were open. It didn't look too bad. The location is good," I added as I sat up in bed.

"Exactly. Now here is my idea. Laila and I thought about this overnight and felt we had to get to you straight away. We would like to go to the *notaire* this morning and make an offer on the place. In your names. I know this might sound bizarre, but if somehow this doesn't work, if you return here and do not like the house, we will buy it from you for whatever you have in it. That's a promise, Ken."

As crazy as that might have sounded, I knew Jean-Jacques and Laila had the money. They'd sold an international chain of boutiques she'd started in London, and owned several Black Mountain properties too, which they said were apartments for struggling church members, though we never saw anyone in them. We had known of how they'd helped the mudslide people in Carcassonne. We had no reason to distrust them. And maybe the timing for something crazy like this was right. Maybe the Mayle and Lenard books had been prophetic.

"Hold on a second, Jean-Jacques, I want to have a quick word with Bing." Putting my hand over the mouthpiece I cocked my head questioningly.

"What do you think?" I asked.

"See if they'll put up the deposit. For the sake of speed and as a . . . test," she said, already more wide-awake than I was. "Check if they can e-mail us photos of the interior, and what contacts they might have with a contractor to take a look at the place to give us an estimate."

"Damn you're smart," I said, and turned back to the phone.

"Jean-Jacques, I just talked this over with the staff . . ."

Bing bounced a pillow off my head.

"We are interested, but it takes a week or more to get money transferred from here. Even by wire. It has to go through Paris, then Toulouse, and all over the place before getting to the Black Mountain bank. And we'd feel better seeing some photos first anyway. Can you e-mail us shots of the interior, garden if there is one, exterior, and see if there is a contractor around who would give you a ballpark on a fix-up?"

"Why would you want a *ballpark*, Ken? What has a stadium to do with this?" Jean-Jacques questioned, confused.

"I'm sorry," I replied, feeling stupid for forgetting the Frenchman wouldn't know our idiom. "That's a local term for *estimate*, a pre-liminary estimate."

"Oh, I see. We call that a *devis*. *Got it*, as you say," he said. "I will do all of that, and by the time you are up for breakfast we will have placed a deposit on the property as well. You will be on your way to having your *stadium*. We'll forward pictures too. Sleep well," he encouraged, then as an afterthought added, "This really is exciting."

"To say the least," I agreed. "I'll check the computer *après midi* your time."

"Perfect. *Bonne nuit*." He hung up.

I looked over at Bing and said, "Done."

"What was the price?"

I stared attentively at the wall. How to frame my reply? Then I decided just to go with the facts.

"I have no idea."

"Let's sleep on it," she said, clicking off her light.

No argument from me.

BY NOON our time we had the house pictures and a promise from Jean-Jacques that he and Laila would be waiting for our call.

The exterior looked good. The façade appeared as solid as we'd recalled it. The stucco facing was not cracked. The windows seemed intact and the folding side-mounted shutters were in good repair. Jean-Jacques had attached notes to each picture. One said the roof was sound and its tiles okay, though not *crocheted*, whatever that meant. Starting a renovation from the roof down was customary, and he'd recommend *crocheting*, which would eliminate the need for annual tile alignments. Hello? After that, insulation could be laid in. Half of that top floor could be left rough as a storage room, the other half finished with skylights for Bing's studio. Jean-Jacques wrote that the second floor was in good enough shape to leave as it was. In the front were two bedrooms with decent plaster, just a lot of wallpaper on top. The rear had two rooms, one average size, the other small, but opening onto a balcony over a little courtyard. One of the four rooms could be converted to a bathroom. No big deal, his notes assured us.

The street level looked a mess. Tiny rooms and one toilet for the whole house. Egads. Nevertheless, Jean-Jacques wrote that knocking down walls, pulling down ceilings, as we had done in Greenwich, would straighten that out. And remember, the way French renovations went, top to bottom, it would be worse before it got better.

The reason the process went that way, he'd explained, was that the debris produced in the upper spaces had to be dumped down the open stairwell. Unlike rehabs in the U.S., where a dumpster can sit out front for months, in French villages there is no room for such monsters in the tiny streets. So the first floor becomes the dumpster. Each week, Fridays usually, the accumulated trash would be hauled away.

After the upper floors were completed, the street level would need its bathroom refinished. Jean-Jacques suggested the cracked plaster ceilings be taken down to expose the old beams, adding atmosphere to the place. The walls could get the same treatment, showing off the stone, Toulousian brick, and heavy wooden posts he said were behind the plaster.

The faxed photo of the kitchen showed it would have to be ripped out, maybe located elsewhere for that matter. The courtyard had a huge kerosene tank taking up most of its space. That would have to go too. And finally there was an abandoned rear building, ownership shared with the houses on either side. It had once been a stable, with tack room and living quarters above. The portion that came with the house could be redone into an office for Kenny, Laila suggested in the notes. If the whole building could eventually be bought and restored, it would make a great studio and gallery for Bing, she'd added. The sketch also showed a narrow lane that had once serviced that building. Since the village was a designated medieval site, the law said the lane had to be protected. Jean-Jacques thought it could be reopened into a charming mews leading to Bing's future gallery and my office.

Very, very exciting. So we placed the call to Jean-Jacques and Laila.

"Ken, Bing, the project is quite doable," Jean-Jacques assured us as soon as he came on the line. "We have a contractor, a *restaurateur* here named Laurant de Gaillac. He has already done a couple of houses for us. While we were awaiting your call, Laurant looked things over. He said the job would take two and a half to three months, depending on the weather. He has a crew available. Starting quickly, the house could be ready for you as early as June. If you give the go-ahead today, he's prepared to fax the *devis* for your approval. He would start on the roof as soon as I have closed at the *notaire*'s office."

Being on our speaker phone felt a bit like being naked in a showroom window. It wasn't easy to crosscheck our emotions with other people listening. Clearly the whole thing was crazy, the timeline a joke, but thrilling. Buying and redesigning a house an ocean away by telephone, e-mail, and fax had to be off the charts. But what the hell, we weren't going to live forever.

"So, do we give Laurant the go-ahead?" Jean-Jacques asked.

"Hey you two," Bing jumped in, "nobody's told us the price. Or even how much for the restoration."

Jean-Jacques apologized while Laila chuckled. Then he gave a number in francs: it was over one hundred thousand. But dividing that by seven, the dollar price was incredibly low. About fourteen-thousand dollars. We couldn't believe it at first, but confirmed the figure with a calculator. And the rehab? Jean-Jacques told us after all was said and done, the entire project, turn-key, would come in for less than thirty thousand dollars, if we didn't do anything to the rear building at this stage. Less than a new car. Holy mackerel! Then the clincher.

"Ken, Bing, look . . . Laila and I have talked this over. Since we are the ones sold on the project, we will do this: We will pay for it all. You pay us back after you get here and feel comfortable about everything. The money is not important. We want you to have a life here with us, doing your painting, writing your books. Making it possible for our friendship and relationship to grow. That is what is important, not a few dollars."

Bing and I looked at each, mouths open.

"Let us get this straight," I said as slowly and as clearly as I could, "you two are offering to buy the house for us, start the renovation with your contractor, oversee everything from there, and hand us the keys on a done deal when we arrive in June?"

Laila jumped in. "The money is so little it doesn't matter. We have so much fun with you two, we only want to make sure that will continue. Pay us when you want to, or never. Just say yes and we will take care of everything. We will have the house ready and waiting. Please say yes."

Bing and I did more staring at each other. My goodness. Talk about the offer you cannot refuse, and from out of nowhere. We really didn't know the Kurtzes well, but they certainly wanted to change that. Incredible.

"Laila, Jean-Jacques, hold on a moment," I said, "we're trying to get over the shock of your offer. We're also checking our consciences, bank book, psychiatrist, minister, our cat, anything for a reason not to do this, but . . ." I looked at Bing, who did another of her French shrugs. "Okay. You have a deal. Start the paperwork. We're ready."

"Oh Ken, Bing," the chorus came from across the sea. "You will never regret this. And . . ." Jean-Jacques paused, allowing Laila to say, ". . . it will be such fun!"

TWELVE

MAD HOUSE DISEASE
BY MAIL

NUMBER 9 rue Basque became a reality in our lives two days later when Jean-Jacques gave the down payment to the *notaire*, locking the house in, with our name on the contract. There would be inspections and title searches as we have at home, but the project was actually under way.

Jean-Jacques faxed us scaled diagrams of each floor and every room in the house. Rooftop, too. The man was amazing, so focused on getting us the place, working out the paperwork, setting up the renovation, and having everything ready for us in June. Turn-key. Risk free. Zero dollars down for us, a figure smack in the middle of my Scottish heritage price range. But why was he so committed to this? In reality, we hardly knew one another.

Anyway, with the material Jean-Jacques forwarded, we had a good idea what Laurant de Gaillac, the contractor, would base his estimate on. Jean-Jacques felt the second floor didn't need anything structural, only cosmetics—paint, wallpaper, light touch-ups—all of which could wait till we moved in. Laurant disagreed. He felt the plaster of the walls and ceilings was not good, and we'd need a second-floor bathroom, so rip it all out. Laila countered that contractors always wanted to add to a project, not subtract. Especially when things were slow. Besides, she and Jean-Jacques had redone two village houses already. Trust their experience. So we had them tell Laurant to forget the second floor except for roughing in basic plumbing for converting one bedroom to a bath.

ACTION BEGAN. The *notaire* papers signed, our names on the deed, and, to ease our consciences, we sent Laurant his *devis* money. Work got under way . . . we were told. Weekly reports started coming in from Jean-Jacques and Laila saying all was on track. Well, more or less on track . . . "coming along," they said. Ahh, hmm.

We cranked up our French lessons. Who knew? Black Mountain might turn into our primary residence. No matter what, we wanted to fit in, not stand out like klutzes.

Then the dollar went on a run against the franc. In just weeks it picked up two points, putting us about 25 percent ahead of where we thought we'd be when we did the final settlement with the Kurtzes. The approaching euro was spooking the franc market. However, coming from Celtic stock, I'd been raised to be leery of good fortune. (Knock on wood. Throw salt over your shoulder. Look out for black cats crossing, that kind of stuff.) So, I wasn't surprised when the international reports told us southwestern France's April weather had gone from surprisingly mild to unusually nasty. Word came that Laurant's work schedule was impacted. Completion was pushed into July. "Maybe later, but not to worry."

Jean-Jacques and Laila assured us we could stay at their place, in the guest house across the swimming pool from the main residence, for as long it would take.

Which sounded reasonable enough until Laila added, "Stay here *all summer,* the whole year! Why care? We'll have such fun!"

"Wait a minute," I said, looking skeptically across the breakfast table at Bing. "Summer? The whole year? Early July is one thing, but what's this stuff about *forever*?"

"I have no idea," she shrugged, "but thank heaven they're offering their guest house."

Beyond the complications of weather, I was beginning to sense there were things going on in Black Mountain we didn't know about. Or maybe didn't understand. I had never been comfortable as a guest anywhere, and an extended stay at Jean-Jacques' estate made me uneasy. I'd never known long-period guest-hood to work.

Weeks passed. The reports we received grew vague at best, though when we talked with Jean-Jacques, he was always reassuring. We could only assume and pray the turn-key aspect of the deal was still in place.

But we did not wait until July or even June. It seemed more prudent to head over in late May to better keep our eyes on things, things which seemed to be growing more and more opaque. We had already learned that the French were rarely on time, so we wanted to keep surprises to a minimum. Before leaving, we spent a week visiting our west coast kids, our east coast kids, saying goodbye to a lot of friends. We telephoned Jean-Jacques and Laila, telling them to expect us. The conversation went from somewhat strained to laughs and talk of "more fun ahead." It was as if the two of them had first hunkered-down, then looked at each other, shrugged, smiled, and threw a "what the hell" in our direction. I think Bing and I sensed all that, uncomfortably. Now the question seemed to be developing, were we total idiots?

THERE WERE no hitches on the flight to Paris. After a drive-by hello to Pierre and Marie-Claude we shot straight down the *autoroute* to Toulouse. Before we knew it, we were rolling under that cathedraled canopy of elegant *platanes* back into Black Mountain.

The whole region we were passing through was the very essence of the spring arriving. Early buds, fields with struggling shoots of green, and the various browns of newly turned earth kept our eyes moving, drinking in the surprise vitality of nature and one season's hint of another. The umbrella-cut sycamores lining the approach to Claude's Café des Fleurs were budding, the trees' new shoots in the afternoon sun seemed to be reaching out to us in welcome . . . welcome home.

We parked in front of the *café* and walked around the corner onto rue Basque. Like kids we reached for each other's hand as our eyes tripped over the cobbled sidewalk to the front door of number 9. I heard a tiny sigh from Bing, drowning out my own as we stood looking at . . . *our house.*

Bing fished in her purse for the key Jean-Jacques had mailed. She started to hand it to me, but I shook my head. This was *her* moment. She'd found crazy Brie the art lady, Black Mountain, rue Basque, number 10, all of it. It was only right she be the one to turn the key to what this new part of our future held.

Nervously she stabbed at the lock. Finally the key slid into the slot. It took quite a twist to click the latch and then, holding our breath, we pushed the door open together, and . . .

"Oh my God!" Bing gasped.

"Oh shit," I said.

"Is it the right house?" Bing asked.

I checked the number under the outside light. "Number 9," I said, wishing it weren't so.

"I want to cry," she said pressing her shoulder against the doorjamb, tilting her head against the chipped dusty paint.

I groaned looking at the heaps of debris and random junk cluttering the place—broken stones, bricks, plaster, piles of sand, crap everywhere. As far as we could see down the hall the place was four feet deep in trash. I wanted to hit something, break something, shout at somebody . . . but no one seemed to be around.

"Ohhhh . . ." was all Bing could get out before a horrendously loud gas-powered generator kicked in. A hundred decibels easy. And in the confined space, *unbelievable.*

"The wires lead up the stairs," I shouted to Bing. "Follow them. Somebody's got to be up there."

"Maybe somebody we can kill," Bing suggested, a bit distant from her Quaker roots it would seem.

We struggled into the front room, picking our way through the debris, down a hallway that, according to Jean-Jacques' reports, wasn't supposed to be there. We tripped and tumbled to where the stairs went up to our left, and looked straight ahead into a dingy soot-caked kitchen and beyond to a set of cracked windows, an unhinged door, and into what was supposed to be a courtyard, but in fact was the residence of the biggest, roundest, fattest piece of junk I'd never wanted to see squatting there.

"The oil tank," Bing said.

Our minds had been full of flattering sketches of what everything was supposed to look like. Our eyes only saw ugly disappointment. No fireplace snuggled into the exposed stone of one living room wall. Not even the frigging wall! Just a cracked plaster mess. No defined living room either. Just piles of rubble, sand, and that damned gas motor blasting away. Sure we'd arrived early, but this was years away from "turn-key." Was it all an issue of *language*? Give us a break.

As we trudged up the stairs, Bing looked close to tears. On the second floor, where we'd been assured nothing needed to be done and we expected to see good tiling and sturdy walls with solid ceilings, there was only crumbling plaster, cracked ceilings, broken windows, and rumbly-tumbly tiles. Had Jean-Jacques been crazy, drunk, or both? Good lord.

It wasn't till we topped the third flight of stairs that anything looked like what we'd expected. The top-floor walls were finished. The ceiling plaster was solid, and tucked neatly between rows of sturdy honey brown support beams were three well-mounted skylights.

A man was standing with his back to us running an electric sander up and down a tree-trunk-sized column supporting the massive center beam running the width of the room's peak. I walked up and tapped him on the shoulder. He jumped about a foot into the air, bouncing his head painfully off the beam. My heart did not go out to him.

"*Bonjour, monsieur. Ça va? Nous sommes les Américains.*" I was trying to be polite while Bing was looking daggers at the guy. Bless her heart.

I must have done pretty well because he smiled, nodded, and launched into a rush of French I hadn't a prayer of following. Which only heightened my frustration with the whole damned situation. I looked to Bing for help, but she only shrugged.

Finally, realizing I was getting nothing of what he was saying, the man mimed he would call someone on his *portable.* I heard the name *Laurant.* My spirits rose. The phone was handed to me. The ringing ended and . . . more tongues. All I could do was stutter and mumble into it. Whatever the hell the voice was saying, I did pick out *tout de suite.* Immediately. I figured whoever was talking to me was on his way. Something had gone seriously wrong. Nothing that should have been done, had been done, and we hadn't been told a word about it. Bing was here to paint beautiful canvases. I was supposed to be finishing my Tom Clancy–type terrorist novel. Neither of us was supposed to be getting caught up in some crazy damn home renovation horror story . . . *again.*

Standing there in the midst of so little done and so much to do, begged the question: With our experience in Greenwich, why did we think this job would be different? There, six months had become two years. Here, three months were looking to become six or more. Our expectations were turning to dust and debris. Yes, the Kurtzes had amassed a fortune by clever business practices and we'd seen what they had done for other people, so we'd believed them. And the books we'd read, especially the long-distance Luberon restoration Yvone Lenard had written about, told us such serendipity sometimes actually worked. Damn the torpedoes, full speed ahead.

WHEN LAURANT rolled up on his flashy red motor scooter, he looked like a typical American-style contractor. (But for the language, of course.) He was wearing engineer boots, a brown leather jacket, and rough-stitched chino pants. He had a round Irish face with sandy brown hair, was well built, in good shape, and about medium height.

Shutting down his machine, he pulled out a bunch of documents from a carrying case strapped to the scooter's rear seat, popped on reading glasses, and leafed through the sheaths, marking the pages he wanted to emphasize in our discussion. As it turned out, however, there was no way to discuss anything. He spoke less English than we did French, so he signaled we go to the Café des Fleurs and see if there was anyone around to interpret for us.

Only the proprietor Claude was there. Bing, Laurant, and I strode up to the bar where he was opening a fresh pack of Marlboros; the American brand, a good omen. Business must be picking up.

"*Claude, est-ce que vous parlez Englais?*" (Do you speak English?) Laurant asked.

Without the slightest hesitation, Claude nodded and said, "Yes."

That was news to me and Bing. The times we ate there during our first time in Black Mountain, he never said one word in

English. And the French he taught me came from hand signals, written text, or just shouting. Had he been pulling my chain all this time or what?

But we all breathed a sigh of relief and Laurant started in on a long ramble, beginning with a few French words I understood, *Dites-il que* ... "Tell him that ..." and then went off on a lengthy and detailed discourse in rapid-fire French. After talking a good five minutes, his index finger stabbing here and there in emphasis on page after page of his papers, he paused, indicating it was time for Claude to give us the translation. Unfazed, Claude wasted no time. Turning to me and Bing, he looked us each in the eye and launched into his own presentation of everything Laurant had said. Word for word. The only problem was that every one of his words was also in French! Yee gads. The bottom line of the whole exercise was that Claude knew one English word: *Yes.*

Recognizing the urge to kill in my eyes, and seeing much the same in Bing's, Claude offered us a round of drinks on the house.

What to do? Finally, armed with the word *demain* (tomorrow) I pidgin-Frenched my way to promising we would have Jean-Jacques along to interpret.

Leaving the *café* Bing's head was down. I put my arm around her shoulder.

"What a mess," I said, my spirits dropping right along with hers. "What an incredible, unnecessary mess."

"Oh Kenny," she said. "How did we ever get into this?"

What could I say? Maybe in the morning we would feel less disappointed, but we sure as hell had to talk with Jean-Jacques and Laila.

THIRTEEN

IS HOME WHERE THE
HEART IS?

T HE KURTZES compound was only a few kilometers west.
Scowling through the sun flooding the windshield as we drove out of
town, all I seemed to see were happy faces. People walking their dogs,
playing with their children, shopping, biking—the whole atmosphere
of Black Mountain was warm and convivial, accommodating.

"Bing, look, everybody seems so happy."

"They probably don't know Jean-Jacques Kurtz," she said, eyes
flashing. "Kenny, that's how I thought we'd be. I saw us unpack-
ing our bags in our practically finished *pied à terre*. A new start.
Ready to take on the world. But now, gosh, look at us. No place to
unpack. No house. It's like we're refugees or something."

I didn't have an answer.

THE GATE of the Kurtz estate was open. We followed a winding driveway of maybe a quarter mile through fields of new hay toward a barn and two large buildings. One was the original farmhouse. The other, country-money-modern, was where Laila and Jean-Jacques lived. We pulled to a stop by the guesthouse. All smiles, Laila and Jean-Jacques hurried to greet us. Which seemed odd. They had to know we would be beside ourselves after seeing the mess at rue Basque.

"Hello, hello, hello," Laila chirped clapping her hands. "*Bonjour, bienvenue,* welcome to your new home here with us! Oh my goodness, I have been holding my breath all day, bursting to hello you with hugs and kisses!"

Laila kissed Bing, then me, then Bing again. I'd never seen her so happy. Nor had I seen such a smile on Jean-Jacques' face as he reached for my hand, sensitive to the American male's discomfort with *mano y mano* kissing. How could they be so relaxed and happy?

They helped unload and stack our stuff inside the kitchen door of the guesthouse, still all smiles. Once that was done they practically dragged us to the main house for *aperitifs.*

"We've got so much to talk about," Laila bubbled.

"I'll say," Bing quipped.

Their place was large. We walked into the *petit salon* adjoining the kitchen, through glass doors open to a wide hallway, into a grand foyer and on into the living room. This was an enormous and modernly appointed cavern with a high-beamed center ceiling and lower vaulted alcoves mirroring the design of the main room. We trekked across what was practically a playing field of carpeted tile to a cluster of sofas and leather easy chairs grouped in front of the stone fireplace, replete with a stack of blazing logs. The heat was welcome. Outside the weather was crisply spring-like, but the stone and tile inside had wrapped us with a chill.

"This is so lovely," Bing commented, her eyes sweeping up and around the *colambaged* walls, the high heavy beams above and the exquisitely detailed array of quality furnishings.

"As you know, normally we keep ourselves in the *petit salon* and its little fireplace," Laila smiled. "But today we wanted you to enjoy more of the house."

"What would you like for *aperitif*?" Jean-Jacques asked, moving toward a drink trolley that looked straight off the set of *Casablanca*.

"Muscat for me," Laila chuckled. "Always muscat for me."

"Bing?" Jean-Jacques asked, as he extracted the cork from a fresh bottle of Laila's favorite.

"That will be fine," she said without a lot of enthusiasm.

"Have you any red?" I asked. "Something local?"

"I have a Corbières I think you'll like," he replied, "but I'm having Scotch. Will you join me?"

"No, no thank you, Jean-Jacques," I said shaking my head, "I'm the designated driver this evening."

"All the way around the pool from here. A challenge," he smiled.

"I don't want to end up in the pool or any more all wet than I already am," I said darkly, but still winning a chuckle from Laila.

"You're so much fun, Ken. You always make me laugh."

I doubted that was going to last.

Hors-d'oeuvres and a second glass of wine for me and Laila, while Bing and Jean-Jacques left it at the one, brought us finally to the eight-hundred-pound gorilla sitting on the sofa next to me.

"The house is a disaster," I said, going at it head-on.

"Yes, it is," Jean-Jacques returned, confirming the obvious but not electing to elaborate. I had taken only one sip but Laila topped me off anyway and recharged her already half empty glass.

"Why?" I asked, my voice perhaps a decibel too loud. Bing touched my arm.

"Complications," Laila volunteered, trying to short-circuit the tension building between me and Jean-Jacques.

"How so?" I asked, my eyes moving questioningly from Laila back to Jean-Jacques. I sensed Bing was proud of me so far. I hadn't grabbed anyone by the throat.

"Laurant has a long-term contract with the *département* that suddenly obligated him to concentrate on the Abbey restoration for the time being and reduce his efforts at rue Basque."

"Why weren't Bing and I told of this?" I asked, feeling my color rising.

"We felt it would only have made things worse," Jean-Jacques said, getting up and moving to the drink trolley again.

"Something stronger?" he asked as he poured himself several more fingers of Scotch. I shook my head, sipping my wine. Everyone was silent for a beat.

"Jean-Jacques," I began again slowly, fighting the impulse to break something, "you know Bing and I are here to paint and to write, not . . . *not* to work on a house. We came last winter to recover from our Connecticut experience. We got a lot done while we were here. Which is why we have returned. Which is also why we agreed to your kind offer . . . *which* we had been assured would be a turn-key operation. *Which* we now learn is decidedly *not* a turn-key operation, which is months away."

"Ken," Jean-Jacques sighed as if laying out *cahier* and crayons for a child. "Dear Ken, Laurant had to divert his people by direction of the departmental government. He had no choice. I made the decision not to bother you with that detail. My reasoning was that your goal in coming here, as you have often expressed, is for writing and for painting. Well, Laurant's situation will not alter that in the least. The rue Basque house will take longer, yes, of course, but you will have the guesthouse here. And you will have Laila and me to help you oversee the restoration. That is not a problem for us. You can set up your computer wherever you wish. I have an extra printer and fax-telephone for you. You will have a complete office to work in and Bing will have more than adequate studio accommodations. We will see to that. So, the job on the house will be done better, because we will all be here together. Laurant's people will finish the work as soon as they are free. You can pop over every day or two to make sure things are as they should be. That was the way I saw the situation *then*. That is the way I see the situation *now*." He made perfect sense. But I knew, sure as little green apples I knew, it was not going to work.

THE NEXT morning the three of us gathered at the Café des Fleurs to meet with Laurant. Laila stayed at home to go over some ledgers relating to their London holdings. Yesterday's linguist, Claude, prepared *café au lait* for four as Laurant motored up on his mini-moto. Greetings were exchanged. Claude retreated to the kitchen. Bing and I stared at Laurant. Jean-Jacques studied the floor.

To get things started, Jean-Jacques briefed Laurant, in French of course, on what we had covered the previous afternoon. As Laurant responded, Jean-Jacques delivered a simultaneous translation. He did far better than Claude.

What Laurant said didn't seem to differ significantly from what we'd heard from Jean-Jacques. Laurant did add that some of his crew would be free the beginning of the next week for rue Basque. The roof and *deuxiem etage,* our third floor, were essentially finished, and he could soon start on the first floor (our second), then our first, their *rez de chaussée.* He believed he could complete everything in two to three weeks.

Then I dropped our bombshell, translated by Jean-Jacques with an uncomfortable look on his face.

"Laurant, Monsieur McAdams and Madame McAdams toured the house yesterday. They have concluded that the second floor must also be redone. They say the walls are crumbling. The ceilings are cracked and falling in chunks. A wall must be removed in the rear section to create a large bedroom, and they would like one front bedroom prepared to be converted into a bathroom.

Overall, they don't know if the weather got in or a miscalculation was made, but a full restoration has to be done throughout."

As Jean-Jacques was delivering that, a slight smile touched the corners of Laurant's mouth and his eyes flicked to mine. As brief as it was, I sensed a moment of contact. But it was short lived. The magic word, *normalement,* made famous by any number of contemporary writers describing the *laissez-faire* lassitude of so many French having to deal with agitated Americans, suddenly popped into the discussion.

"*Monsieur et Madame MacAdams, normalement . . .*" Laurant began and Jean-Jacques picked up the translation,". . . a restoration progresses from the roof, then to the top floor and downward in logical order to the street level. The various system installations, water, heat, electric, etc., are coordinated with the contractor or *restaurateur* during the process. These are installed in a logical sequence, once the old walls have come down and before the new ones go up. For whatever reason there have been none of the trades on the job so far, even on the top floor. No plumbers, no electricians, no gas or furnace people either. *Normalement* I would have used my subcontractors for this work, but Jean-Jacques said *you* would bring these people in as necessary. The *devis,* the estimate, I originally sent you had all of this in it. However—"

I interrupted, asking Jean-Jacques where *were* the tradesmen he'd told us would be working on rue Basque?

"On other jobs," he answered simply. "Plumber, electrician, gas installer, are all on other jobs. Things have turned around in Black Mountain. Winter had a mild spell after an early cold snap. Spring work has been moved up. We got caught in the middle."

I looked at Bing. Bing looked at me. Our eyes said all that needed to be said. We had been screwed. Which meant, like it or not, we were now out of the art world and again into the world of house rebuilding. We'd both been down that damn road before.

But never before because of the actions of a friend. What the hell was going on?

Reaching for a straw, I asked, "Jean-Jacques, you'd mentioned a plumber you use on your London properties. Aren't things slow over there? Could we get him here?

"Cork," he said, nodding.

"For a plumber, the name sounds appropriate. Can we give him a call? See if we can get him here for a hellish week of work? Water and gas. Same license, right? We'll put him up at the Abbey Hotel. Food, grog, everything on us. We can pick him up at the Carcassonne airport. Ryan Air has ridiculous rates from London, right?"

Jean-Jacques took over again, in French this time, explaining to Laurant how we'd get plumbers in from England, perhaps over the weekend. Laurant brightened and promised to have as many of his people as possible on the job Monday. Bing and I felt some energy in the room. We were going to hit this like other Americans hit Normandy, but we would finish it one hell of a lot faster. Hopefully.

We rang up Cork in London. He and a helper *could* make it. His price for the job would be about half what the *unavailable* local Frenchmen demanded. A candle of hope began to flicker at the end of this absurd tunnel we'd gotten ourselves into. But, BUT . . . the bottom line of the whole horrible exercise was Bing and I would become, at best, sub-contractors again. Or grunt laborers. No longer artists. All of it in another country with another language, living in someone else's house. And none of this addressed the issue of six-month visitor visas, *les cartes de séjour*. Would time, like everything else, run out on us?

"I think I'm going to scream," Bing said as we started to the car.

"My *inner bitch* hasn't stopped screaming since we opened that damn front door of number 9 rue Basque," I sighed, shoving my fists deep into my pockets, kicking stones as I shuffled along, head down, feet heavy.

FOURTEEN

TRANQUILITY BASE?

T HAT AFTERNOON, back at the Kurtz compound, Jean-Jacques and I stacked firewood, a wall of it by the kitchen door of the farmhouse. Despite summer coming on, Black Mountain's thick stone buildings still held a lot of winter chills. Besides that, the calendar and the weather seemed out of synch. When it was supposed to be cold it was warm, and vice versa. So everyone had a lot of logs ready to burn.

Our guest farmhouse had a large fireplace in the kitchen, but unfortunately it laid a smokescreen throughout the house before it got hot enough to draw. To counter that, we had to crack open a door, letting in more cold night air to produce heat. Another instance of one step forward with at least one back.

For the two hours Jean-Jacques and I stacked wood, he gave me more insight into French living, encouraging my taking a longer view of things, using the stacking as an example.

"Ken," he said, "we are stacking wood not only for now, but for next fall and next winter. Why do the job twice? The long view is the right view."

"You're telling me our house won't be finished until next year?" I asked, hoping he'd only been speaking figuratively.

"When Germany attacked in 1940, the French newspapers said the war would be brief. They were correct, but not in the way they thought. Even with Paris occupied, England expected victory in a year. The year 1940 became 1945. One never knows," he concluded.

"Jean-Jacques, I had a forty-year career in aviation, whether I wanted it or not," I said. "Now I'm finally into what my life was *supposed* to be about. Bing too, but we're both running forty years behind. At this stage we don't have room for these miscalculations."

Jean-Jacques paused for a moment, digesting my remark, then offered, "Life's experiences never quit, only *we* quit. They are the well from which we draw the water of living. The unexpected can be our greatest treasure. We might find ourselves on a different path than the one we set out to follow, but as your friend Pierre said that night at dinner, the important thing is that our differing paths still move us in the right direction. *Toward the Kingdom.* A phrase I like. So, consider yourselves to have stepped onto another path, and follow it with anticipation. Not anger. What seems a setback might in fact be the best thing that could be happening to you right now."

"All well and good," I returned, "but that house on rue Basque can be the metaphor of Bing's and my new life together. We'd expected it to be a door to our futures. Our turn-key futures at that. But when we opened the damned thing, all we saw was disaster. That's not what we are here for," I said, banging my fist against a log.

"Ken, rue Basque *is* the perfect metaphor for what you and Bing are doing. And like everything else in life, things happen, things change. Why let it upset you? All of this just adds new dimension. The book you are writing will still get written, probably with more insight. Bing's paintings will be completed, but with greater import. Look at these unexpected experiences as things to *embrace*. Don't be so obsessed trying to *press on* with what no longer is. Welcome change. Enjoy its surprises."

"Enjoy this," I muttered to myself.

L A T E R   J E A N - J A C Q U E S and Laila went off on their proselytizing rounds knocking on doors. They drove one of their two big Mercedes. As insightful as Jean-Jacques could be, he could also miss the fine points.

Dinner, anyway, was terrific. I felt obligated to display my native American grilling skills and I think I did rather well. I cut up a chicken, sprinkled on my secret garlic-salt, garlic-pepper, garlic-garlic formula, added a drop or two of lemon and white wine . . . the latter mostly taken internally . . . and plunked it all down on a barbecue of charcoal chunks and mesquite shavings. The French might know everything there is to know about kitchens, but outside, on the grill, Americans rule! (No matter what the Aussies say.)

I don't know if it was the wine, the blown-off tension, or what, but our time around the dinner table was nothing but laughs running to tears. I was the brunt of the funniest stuff, telling story after story of my own linguistic screw-ups. The time I welcomed people with a hearty *au revoir*, rather than the more traditional *bonjour*. Or my sunny morning *bonsoir!* And of course my comment on the baker's *pretty colored horses on his head.*

Bing couldn't resist telling of the time I asked the butcher for *poulet seins*, which I thought meant chicken breasts but was closer to *chicken nipples.* Or the time I didn't have my little red dictionary along when I was trying to remember the word for eggplant. Distracted, and I'd thought muttering under my breath, I came out with *merde*. The clerk advised me with a smile that he was sorry but they fresh out of *shit*.

So many funny McBumpkin Abroad stories. It was a relief from the tension and anger we'd been struggling with these past days. Maybe there was something to what Jean-Jacques said after all.

THE NEXT morning we were up early and off to Black Mountain. Laila and Jean-Jacques were not early risers, so we didn't wait to have breakfast with them. It was chilly, but after picking up *café au lait* at Claude's and croissant from François and Caroline's *patisserie* (now with better quality farina and a match for the other shop run by the grumps), we sat on the wall of the fountain in the village square sipping and munching. The bread was *so* good. The coffee *so* good. The air *so* fresh. Our hearts crinkled with the joy of how wonderful even a simple morning could be here. How at home we could so easily feel.

A white van drove up and around the fountain, stopping across from us. The legend on its side caught my eye. LAROUSSE ET FILS, PLOMBIERS, ÉLECTRICIENS, GAZ ET MAÇONNERIE. The list of skills these guys had was impressive. Plumbers, electricians, gas system installers, and masons. Busy fellows.

Two men, probably the father and son, swung out of the truck, opened the rear doors, hauled out their toolboxes and other equipment, and walked to one of the houses diagonally across from number 9. Why was I finding this so interesting?

Again my eyes wandered back to the name—LaRousse. Could that be *Christophe LaRousse*, I asked myself? If it was, his being there could be very interesting indeed.

"Bing. Check the van," I said, motioning with half a croissant. "Does that name mean anything to you? *LaRousse . . .*"

As she thought about it, the two men got to the door of the house, unlocked it, and stepped inside.

"LaRousse. Wasn't that Christophe's last name, the plumber Jean-Jacques originally said would do our place? Electrical too? I am sure it is. Laila said his father worked with him on the masonry and the two did all kinds of other stuff. Like it says on the side of the truck."

"Exactly, but why did they go into that house and not into our house? Whose place is it?"

"We can ask Jean-Jacques," she offered.

"Right," I said, getting to my feet and collecting paper napkins and our cardboard cups for the trash container on the way to number 9 rue Basque.

WALKING INTO our place and again being hit by the mess, the French word for trash popped into my mind: *poubelle*. This was Château Poubelle. Oh Lord, what to do? Where to begin?

We trudged to the third floor. At least some work had been done there. Then Bing pointed out something I'd totally missed.

"There's no electricity, no wiring," she said, after checking the baseboards.

"Oh man," I groaned, wondering why LaRousse & Fils hadn't been here and put lines in. Bing pulled out a pad and pencil and started writing. The plastering should have been done after the wiring was in, or at least grooves cut where and if baseboards would go on. This whole top floor's plastering would be one of those "begin again" deals. Great.

Looking at the stairway next, we saw the risers were a mess. Sanding, staining, and preserving were jobs we did not want to do, but could do. Then down to the second floor, where Jean-Jacques had only seen the need for spit and polish, it looked to us like broken windows had allowed the weather in, turning the plaster to powder. When had so many windows gotten broken?

When was the last time Jean-Jacques had been in the place? What did this say about our weekly progress reports?

"Kenny, look here," Bing said, pulling at a strip of wallpaper. "This is the sixth layer I've gotten off. I think the paper is the only thing holding the wall together."

All the second- and first-floor walls were equally covered with layers of wallpaper. We'd have to pull it off, but at least we would get wiring in before there was plastering done. Then it occurred to me, without Jean-Jacques by our side, how were we going to communicate with Laurant or his troops once work began? When the plumber, Mr. Cork, rolled in from London, he'd be speaking English, but that was only a partial plus. What would his relations be with Laurant's men?

About eleven o'clock, we returned to the compound and asked Jean-Jacques to call Laurant to establish some sort of work schedule. Needing Jean-Jacques like this made both Bing and me feel horribly dependant. We were going to have to get a French teacher. We'd been working as best we could with tapes, but that was nowhere near enough.

At least during the phone conversation I understood Jean-Jacques asking Laurant, "How long to finish the second floor?" Then he scribbled on a note pad for us to read, "Two to three weeks."

We nodded and I asked, "*Le rez-de-chaussée*?" (The first floor or street level.)

"Two to three weeks." More Jean-Jacques scribbles.

For the hell of it, through Jean-Jacques, I asked Laurant how long to redo the courtyard and back building. You guessed it, *two to three weeks!*

In America we call that *blowing smoke*. So, my take on the whole thing, and Bing agreed, was that two to three weeks meant three to four, which, when applied to the second floor and the first floor and the courtyard (including the back building), added up to an easy three months. And any fool who's ever dealt with contractors anywhere on the planet knows three months means four, minimum. So, with us on-site to keep things moving forward, it was clear I would not write one damn word of the book, or Bing paint one damn canvas for her new collection, before our visas ran out. I was fuming, as much with myself as with the whole stupid situation. To any outside observer, it was probably clear from the get-go that we were not dealing with Brigadoon here, but more accurately Cloud Cuckooland. Greenwich had been a mess, now Black Mountain looked to top it. What on earth could we have been thinking?

"Kenny, it's not the end of the world," Bing said, taking my hand as we walked back from the Kurtz kitchen and around the pool to our guesthouse. "Somehow this will work out . . . even in our favor. Two or three weeks, months . . . that's nothing. We've got the rest of our lives ahead of us. What's that phrase we hear all the time? *Bon courage*. Take heart. That's what this is all about. We've just got to take heart."

"Bing, I love ya darling, but trust me . . . all these projections are total bull," I growled, pushing through the kitchen door and shrugging off my coat. "You know that. I know that. Let's be real."

"Please, don't snap at me. We are on the same team in this . . ."

"Well damn it, I've already heard the calm waters, distant horizons, and vastness of life crap from Jean-Jacques," I fired back. "I don't need more of the same from you."

As soon as I said it, I regretted it. I tried to reach out to pull Bing to me as if to take it back. But she wasn't having any of that. She retreated a couple of paces, putting out her hands, palms up like a third-base coach's "hold up" sign to the runner. I'd taken one step . . . then I stopped.

"Kenny, understand this. You cannot talk roughly to me and then expect me to fall into your arms as soon as you realize you've been a jerk. So just stay away. I need space. And some quiet."

She turned and walked out of the kitchen. I could hear her go up the creaky stairs, walk down the hall to our bedroom, then there was the faint click as she pulled the door shut.

I guess that was our first fight. In a way I wished it had been louder and longer, like I was used to as a kid listening to my parents doing battle. Bing's walking away in silence bugged me. Actually, it only made me angrier. I grabbed my coat, opened the kitchen door, and when I pulled it shut . . . I slammed the shit out of it.

FIFTEEN

AS THE FAN TURNS

NOT ONLY is silence one of Bing's tools against whatever and whomever, she also uses meditation to help right her ship, if and when it lists. She usually sits an hour most mornings, but that particular afternoon she needed another session to deal with my being an ass.

For me, throwing a leg over a Harley and riding into the sunset does much the same thing. The throb, pulse, and rumble of those grand old engines soothes my soul. But we were not in Connecticut, and nobody around Black Mountain had a Harley that I knew of, so I was left pacing through Jean-Jacques' fields, grinding my teeth for being a jerk and cussing louder and louder the farther I got from the house. I was galled to think what a mess our great turn-key deal had turned into. A turn of the key into freaking Château Poubelle!

THE NEXT day, letting our storm clouds pass and at Bing's suggestion, we took another run at that sweet house we'd drooled over, La Maison Framboise. Since it was totally rehabbed, it was a way out of our mess and to still stay in France. Jean-Jacques' deal had never been rescinded. We could withdraw anytime. Maybe that time had come.

Trudging back into the Black Mountain *notaire*'s office, we unfortunately learned nothing had changed. The little old lady still refused to give any garden or any other rights to a buyer, foreign or domestic. Back to square one, so Bing and I discussed whether or not we should call Jean-Jacques on his offer to buy us out at any time.

That evening, at six PM at their estate, we walked around the pool to the big house for *aperitifs*. I didn't know about Bing, but I felt like a peasant coming to his lord, hat in hand. But the issue had to be addressed. What we had been promised had not happened. We had a right to pull out. So be it.

As Jean-Jacques took a bottle of muscat in one hand and his silver with gold inlaid *tire-bouchon* (corkscrew) in the other, I got to the point.

"Jean-Jacques, when this project began, you said if Bing and I were unhappy with it anywhere along the way, you and Laila would buy us out. Does that still stand?"

My question came just as he drove the screw into the cork. With a B-movie flat-eyed glance in my direction, he started to twist.

"But Ken, you have not paid me for the house in the first place. I understand you paid de Gaillac the start-up fee, but so far the bulk of the money has come from Laila and me." There was an edge to the way he said this. I felt my gut tightening.

"Jean-Jacques—" But before I could say anything more, he interrupted as if he'd not paused in the first place.

"And things have changed. Unfortunately, we have run into some problems in London. Too complicated to go into, but some previously trusted associates have been tampering with the accounts. Rather than continue our financing of rue Basque, we are going to have to ask you for the money we put up to the *notaire* starting things off. Sorry."

The screw was tight into the cork now. He applied pressure, levering it from the bottle with a *pop*!

"Muscat," he said, though to me it sounded a bit more like *touché*. We'd been had.

Dinner was not the laugh *fête* of the night before. When I started talking about what Bing and I had run into at the house and what our to-do list indicated, the best way to proceed and so forth, Laila said, with a roll of her eyes, "Can't we talk about something other than the house? We had such fun last night. Ken, be *funny* again tonight."

I wasn't funny, though I thought a lot of what had been going on certainly was. Why had the Kurtzes pushed us into this in the first place, enticing us into buying number 9, only to suddenly bail out? Originally they'd said the money was of no importance. It was not a large amount, tiny actually. It could hardly make or break the fortunes of such a wealthy couple, no matter how dire the London situation. What was going on?

Before leaving to return to the guesthouse, I wrote them the check. I didn't see how we could do otherwise. They were reneging, no question about that. A somber moment, almost embarrassing, but for the sake of the friendship, shredding as it was, we weren't about to fight over it.

LATER, TUCKED under the covers, Bing said, "I think it will be too tense to stay around here for the weekend. Why don't we drive to the Mediterranean for Saturday night? Collioures is a wonderful arty village by the sea. Let's go there, just get away."

For me, being behind the wheel of a car was second best to hanging on to the handlebars of a bike. The plumbers wouldn't land in Carcassonne until Monday. We didn't have anything holding us back. We needed time to think. What the hell.

"Great idea. Let's do it," I said, reaching for the bedside light.

"I'll set the alarm for six," Bing said, throwing back the covers with a big smile lighting her face.

EARLY UP and out on the road. We would stop for coffee and croissants somewhere along the way. The spark of anticipation soothed the day's wounds and eased the weight of our growing mistrust and confusion.

As I said, I like driving. Bing likes navigating. And she enjoys picking spots to stop along the way. I'm perfectly happy just to point the car in any direction and step on the gas. In France, I didn't care where we went, since every bend in the road led to another treasure, another pleasant experience. About an hour out, having finished a delightful *petit-déjeuner* at a large *aire*, or roadside eating and gas stop, near Carcassonne, we set off to investigate some of the smaller roads leading to . . . who cared?

As we motored contentedly along, I asked Bing, "Do you realize how our bodies are in total synch?"

She raised an eyebrow. "What's that supposed to mean?"

"Simple. You never have to go to the potty before I do, and vice versa. Think of how important that is. For compatibility."

"I haven't thought of anything else all morning," she said dryly.

"Okay, picture this—two people traveling the roadways of life together. That should be a time of wonder and joy. But what if the two have different-sized bladders?"

Bing looked over at me like I was out of my mind.

"What if one of them needs to stop while the other doesn't? One person would start to feel embarrassed, inadequate, filled with doubt, while the other would feel superior, perhaps start to gloat. What would that do to a marriage?"

"I think I need to stop," Bing said. "You put peeing on my mind. I've got to go, *quickly.*"

"Good. Me too." What had I done? "Keep an eye out for one of those *pissotière* in the next village."

I often gave thanks for the French system of laying out villages. No matter how small, there's a post office, bus stop, telephone, perhaps a *patisserie,* but definitely a *pissotière.* We were somewhere beyond Narbonne. The village we'd entered was dark and rustic, a Visigoth leftover perhaps.

I drove up beside a fellow pushing a baby carriage, probably his daughter on a tricycle ahead. I *bonjour*ed in my best French and he smiled. I asked, "*S'il vous plaît, monsieur, où est le pissoir?*"

No problem up to that point. Then he answered. Good heavens, he sounded like a chopper pulling away from a light. The rumble. The throaty roar, but I heard no discernible words. Amazing. He nodded and indicated a left down an even smaller side street. I flagged down another fellow. Much the same thing.

"Kenny, this is getting serious. I need to stop," Bing said.

"Tell me about it." My eyes were misting.

Stopping anywhere here for a *rustica* was out of the question. Too many people. Then, by the grace of God, a saint on a bicycle rolled up beside my open window. He must have been trailing behind and figured out our problem. He indicated for us to follow.

He was fast. It was like the Tour de France down the cobblestone street. From the way he sailed through stop signs and barreled through intersections, it was clear he knew bladders. Finally, with a jabbing motion, he pointed to his right for us to turn down the next road at the approaching intersection. I waved my hand out the window. Yes! Understood! We could take it from here.

He pumped his fist and was gone. What a guy.

After the corner we came skittering into what appeared to be an abandoned bus terminal. On our side of the road facing an empty bus was the *pissotière*! Hallelujah. But it was a one-holer, without a door!

What to do? Think Marine Corps.

"Everything's going to be all right, "I assured Bing. "I'll run the car tight against the wall. You'll be able to open the door into the toilet. I'll leave the car there as a door while I run across behind the bus."

Bing had just enough space to twist out and get down to business while I pulled on the brake and switched off the engine. She was home free and I was on my way. Voilà! Mission accomplished.

When I got back to the car, Bing was comfortably sitting in the navigator's seat, map in hand, a smile on her face. She turned to me as I got in, but before I could reach for the ignition key, she held up her right hand, palm open, and we smacked off a cracking high five. We had just scored another team victory in the never ending War of the Adult Bladder.

EARLY SEASON in Collioures, a Mediterranean fishing village filled with artists, galleries, and charm, had been a necessary respite. Welcoming a weekend's separation from the chaos of rue Basque and the questions surrounding Jean-Jacques and Laila, we'd recharged our batteries.

We got back to the Kurtze's farm late Sunday evening. As we started in through the estate's gate, Bing sighed. "Their lights are on. In Jean-Jacques' office. It looks like the two of them have their heads together in there. Something's going on."

"They're always up late," I said.

"But not usually in the office. I'd love to know what's happening."

"Strange people," I said. "All the church business, proselytizing and at times really helping people, but now this. When we first met them, Jean-Jacques said something I had assumed was just a joke. He told me that you and I were worth five thousand francs apiece to him if we joined their temple. The way they're acting now, maybe he wasn't kidding."

"Who knows?" Bing replied. "But who cares either? I just need a goodnight's sleep."

"Here, here."

But our malaise wasn't over yet. Turning the light on in the kitchen, we found the floor a couple of inches deep in water. Had we left a faucet running? Had the toilet overflowed? What had we done to cause *this* mess? After wading around I found a pinprick hole in the copper cold water pipe under the sink. Not uncommon. This will happen when cheap copper pipes are attacked by acidic water for twenty, thirty years. But why now?

I'd done a lot of plumbing over the years. Built my first house myself (another book in the pipeline, no pun intended) and renovated others, so I was able to shut down the sink's cold water, squirt a dab of all-purpose glue on a plastic disk I cut from a cup, press that over the tiny hole, and then torque it tight with a piece of wire and pliers I found under the sink. I wrapped duct tape tightly around it all and turned the water back on—no more leak! Since our plumbers would come into town the next day, I'd do a real fix using their stuff. I went to all this trouble in case Laila or Jean-Jacque came in to that kitchen while we were away and needed to us the tap. (Guest's paranoia.) For the night, I shut the line off again, then Bing and I spent much of the evening sopping up and squeegeeing the whole mess dry.

Oh how I hated being a guest . . .

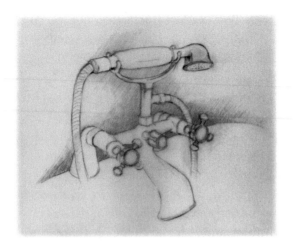

SIXTEEN

IF IT DRIPS, CORK IT

MONDAY MORNING I drove to the airport at Carcassonne to pick up our British plumbers. Bing stayed behind hoping to sketch some horses in the nearby fields. Anyway, the car would be full with me, Mister Cork, his helper, plus their tools.

The day was clear and brisk. A shade under 50 degrees Fahrenheit. Where was summer? Most of the people arriving from England looked to be French nationals returning from weekending in London. Most wore jackets or sweaters. Though southwestern France has short and generally mild winters, as I've said, even late spring was unpredictable. Very warm one day, freezing rain the next.

Mr. Cork and his youthful assistance, Leathan Bobb, whom I

assumed to be Bob Leathan (the French put the surname first), had not gotten word about the chilly weather and descended from the aircraft in brightly colored Aloha shirts. Though Mr. Bobb had on dark slacks, his employer had donned neon bright Bermuda shorts and work boots. I prayed he plumbed better than he dressed.

Their personal luggage was minimal, though each had a crushingly heavy metal toolbox displaying large stickers announcing—IF IT DRIPS, CORK IT! NIGEL CORK, PLUMBER TO THE KING. Nigel later explained that his royal service claim was based on his grandfather's drunken boast of having once been called to Buckingham on short notice. No word on what year it was. Anyway, for now it's "God save the queen."

"Sunny day," were his first words to me. "You must be the Yank. I says to Leathan here, that bloke's the look. And I was correct, wun't I? Nigel Cork and my assistant Leathan, at your service."

His handshake was firm. I felt that made him trustworthy. "Ken. Just call me Ken, or Mac if you like," I said, turning to the younger man.

"I'm freezing me bluddy arse uff," the lad announced, his hands as close to his sides as they'd go.

"Stoop whining, Leathan, and shake Mr. Kenny Mac's hand," Cork directed, green eyes sparkling from under bushy brows. Cork's head was covered with a thick thatch of gray hair aggressive in its commitment to growth. Other than a nose with a small crook to it, he was a handsome man: about my height at five-ten, sturdily built, and clearly impervious to the weather.

"Mr. Leathan," I said, holding out my hand to the young fellow.

"Bobb," he said, pressing his gnarly, calloused one into mine.

"Do you go by Bob or Robert?" I asked, wanting to get off to a good start.

"Leathan," he replied, squinting a bit.

"But not Mister Leathan, I gather," I said muddlingly.

"Mr. Bobb it is," he explained, leaving me totally confused, much like Lou Costello in his famous "Who's on First?" routine.

"Is your car nearby?" Nigel asked, bailing me out.

"Not far. Haul your stuff to the curb. I'll meet you there in a couple of minutes," I said, setting off at a half jog toward the parking lot.

We'd gotten the big metal tool boxes in, but the lid wouldn't quite close. Fortunately, I had a couple of bungee cords to hold the trunk lid from bobbing up and down. Young Mr. Bobb, whom I finally figured out to be Leathan Bobb, was in the back seat leaning on the small suitcases. By now he was tightly zipped into a parka the color of gangrene.

Nigel was a rock. No jacket for him. No way. He saw this jaunt to southern France, with pay plus expenses, as a vacation. And he would treat it as such. Sunny skies. A Yank with money—which was his definition of Yanks anyway—grog with football or rugby on the tellie evenings, wife nowhere near, Froggie food hopefully not too bad; all in all a pretty good time ahead no matter how you cut it. Right, mate? So he'd worn his party shirt, and he'd brought one for Leathan too.

I put the Brits in the Abbey Hotel, within walking distance of the house. Happily, since Bing and I now owned property in Black Mountain, the hotel gave us a discount for guests we lodged there.

Once the two had laid in their stuff, we took them and their toolboxes to number 9. None of Laurant's men had shown up yet. I was not pleased. But we made the best of the time doing a lot of measuring for lying in pipes. Mr. Cork was efficient. Using an oversized notepad, he drew diagrams of the water and gas layouts. He checked the soil, found it acidic, so said to forget copper, he'd go with the new semi-rigid plastic for the sub-floor feed. Never rot. Never give out and was the latest thing approved by the EU. The water company would love us for it, he added.

Leathan did the legwork, running everywhere with his end of the tape measure, much like a dog on a friction leash. Cork jotted down the numbers with his fat, flat pencil probably left over from the battle of Britain. Street floor. Second floor. Third floor. Out back across the nasty little courtyard to the hell-hole rabbit hutch that would one day be my office. I was amazed how quickly these two men specked things out. Then, working from the diagram, Cork jotted down all the pipe Ls and Ts and 45-degree fittings he'd need; couplings, shutoffs, faucets, sinks, showerheads, tub; the whole *schmere.* Bing, bang, boom. He was good.

When the last required coupling was recorded, he tore off the sheets, handed them to me, and with a smile said, "I hope you speak some Froggy. I'll need this stuff first sparrow hop in the morning."

Speak some French? No sweat. Right. Say a prayer.

R E V E L ,   W H E R E the Saturday farmers' market was, had two plumbing supply houses. The first was very U.S. looking—big windows, advertising all over the front, slick and impersonal. I expected a place like that wouldn't be interested in trying to sort out a foreigner's bad babble, so I poked around for the kind that would put an arm around a mumbling American's shoulder and walk him through the ordeal. Happily, on the road to St. Félix, I found what I was looking for. It was half the size of the other, a bit beat up, with plumbing trucks out front looking like they'd seen better days; I sensed I could make it there.

Bing had prepped me. Early that morning we'd dug into our dictionaries for the nouns I'd need. Pipe (*tuyau*), faucet (*robinet*), wire (*fil*), bathtub (*baignoire*), wash basin (*lavabo*), everything Nigel Cork had listed. I figured I had enough verbs left over from

BON COURAGE · 145 ·

an old high school text we'd thought to bring along to really put those nouns through their paces.

Confidently swinging through the door into the shop, I felt a bit like Duke Wayne. The two men behind the counter turned toward me, as did the three or four plumber types in front. I could hear a pin drop. My confidence fell with it.

The fellow first in line was stout and short, not much taller than the counter. He had a wet cigar hanging from the corner of his sagging mouth. The guy next to him was tall, thin, and sported the kind of beak that would make a heron proud. Behind those two was a fellow wearing an eye patch, and another so heavily bearded he looked like a giant pussy willow. For a moment I thought I'd walked onto the set of that bar scene in *Star Wars*.

Thinking back to our first day in Black Mountain, the lunchtime at Claude's, it occurred to me to *bonjour* the shop. I did, and it worked. Everyone *bonjour*ed in return. Camera, action, and business rolled back to normal. Unfortunately though, when my turn at the counter came, my mind went blank. No nouns, no verbs, consonants, zip, zero, nada.

"*Monsieur?*" the proprietor asked.

"*Bon . . . jour,*" I managed again.

"*Bonjour,*" he returned, raising an eyebrow. "*Oui?*"

"*Je suis American,*" popped out of my mouth.

"*Et je suis Français,*" he countered.

This was not going to be easy.

"*Mon Français est très pauvre,*" I said.

"*Mon Français est très bon,*" he replied, leaving me in a linguistic cul-de-sac.

After a moment or two of looking like that damned deer in the headlights, I started reciting my store of nouns. *Robinet, tuyau,* the whole lot. But no verbs. I'd forgotten my verbs! I pulled out Cork's diagrams, sketches, measurements for lengths of pipe (plastic) and joints (brass), Ts and Ls, all that sweet stuff (thankfully in centimeters and millimeters). There was a nod from across the counter, putting hope in my heart.

To formalize what was to follow, the fellow gave me his full name. I thought his first name was Roget, pronounced *Rog-jeh*, because that came last. He introduced the other man simply as *Bernard*. That gave me the pecking order, so I made the boss *Monsieur Roget* and Bernard, *Bernard*.

The two swung into action. They zipped into the parts bins and equipment lockers, hauled down large rolls of plastic pipe from a loft, actually jogged from one end of the storage area to the other and back to the desk again, stacking boxes and crates of stuff we needed by the front door. It was like watching a ballet. When everything was assembled, a lot of arm-waving, cheek-puffing, and air-blowing followed—which I deciphered to mean they would deliver everything to rue Basque by 8 AM the next morning. Fantastic.

It was my turn to smile, shrug, and pencil-sketch where our house in Black Mountain was. It was an embarrassing process to have to go through, but it got the job done. Oh joyful day.

❧

SEVENTEEN

WORKING . . . IN FRANCE

T UESDAY MORNING things finally started in earnest at the house. Bing and I were at number 9 by 8 AM. For a moment I was a little put out that none of de Gaillac's troops had arrived, but Bing made the point I missed.

"Kenny, Black Mountain is a village. Everything is packed closely together. Start hammering before people are up and you would break the social contract. Laurant's people probably won't be around until nine."

Why wasn't my mind so logical?

Bernard, from the plumbing shop, arrived to deliver our stuff only moments later. We were putting our key in the front door as he drove up in a goofy little truck, the kind Inspector Clouseau drove into swimming pools. A moment later, Nigel Cork came with Leathan in tow. Everyone pitched in unloading, and in no time the plumbing job was ready to start. And at nine, as Bing predicted, Laurant's crew rumbled in.

As Nigel and Leathan laid out their day's work, Bing and I went to introduce ourselves to Laurant's men, top dog down. Figuring who the foreman was took some detective work. Four were dressed mostly in blue, France's worker color, but two of these were too young to be foremen. One man had on blue trousers and a white wool sweater: age alone made him a candidate for chief. But there was another fellow in his mid-thirties wearing no blue at all. Above his gray chino slacks he had a red cotton sweater with the old English lettering announcing UNIVERSITY OF PRINCETON, as opposed to the "Princeton University" many know and love. Chances were he had not bought it at the campus store. But he did have the look of a foreman.

We'd already learned etiquette's importance here. When asking directions one started with *bonjour,* then *s'il vous plaît,* before getting to the meat of the question. This indicated you were *bien élevé*—well raised. Americans are so used to just blasting away with our "Where is this or that" right off the bat that we grate on French sensitivities. So, addressing a subordinate as the chief in front of the man actually in authority could quickly sour relations with these guys. We wanted to get it right.

Going with age, I walked up to Monsieur White-wool-sweater, put out my hand, and said, *"Bonjour, je m'appelle Ken et ici est ma femme, Bing."*

"Bonjour Monsieur et Madame, je m'appelle Antoine . . ."

Bing and I both missed his surname, which got lost in the blur of his thick Spanish/Tarnese accent. He had an eyes-lowering roughness about him, as if he didn't like having to talk to a foreigner so early in the morning, or perhaps *ever* for that matter.

While Bing and I bumbled along, I found it interesting that

everything he said to us seemed directed exclusively to me. As if Bing didn't exist. The other men acted the same way. Why was that, or was it just my imagination?

Then the young man in the University of Princeton sweatshirt stepped up to shake hands, introducing himself as *Eric* somebody, another surname promptly forgotten by yours truly. And the other two fellows were introduced, their names also lost to thick accents.

I went over and grabbed Cork and Leathan, having to half-drag them across the room to meet the Frenchmen. Clearly both groups were reticent to mix, each studying the other suspiciously. *What the hell are English plumbers doing here?* I could read in the Frenchmen's eyes; as well as the reverse, *What the hell are we English plumbers doing in the land of Frogs?*

Linguistically, Cork and Leathan were even more challenged than Bing and I. Nor could the Frenchmen speak any English. All of which indicated we'd assembled a crackerjack team capable of roughly zero communication. It was going to be interesting to see how this fiasco played out.

Eric, we learned, was the foreman. Antoine, however, a long-time friend of Laurant's, had elder statesman status, further smudging the lines of command and control.

"Fun days ahead," Bing said with a wry smile.

During the introductions I realized we needed a way to keep names straight, so I decided to make up my own for everybody. Eric with the red sweater conjured Eric-the-Red. I could remember that, or Monsieur Rouge, which I sometimes shortened to just Rouge. For some reason I had a devil of a time remembering Antoine. With my new tactic in mind I gave him a job-related name, Placo. Antoine was the *placoplâtre*, or drywall specialist.

One of the two young men was Bruno. Early on he impressed us with the way he took the crappiest jobs and never complained. He'd even smile as he did the work, efficiently and well. So, feeling sorry for the guy, I said to him one time, "Bruno, you get all the bad jobs, but you do them very well. Truly you are number one."

He'd smiled, nodded, and said, "*A votre service toujours, Monsieur Ken.*"

The names stuck. Bruno became *Numéro Un, or Number 1.* When he had another guy working with him, the subordinate became *Numéro Deux, or Number Two.* (Of course, when Placo had a helper, he would be called *Placo Deux.*)

This made every thing easier, and everybody seemed to get a kick out of the forgetful American. What grew to be especially charming about the whole deal was, after a few weeks, Bing and I overheard conversations that went something like this—*Hey, where is Rouge? Oh, I saw him with Placo. No, Placo is with Placo Deux. Hey, Numéro Un, where is Rouge?*

After a week side by side with the two camps, it was clear the English and the French work differently. There are those who say people from northern Europe, along with Americans, Canadians, and northern types, tend to be linear and result-oriented, while the French, Italians, Spanish, and others from southern Europe are more conceptual, philosophical, and emotional. Working with both groups seemed to confirm it.

Nigel and Leathan hit the ground running. That first afternoon they'd written down all the materials for me to fetch. If I did my job they could do theirs. They were there at eight sharp from day one, every day, until the job was finished. They worked straight through with only a sandwich for lunch. Finishing at eight in the evening, they'd walk to the hotel for showers, and then back to Claude's *café* for food, grog, and the tellie. And they completed the project a day early—seven, not eight. They took their pay and clocked out in what amounted to one-fourth the time Laurant had estimated for the job. Then, after a big goodbye dinner at a fancy restaurant, they got on their plane and were gone, with a "Thank you very much. Call if you have anything more for us.

Cheerio." The French crew had a different playbook. Their day started at nine. Then everything stopped dead in its tracks at noon, just like it had at noon that first day we arrived in Black Mountain. The men went either to their homes or to the kitchen and lounge Laurant had added to his depot for their comfort. After two hours of food and relaxation, they'd be back on the job, working until 5 or 5:30 at the latest. That meant the best we could expect from the French crew was six and a half hours a day. But that wasn't all.

After I got on Laurant's case about how slowly things were moving, he drove me to his office. Unrolling a scroll of paper on a long drawing board, he tacked it down so I could see a full four months in one sweep. He took a red pencil and shaded the weekends. He did the same with the holidays. I was amazed to see there were about as many holidays as weekends! It got worse. The day of the week each holiday fell on was important. The Friday and Monday ones obviously led to three-day weekends. But, and this was a *big* but, the Thursday and Tuesday celebrations of anything from National Dog Collar Day to Kiss a Toad Tuesday meant some work weeks maxed out at three days. Then—*vacations*. Every worker gets six weeks. So, in those four months, on top of everything else, a third of Laurant's work force was off the property for a month and a half. And the government was talking about adding another two weeks to that.

One day, with the help of Jean-Jacques, Laurant summed it all up, saying, "Monsieur Ken and Bing, this country is only for the workers. We small businessmen have no chance. I am stupid to keep trying. These crazy rules make it impossible to get things done, and then they tax away my profit to pay for all the worker benefits. I have no vacations. I have to be here all the time to keep things going. If I leave for a week, *nothing* gets done. Of course, as you see, the work hardly gets done anyway. No one cares. Everyone thinks I am crazy for getting upset. They say I act like an American! I should say to hell with it and just be another worker who the government makes sure does not have to work. I should go to America. But I don't speak English. I have seen you two learning French. Nothing is impossible . . . except perhaps running a business in France."

But we saw rainbows too. I doubt any country has been as successful with quality-of-life issues as France. Other than small businessmen like Laurant, the people are laid back, comfortable, and confident of the lives ahead of them. They don't have the kind of money Americans have, but they don't need it. Their future, their old age, is safe—so they feel secure, and with that security comes peace of mind.

Though taxes are high, their healthcare system sees them through. Because one generation is not dependent on the next for financial support, there seems to be a tighter weave to the fabric of a village's life than we experience in the States. A case in point is the daily scene at the fountain in Black Mountain, which is circled by comfortable benches. Across from it is a retirement home—a beautifully restored place, well run, with reportedly the best wine cellar around. Each day as we passed we would see old folks sitting on benches, or even up in their windows, watching their children's children riding their tricycles, roller-skating, or playing bounce-ball. They talked together, called out to one another, laughed and shared stories; three generations enjoying each other's company. Real community.

The village's shopkeepers ran stores their parents and grandparents had run. We met people whose histories went back beyond Charlemagne. Surrounding Black Mountain were farms that seemed to predate time itself. Rich soil. Rich farmers. Animals, crops, fields, and streams so alive we felt bathed, immersed in it all. Songbirds everywhere, part of the flowers' bloom. So much life in sync . . . except for Laurant's and mine.

EIGHTEEN

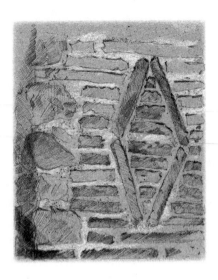

AND THE WALL CAME TUMBLING DOWN

A COUPLE OF days after Nigel Cork's arrival, Laurant's men started whacking out the second floor wall between the two small rooms overlooking the courtyard. This would give us one good-sized master bedroom. The ceilings had to come down too, to expose the old beams and give it all a medieval flavor. We tried not to think about the storm of mouse droppings that showered down on us as we worked without masks. Greenwich all over again.

Laurant had a dump truck run up onto the sidewalk in front of the house, blocking as little of rue Basque as possible. Numéro Un (Bruno) and Numéro Deux would shovel the piles of razed plaster out the windows into the truck below. Of course Bruno was expert at it, arching his shovels-full neatly through, hardly brushing a window frame. Deux, however, was a novice. At one point his shovelful slammed smack off the bedroom wall. The mess it made of the wall wasn't important because Placo was going to replace it anyway, but it was a harbinger of things to come. A short time later, another wayward toss took out six panes of glass from one window, which crashed down into the truck below. Though Deux got a lot of criticism from Bruno, and damn near a shovel on the head from Bing, he managed to do the same thing again later, taking out the six panes of the adjoining window. After that, Bing, getting gently into Rouge's face, got Deux reassigned.

By the end of our restoration, twenty-seven panes were broken. Though the cost of damage like that got adjusted, Laurant was shorthanded. It fell to Bing to replace them. A miserable task. The glass had been set in mastic about one-hundred years ago, which had hardened to stone. Trying to chip the stuff out, working around the imbedded glass's sharp edges, caused her lots of cuts. But she hung in there. Laurant had Bruno. I had Bing.

As bad as things were, at least we were learning more French every day. Especially how to curse. The first real opportunity for me to show my stuff came when we found two novice painters I had hired were grossly incompetent. Laurant's people were busy on the second floor, and with the third finished but for wiring, painting could start there. A pair of young apprentices working next door offered to do the job. Cheaply. Since *cheap* is my second favorite word next to *free*, and despite Bing suggesting caution, I hired them.

I'd already used the same criteria getting an electrician. The La Rousse & Fils truck had stopped in front of the house up the street a few days earlier and I'd grabbed Christophe, the son of La Rousse, and asked if he could handle the electrical work. Though very busy, he agreed to fit us in around the edges for *d'argent liquide* (cash). He said that way would be *meilleur marché*— cheaper. Hired.

The first day and a half our (Bing would say Kenny's) painters seemed to know what they were doing. They spread tarps, gave us the names of the required supplies, and told us where to go for them. Bing and I dutifully hit the road to get what was needed, just as I had for Cork.

A couple of towns away there is a home supply place called Monsieur Bricolage. Though we'd felt marginally confident heading there, once walking the aisles we were like babes in the wood. It was frustrating not being able to ask questions properly, much less understand the answers we'd get when we tried. Then we met Madame Bricolage, which is the name Bing gave her.

Mme Bricolage, actually Blendine, spoke no English, but she seemed able to read minds in any language. Suffering our sputters and waves, she'd take us by the hand, march us around the place, aisle by aisle, until we had everything we needed. What a dear person.

With that mission accomplished, we returned to rue Basque and found things humming. Or *crashing* might be more accurate. With the second floor interior wall smashed down to allow for the master bedroom, the first floor was undergoing the same treatment. But dangerously so.

As I opened the front door and Bing started in, her attention was elsewhere. I was behind, looking over her shoulder, and saw Numéro Deux's raised sledgehammer start its backswing straight for Bing's head. I grabbed her belt, yanking her back. The sledge missed her, but not by more than an inch.

"What *are* you doing?" she said sharply, eyes flashing as she spun back toward me. "I *do not* appreciate being jerked around. Stop it."

"Bing, you nearly got your head caved in," I tried to explain. "Deux's sledgehammer would have done the job if I hadn't pulled you back. Give me a break."

"I'm just telling you I'm not a dog on a leash. There are better ways to do these things."

She hadn't seen how close she'd come to being seriously hurt, so nothing I said now would make a difference. I shut up and walked past her carrying the box of paint cans, brushes, turpentine, tarps, and caulking to the painter boys waiting upstairs.

Reaching the top of the stairs, I saw that Christophe the electrician was there too. Of course he was shaking his head at the way the lads were working, as they in turn were shaking their heads at the way he was doing his.

Bing came up beside me. I wanted to put my arm around her, but I sensed she was still in her "need space" mode. We both just stood trying to decipher the repartee. Then the church bells rang. All conversation stopped. The three started past us. We could hear the thump of equipment hitting the floor below and the scrape of boots headed out to the street. Lunch time. All France stopped in its tracks.

Before anyone reached the stairs I offered, *"Déjeuner?"*

Christophe declined. Like most French workers, he went home at noon. The paint-splattered boys, however, were happy to join us. A free lunch was a free lunch.

Sitting down at Claude's they explained, as far as we could understand, that Christophe wasn't respecting their request that he not bugger up what they had just sanded and primed. They felt he should string his wires where they *hadn't* yet worked, not the other way around. We would crosscheck with Christophe. Of course we could have misunderstood what they were trying to tell us, but Bing and I promised, as best we could, to check things out. Where was Jean-Jacques when we needed him? Especially since he said he or Laila would be there every day.

Laurant de Gaillac appeared about 2 PM. We'd taken a liking to the man's style, the way he worked hard to figure out what we were trying to say. He sorted through our mismatched subjects and verbs, finally realizing much of the time we were actually trying to be funny. He'd say something. I'd muddle through what

I thought was a great comeback. He'd stare blank-faced at me for a good ten count, rearranging my babble into real French . . . then crack up. Big booming laughs followed by retelling my latest witticism to someone else. There'd be a second round of howls, making me feel quite the comedian. I suspected Laurant prettied-up my stuff. Probably he was the real comedian, truth be known.

Neither Laurant nor Placo thought our choice of painters was a laughing matter, however. They took us up to the third floor and pointed out the sloppy priming. It was true. I hadn't been paying attention. Too busy with everything else. So we had a talk with the boys. They shrugged. SHRUGGED! Now *that* got me going. Bing had put a hand on my arm. I counted to ten, and then I explained that all their work would have to be done professionally or we would find others to do it. Simple as that. I thought they got the picture. The next day or two would tell.

THAT NIGHT, driving through a steady rain back to the Kurtzes, Bing asked the obvious. "Kenny, where has Jean-Jacques been? He said he and Laila would be on-site a lot. He's the linguist. Where has he been?"

"I asked myself exactly the same thing this afternoon. Maybe their problems in London are worse than they've been letting on. Laila is always on the phone, or going over the stack of ledgers they have. I don't think she goes door-to-door with Jean-Jacques anymore either. What the heck is going on? The whole deal is getting weird."

"Maybe setting us up in the guesthouse is their extra mile," Bing said with a shrug.

I flipped from high beams to low because of the thickening fog. "If they hadn't made all this so attractive I'd agree with you, but that's not how this whole exercise started. They promised a lot more."

"You're right about that." She nodded as we approached our

turnoff. "They talked us into this no-risk adventure, but now they're pulling the rug out. It's so strange."

As we drove through their gate, a heavy rain started slanting through our headlights. I found myself hoping Jean-Jacques and Laila wouldn't see us. This seemed typical of the way long-term guest situations work out. No question our relationship with the Kurtzes was souring, but I didn't think it was our doing.

"You know," I said, "If we'd known what we'd be getting into, don't you think France would have been for vacations, not a place call to home? We certainly aren't the artist and writer in residence we'd thought we'd be. Not by a long shot."

"I know, Kenny. Oh how I know," she said looking away from the lights of Jean-Jacques' office dimly flickering through the rain.

THE NEXT day, our chastened pair of painters started cleaning up their over-runs, drips, and splashes. I watched, encouraged, as they scraped off the old paint and started rolling primer on the walls over the stairs to the top floor. But the stuff they were using looked different. Not the water-based latex I'd expected. Bing and I ruffled through our little red dictionaries to ask what was up.

"*Quelle peinture utilisez-vous? Latex ou l'huile?*" (Which paint are you using? Latex or oil-based?) Bing asked.

"*Huile*," (oil) they replied.

"Why?"

They said it bonded better to *le torchis*, the ancient adobe-type material many of our walls were made from. (Some of these had the actual hand prints of the medieval laborers, indicating the work might have been done as long as seven hundred years earlier!) They said the crumbling old material would re-bond with the oil-based paint to form a stronger, more solid wall. That seemed to make sense, especially if you didn't know a damn thing about ancient *torchis* walls.

Just before noon Laurant stopped in again, striding authoritatively through the place, checking on what was and what was not going on. He seemed particularly interested in the painters' work at the top of the stairway. My heart sank as he shook his head. What could be wrong? He didn't want to speak where the painters could hear.

Out in front of the house, Laurant looked Bing straight in the eye, ignoring me, as was his particular custom, unlike the other laborers who only addressed me, and said, "*Ces types sont fous.*" (These guys are idiots.)

After the usual spin through our dictionaries, we figured out that Laurant was telling us the walls of the third floor were plaster over *torchis*, a combination that breathed. The oil-based stuff they were using would act as a seal, making everything weaker rather than stronger. The painters didn't know what they were doing. "Get rid of them," he said.

The way Laurant directed his entire conversation to Bing when I was making the responses for our team was starting to irritate me. Admittedly, Bing understood French better than I did, but I did most of the talking. My ego was bruised. He said we should let these guys go. Of course I was the one who hired them, so that was another pin in my cushion. I was trying not to get in a huff or to wonder if charming Laurant was starting to have a thing for Bing.

So what happens next? We'd started toward Claude's for lunch, but M. Rouge came running out, making it very clear we had to get back to the house. When we got to the bottom of the stairs, Rouge pointed up. Oh shit. The whole stairway wall had collapsed! Where a wall had been was now just a skeleton of columns and cross-beams.

As Bing, Rouge, and I stood staring open-mouthed at the mess above, our two painting men came striding through the front door, back from lunch and eager to continue . . . screwing up.

When they saw the mess, they were as shocked as we were. That spoke for itself: Laurant had seen the mistake they were making, but they hadn't a clue. These clowns had to go. No doubt about it now.

Out with the dictionaries again. Bing and I put our heads together to produce a reasonable dismissal announcement amounting to: "If you want any money at all, you will clean the mess off the stairs. Get it down to the *rez de chaussée* for the truck this afternoon. After you collect your brushes and everything that is yours, leave. We will pay you for the time you worked, but nothing more. And never ask us for work again."

They weren't happy and apparently said some nasty things because Bruno looked to see if I understood. When it was clear I didn't, he walked up to the leader and started bouncing the flat of his hand off the young man's chest, shoving him back against the wall, getting severely into his face. I couldn't understand the words, but from the expression on the painters' faces, it was clear they would watch what they said or there would be teeth lost. Bruno stayed close behind the two of them until the stairs were cleared. Bruno was nobody to screw with, and I thanked God he was in their faces, not mine.

NINETEEN

EXPULSÉ

O VER THE next week the quality of life at Chez Kurtz plummeted. The leaky water pipe (which I'd finally fixed) started things off. The malaise that produced (as if the break was our fault) was compounded next by the fax machine they lent us screwing up and blocking one of their phone lines. We were unaware of it until I went online with my laptop and wiped out Laila's other line while she was talking to London. Jean-Jacques stormed around the pool, banged on our door, and reclaimed the fax and printer. Big-time paranoia was now in place. It was like being kids in another kid's sandbox. His pail. His shovel. Nothing actually ours so that every little screw up had our names on it.

"Bing, do you think we're burning too much wood? I mean,

considering it's supposed to be nearly summer?" I asked one morning as I dumped an armload of logs next to the kitchen fireplace.

"I have no idea how much is too much," she said from the sink, finishing the breakfast dishes. "Most nights have been rainy or cold. If we don't burn wood it means turning on the electric heaters. You know what Jean-Jacques said about how expensive they are. There are a couple forests of logs stacked by both houses. We can pay for what we use if it comes to that."

"Yeah, I guess," I said, my eyes scooting back from the wood to the tiles of the kitchen floor. "Oh, oh. Bing, check the black marks on the tiles." They hadn't been there after we sopped up the flood.

Taking up the dishtowel, she looked at the floor.

"The soles of the new boots," she said, nodding toward my feet. "I'll bet that's why they were so cheap. Soft rubber. It shouldn't be much of a problem to clean up though," she concluded, then added, "There's cleaner and a stiff brush under the sink."

I'd been standing in front of the raised hearth looking at the floor. When Bing mentioned the stuff under the sink, I turned just as she turned, my elbow bumping hers, and CRASH! A vase she'd just dried hit the floor.

"Oh no," Bing moaned, "that was the vase Laila put the flowers in when we arrived."

"One of her favorites, naturally," I said. "She found it at a brocante someplace. We'd better start hitting the brocantes; after I fix the floor, and deal with the wood supply, and pay for our telephone calls, and do a better job on the water pipe, and—"

"Kenny, stop it. You're making mountains out of molehills. Relax," Bing said a little testily, reaching for the dustpan and broom. The tone of her "relax" irritated me, but that could just have been my paranoid imagination, along with my vision of Laila knocking on the door any minute asking for her vase back, like the fax machine, and printer, and telephone before it. So, to make amends, I took the broom and, unbelievably, managed to knock a ceramic pitcher of honey off the counter.

We spent that afternoon and several more searching *brocantes* for a matching vase. Without success. Which I think added to my growing distraction because, a couple of nights later, I forgot to crack open a kitchen window to help the fireplace draw. Ah yes, I filled the whole damn guesthouse with smoke. Shades of the rue Basque fireman's folly. Though this time without big red trucks, thank heaven. The smoke wasn't visible. Prayerfully, the Kurtzes were none the wiser.

I spent the next morning cleaning up soot. This was no way to live, and no damn way to finish my novel, or for Bing to create a canvas either.

SURPRISINGLY, INEXPLICABLY, Jean-Jacques and Laila started acting warmer again. The night after the smoke incident we were invited to the main house for roast duck. Always a delight. Jean-Jacques was an excellent cook, having attended the Cordon Bleu some years before. The conversation was vigorous again, too, which led to some insight as to why we were, temporarily at least, returning to favor. It turned out Jean-Jacques was giving the sermon at his church that week and a group of senior elders was coming to hear him. He wanted to use us as sounding boards.

His topic was "Why We Don't Celebrate Christmas." The fact that it was almost June made it a strange time to be concerned about such things, but what did we know? He really got into it during dinner, reciting what seemed a memorized soliloquy about the terrible travesty Christmas celebrations actually were.

"The Wise Men were not the Magi as they've been historically popularized," he said. "In fact they were astrologers, magicians, diabolic frauds in leagues with Herod! They were his agents sent to find the Christ child and then report back."

I can never stay out of an argument, so I reached behind me and picked up a Bible he had lying on the coffee table. Opening it, I read aloud, *"'They bowed down and worshiped Him. Then they opened their treasures and presented Him with gifts of gold and incense and myrrh. And having been warned in a dream not to go back to Herod, they returned to their country by another route.'* That doesn't sound like they were conspiring with Herod to me," I said.

Jean-Jacques just blew that off as "Irrelevant."

Hmm?

"And Ken, December 25th was not the actual date anyway. The birth probably was in September or October. So the whole celebration is really just an extrapolation of pagan festivals and should not be paid any attention."

In my new role as amateur street theologian, I put my two cents in on that too. "Who cares what the actual date was? If that were important in itself, it would be in the Bible. The *fact* of the birth is what is important. And how it fits into what the early prophets had heralded. A new Covenant *literally* was being born . . . one in which God later sacrifices His Son, not a lamb as in the old. Abraham had been spared giving up Isaac. God, however, does not step back from such a horrific affirmation of *His* love for mankind."

"Only Easter, the Resurrection, should be celebrated by Christians," Jean-Jacques announced didactically.

"Without the *birth* of Christ, there's no death from which to be resurrected, so doesn't that birth constitute ground for celebration in itself?" Bing asked. I wanted to run around the table and hug her.

We went back and forth on this and other scripture, succeeding only in establishing how far apart our understandings of the Bible really were. By the time Bing and I left, our relationship with the Kurtzes was again tumbling downhill. We had failed as sounding boards of affirmation. Back in our slightly smoky bed, however, Bing said she'd been proud of me and felt good about both our performances. Amen.

IT TURNED out that Jean-Jacques' sermon was part of a larger and much-heralded event for his local congregation. A dinner after services was planned at the main house too. To our surprise, Bing and I were invited, though as things developed it would have been better if we had not been.

At their temple hall the congregation was warm and friendly. Despite our rough French, people chatted encouragingly with us. Finally, as we moved to our seats, Bing gave a little tug on my sleeve and asked if I'd seen the young woman sitting conspicuously alone in the last row? I glanced in that direction, noting a haggard, almost fragile, yet attractive woman there. Bing described her as looking like a broken-winged bird. Then the service began.

When it came time for the sermon, as best I could follow it, Jean-Jacques seemed to make the same points he'd made in English the night before. The reception here, however, was far more positive. The invited leaders seemed pleased, nodding as the points were clicked off, almost as a catechism. Fortunately, I wasn't able to understand enough to cause my blood pressure to rise. Bing and I made it through the service, and the Bible class that followed, without doing or saying anything untoward.

The dinner later at the Kurtzes' was another story. Though it started warmly enough, once we'd sat down at the table things quickly went frigid. We hadn't been seated very long before Laila, smiling brightly and speaking in English, asked, "Did everyone notice the woman sitting alone in the last row?"

"I did," Bing said. "I wondered if she was ill. She looked so sad, like a broken-winged bird."

As if what Bing had said was *good* news, Laila gave a slight chuckle, nodded, and with her eyes moving brightly around the table said, "She *should* look sad. We are *shunning* her." Reaching for her wine glass, she looked at Bing, then over at me with a slight lift of her glass.

"Shunning her?" Bing questioned, looking nonplused.

Isn't that something out of the Middle Ages? I wanted to ask but held off.

"Oh yes," Laila said. "She has sinned and we are admonishing her as scripture directs. One member of our congregation drives to her house two nights a week to bring her to class and services. But he doesn't speak to her. Until she repents with full confession before the whole Temple, she will continue in this state. Would you like some butter with your bread?" she asked me, turning from Bing.

Bing was sitting across from me. She looked like she was holding her breath, ready to explode.

I couldn't keep my mouth shut. Looking around at everyone at the table, in French I apologized for having to speak English, then said, "As I understand it, the New Covenant was supposed to have brought love into the world of human affairs. And that the unfulfillable nature of the Old Law, its hundreds of requirements, inflexibility, and cold oversight, had led to a judgementalism which Jesus was sent to change; and in so doing change the relationship amongst men to one based on love's sacrifice and service." I went on to challenge them, as men and women of God, to review how the Father had given the Son, and in turn, how Christ had dealt with those who sinned. The Samaritan woman at the well. His association with suspect tax collectors and ne'er-do-wells. What He said in Luke about judging others. The admonition to forgive almost without end; and of course I referenced the time when He ate at the Pharisee's house and the harlot washed His feet with her tears and dried them with her hair. In all of these examples, kindness, wisdom, love, and forgiveness were the common threads.

So, looking around again, and catching each of these leaders' eyes, ending with Laila herself, I said, "You are all men and women of God. In His service. Therefore each of you must ask yourself, if Jesus Christ had been in your temple tonight and saw that woman, what would He have done? Would He have shunned her? Or would He have gone to comfort her, embraced her, with forgiveness and love, asking only that she go and sin no more? That's the question. The answer is in your hearts . . . and in that Book." I gestured toward the Bible that lay open between the candles in the center of the table.

Then Bing and I got up, wished them all a good evening, and left.

Crossing the way to the guesthouse, Bing slid her hand into mine and said, "Remember when Pierre and Marie-Claude were here for that frosty dinner? How Jean-Jacques said something about *if ever I am wrong in my faith I want it pointed out to me from Scripture.* Well, that's exactly what you did tonight. It will be interesting to see how he deals with it."

"My gut tells me it won't be well," I said, putting my arm around her shoulder. "But at least we fought the good fight."

WE DIDN'T see Jean-Jacques and Laila for three days. (An ecclesiastically appropriate number, I would say.) They'd had to go to a follow-up convention in Avignon. When they returned, however, they telephoned our cell phone and asked me to come over. I gave Bing a hug. We both sensed this would be a difficult confrontation.

It was raining, not a downpour, just steadily. I pulled on a jacket, turned up the collar, and trudged around the pool to their back door.

For as long as we'd known the Kurtzes, that door had been open to us whether they were at home or not. This evening, however, Jean-Jacques stood in the doorway, framed for Bing by the backlighting of their kitchen. She said later she was surprised that I wasn't welcomed in, even more that I was left standing in the rain.

Jean-Jacques was a fairly large man, round-faced. Back home he'd be referred to as "beefy." As I approached, the way he filled the doorway told me he wasn't about to move aside. He was not smiling. His expression was blank, eyes dull, not friendly.

Laila, who never cooked, was at the stove some distance behind Jean-Jacques. There was a spatula in her hand that she was using to prod something in a skillet. She was in profile to me and never turned her head in my direction.

"*Bonsoir*, Jean-Jacques. You want to talk?" I offered non-committally.

"Yes," he replied, his hands going up to the door jams, not shaking mine. "We need you to leave."

I didn't say anything, just looked him in the eye until he added, "Many things have changed."

"When do we have to be out?" I asked.

"Tomorrow," he said.

"Tomorrow is Saturday. To find a place to stay on Saturday could be very difficult. Give us the weekend to relocate."

He didn't say anything for a moment, and then turned toward Laila. "He wants until Monday, Laila," he called.

Without looking in our direction, and after a pause of her own, she said, "All right."

Jean-Jacques looked back at me, still expressionless.

"Can we leave the furniture we bought in the barn till we finish the house?" There were a half dozen pieces, several quite large, that we'd found at various *brocantes*. If they couldn't be left there, we'd really be up the creek.

Jean-Jacques turned toward Laila again. This was very strange. It was as if the two of them were rehearsing a bad play.

"He wants to leave the furniture in the barn."

Laila didn't pause on this one. "No," she said, short and sweet.

Jean-Jacques turned and walked to a table not far from the door. He didn't invite me in. I started to leave when he called, "Ken, wait a moment."

I turned as he returned to the door. For an instant I hoped he wasn't going to soften and offer some explanation, or even an apology. It was too late for that. I'd had enough.

Jean-Jacques had some papers in his hand, which he held out to me.

"These are the costs of the wood you have burned and your telephone usage. I will have bills for the electric and gas at the end of the month."

I took the bills without looking at them as I turned back to the warm glow of the lights from the guesthouse kitchen we would soon be leaving. On the short walk through the rain it occurred to me that Jean-Jacques' sermon had, in one sense, been fairly accurate: he and his people really don't have Christmas . . . ever.

TWENTY

DOWN A ROAD LESS TRAVELED

T HE STATUE of Liberty, designed by the Frenchman Frédéric-Auguste Bartholdi, was dedicated to the homeless huddled masses yearning to be free. It didn't escape us that there was some irony in the situation we found ourselves in—evicted, huddled, and yearning for the artistic freedom promised by a Frenchman who was himself actively shoving us into that huddled mass status.

As Saturday's dawn was breaking, I fantasized about going to *la mairie*, the town hall, which was open till noon, and applying for village idiot status. Perhaps there was a Ministère des Idiots du Village that would put a roof over our heads. There was one for everything else it seemed.

Other than hotels, where could we live? Bing grabbed a phonebook and discovered *gîtes*—country rentals available by the week or month—a booming business in a country perpetually on holiday.

As I'd mentioned earlier, one gets the feeling the goal of the French government, certainly the politicians, is to have 365 workfree days per year. They're about halfway there right now. Even the educational system helps. Schools are out much of the time, though each *département* has specific control of its breaks, which are coordinated with the adjoining jurisdictions. For the area around Black Mountain, three different school systems could be vacationing one after the other driving local *gîte* prices to high-season levels three times longer than elsewhere. Having so many families looking for places could make it difficult for us. Plus trying to negotiate in French over the telephone . . . good grief, we were in way over out heads. We needed a linguist who knew something about this kind of stuff—and knew about something huddled masses too.

"Adrian. He'd know about *gîtes*," Bing suggested. "And if he has the boat back at Port Lauragais we might even stay on it for a few days while we get located."

I was glad Bing thought to call Adrian. We'd been so focused on the mess we were in we'd lost sight of the far worse mess he was in. The phone had a speaker button so Bing and I were able to jump in together once we had him on the line.

"*Notre cher ami*," we began, quickly exhausting our tip-of-the-tongue salutations. "How have you been? Is your family all right? We tried to reach you before we left for the States. And now, amazingly enough, we are back. We've been very worried and felt guilty for losing touch."

The barrage of questions and confessions gave Adrian his own opportunity to apologize for not responding to our messages.

"Dear Ken, Bing, I owe *you* the apology. I destroyed your special honeymoon," he said, real concern flooding his voice. "I burdened you with worry for my family troubles. I did not get back to you only because I had nothing substantial to report, and that would have added unnecessarily to your concern."

"What news do you have of your son?" Bing jumped in.

"It took me forever to find him," Adrian said. "He really had run away. I found him in Paris. He'd hitchhiked. He has an older friend there who had been giving him bass, bass violin, lessons last year. So he made the decision to get away from the craziness and go to Paris to become a musician. I got him a room near the conservatory and, through some friends, was able to get him enrolled. At least now he has a focus and a goal. Realistically there's nothing healthy here for him. He made the right decision. I'm supporting him on it."

"Oh Adrian, that is wonderful," we said in unison. "Are things better with your wife and daughter?" Bing added.

"Yes to Aimee. She has gone to Nice to stay with her aunt. They get along well. She will be working in their restaurant until the next semester begins. I am so thankful my sister volunteered to help," he said, obvious relief in his voice.

"I wish I could say things are going as well for Aimee's mother," Adrian added, his voice tightening. "She is under intense psychiatric care, but I doubt she is making any progress. I cannot help. The more I try, the more it seems to drive her to the edge. All I can do is work on my boat and do what I can for my kids."

"Adrian, I'm so sorry. Perhaps—" but he cut me off before I could finish.

"How are you two? Have you been in France all this time?"

"It's a long, long story," Bing jumped in. "We had a death in the family, returned to the States. Then got a call on a house in Black Mountain. Bought it site unseen. Thought we had a turn-key restoration. Did not. Had a falling out with our friends here.

And now we're kind of homeless. Oh, Adrian, it is has really been a mess."

"We think we need a *gîte* to see us through till the house is finished," I took over, "so we thought you might have some ideas?"

"Hmmm," he said. "I do think I can help. When I was in Paris I stayed with a friend there, a lawyer, who has a working farm not far from you, with a rental house on the property. Actually it is a large building with two very well-equipped apartments. He uses one on weekends, from time to time, while renting the other. Both are quite spacious and lovely. Give me a few hours. I will get to him. Call me back this afternoon. If nothing develops with him, you can stay on the boat with me for a few days. I owe you anyway, and I don't have a cruise until next Friday."

"You are a lifesaver," I sighed. "Thank you so much. We're trying to make arrangements for storing the furniture we've accumulated. It will take a couple of hours to sort that out, then we'll call you back."

"Thank you so much, Adrian," Bing added, equally relieved. "You are really pulling us out of a mess. Thank you, thank you."

LATER THAT morning, we drove for one last time down Jean-Jacques and Laila's long drive, past the fields and through the gate. Bing had left a framed sketch she'd done of the Kurtzes main house in the kitchen along with our check for telephone time and firewood. I thought a box of horse poop might be appropriate too, but Bing launched into a treatise on how she had been raised and how she was sure I had been raised, and that the right thing to do in a situation like this was to say thank you for the kindnesses we had received and let the rest go. The fact that those kindnesses had been withdrawn was not the issue. We were making it clear to Jean-Jacques and Laila that we were *bien élevé* and knew how to act properly.

I knew where she was coming from, but I wasn't happy.

"Bing, don't be such a saint," I said. "These people have messed us up big time. And I have no idea why they did it. Maybe it started with their proselytizing. You know, in their reading of scripture, Book of Revelations, they come up with some kind of numerological business about 144,000 select souls who will make it to heaven. I think this whole deal was designed to bring us into the fold. When I shot my mouth off about the shunning, we were counted out. I guess with these folks, if you are clearly not of the 144,000, you are *way* out. Maybe we're being shunned too. Which doesn't bother me in the least."

"I agree," Bing said, "but I'm not going to let them make me a lesser person. It is time to forgive and forget."

"That does not make me feel very warm and fuzzy."

"Get over it."

"Bing, my love, if you really work at this you might be able tick me off."

She went silent. Her emotional doors closed. I gritted my teeth, mouth shut.

Moving on . . . we still had the furniture problem. Anton and Trakya might be able to help. He had the trailer. Hopefully we could hire him to help move everything out of Jean-Jacques' barn to wherever. So, arriving back in Black Mountain, we told them what had happened. Trakya's reaction was interesting.

Popping her fists onto her hips, she shook her head, saying, "I never trusted that man. He would drive over here whenever I had a baby to change or a dinner to prepare and tell me all about how wonderful Jesus is. I don't need him to tell me that. I already know it. All I needed was for him to go away so I could get my work done. I thought he was slippery. Like a snake."

Then Anton piped in, "Jesus rode on a donkey, not in a Mercedes."

Which sent us into peals of laughter.

"Anton," I chuckled, "I thought Germans had no sense of humor."

"True, my friend, but, as I keep telling you, I am Austrian. We are naturally funny people. Our national anthem is about little plants and their flowers. That is *very* funny. Yah."

This only added to the hoots.

"You will need my trailer to haul your furniture. I will also give you my back to use, if we have beer later," he said smiling.

"That would be wonderful," Bing said, loosening up and taking my hand.

"Great, but our next problem is where to put the stuff?" I said. "If you could help with a phone call, I'd like to ask Raoul at the *bocante* near Saint Félix if we could store it there until the house is done."

"No problem," he replied, "I will call. He will say yes. I know him. We will take everything there."

And Trakya told us not to worry about where to stay either. "If worst comes to worst," she said, "we have sleeping bags for you to spend the nights in front of our fireplace. You can be Gypsies like Anton and I were for so long."

They were being so kind. I could feel a lump starting in my throat.

"But first, *gîtes*," Trakya said.

Before she could get started in that direction, though, Bing jumped in with what we'd accomplished with Adrian.

"I think we are all right," Bing told her. "Our friend on the boat at Port Lauragais is talking to a friend who has a place near here. He thinks that will work out, but if it doesn't, we can stay on his boat until the end of next week. That should give us time to settle somewhere."

The pieces started to fall into place. Raoul had no problem with our leaving things with him. Astutely enough, he figured the more time we spent in his barn full of antiques, the more we'd think we needed to buy from him.

When Anton and I got back to the Kurtzes barn, the storage door was unlocked and Jean-Jacques was nowhere in sight. In fact, he and Laila had been conspicuously out of sight since they announced our eviction, though their cars were parked out front.

Between the trailer and Anton's old Mercedes wagon, we were able to get everything in one load. Bravo. The ride to Saint-Félix-Lauragais took only about thirty minutes. We spent another twenty unloading.

Raoul and Evita (whose name I *could* remember), like Anton and Trakya, were two of the nicest people we'd met our first time in Black Mountain. They were so sweet, putting up with our poking around their barn full of old stuff, haggling over prices, and not buying enough, by their estimation.

Many of the items of the furniture had been bought from Raoul in the first place. After unloading, Raoul led Anton and me to the far end of the barn to the section he'd turned into an apartment, where he and Evita lived. He stood us in front of a huge glass vessel he'd dug up when he was getting ready to lay a slab for his kitchen floor. It was balloon shaped, with lots of bubbles entrapped in its thick green glass. Really old. About a meter in diameter at its widest point, it tapered to a regular corked opening at the top. It was a quarter full of . . . whatever. Raoul's eyes twinkled as he had us lift the thing onto an old carriage seat, settling it against one of the curved armrests so it wouldn't roll off.

As he worked the cork free, Evita arrived carrying brandy snifters on a tray. Without ceremony he sloshed about an inch of the stuff into each and handed them around, then nodded for me to take the first sip. How long had this stuff been buried? How many generations of Raoul's family had lived over it since the burial? Maybe it was a leftover from Bonaparte's quartermaster corps?

Does brandy, or whatever it was, turn to cyanide over time? Why was I first? But what the hell, I lifted the snifter like I knew what I was doing. Held it to the light like the big guys do and then lowered it to sniff. Wow. As the old sinus passages were torched, my eyes teared. All three were smiling at me. Anton chucking his chin up, urging me to sip. Even Evita was fluttering her eyelashes for action.

"Okay, here goes nothing," I said. Down the hatch and then . . . *kaboom*, it hit bottom. Napalm. "*Bon*," I whispered, hardly able to breathe.

Raoul gave me a respectful nod and lifted his glass, as did Anton and Evita, then the three popped theirs down without a hint of the plumbing problems I'd had. What could I say? After the initiation, or whatever it was meant to be, Raoul led the way into their snug kitchen. A charming place. Small interior stone walls defined alcoves where the appliances were tucked. One for the fridge, another for the *Cuisine à Simone* gas stove. The fireplace was also of stone, with a huge squared log for a mantle. A few embers smoldered as evidence of their struggle against the hilltop's windy chill. We sat around the antique wooden table in the center of the room, in front of the French doors. From my chair I had a commanding view of the valley below, and in the distance, the magnificent snow capped Pyrenees. With the Mediterranean Sea distant to the east and the Atlantic west of us, the region's weather is so changeable it wasn't a surprise to watch the fingers of a cloudy sky start reaching toward the mountains. That view blurred as a light rain began falling. Now the kitchen's warmth was especially welcome.

As if the ancient brandy hadn't been enough, Raoul opened a bottle of Gaillac. Red wine seemed the answer to every hitch in a Frenchman's day. Then the shop bell rang and Evita excused herself. With the three of us left to our own devices, Anton and Raoul sipped and chatted about the crazy weather, what it was to raise kids nowadays, and the price of petrol. I was mildly surprised to find I understood a lot of what they said. Suddenly I was filled with the marvelous realization of where I was—sitting in a restored medieval kitchen with stunning views, listening to people talk about everyday things in another language and actually understanding them. Was it the buzz of booze, or was progress being made?

TWENTY-ONE

COWS

WHEN WE got back to Black Mountain, Bing had good news. Adrian's Parisian friend had three weeks open at his place in Soual, just twenty kilometers (about twelve miles) from Black Mountain. We would have to pay the high-season rates because of all the departmental school vacations, but so what? We'd have a roof over our heads. However . . . we would have to pass an interview.

"Tell me you're kidding, Bing," I said. "This isn't the Upper West Side. We aren't trying to get Buffy and Brie into preschool. We just want to rent a few rooms. How the heck are we supposed to have enough French for an interview?"

"Adrian said it won't be like that . . ."

"What does *that* mean? Is this one of those *what's the meaning of ' is'* deals? I'm not running for president. I just want a place to sleep, for heaven sakes."

"Adrian says the owner's agent, Madame Rigale, is required to get a look at us. Make sure we aren't leftover hippies or something. We give her a couple of checks—one for our time there and the other for damages," Bing explained. "It's the same back home. The bad news is they have people coming in behind us so we'll have to go somewhere else in three weeks. We're beggars now, Kenny. You know the story."

"Okay, whatever. But you do the talking. My vocabulary doesn't include house care. Tell her I'm deaf or just extremely American. She'll understand."

"Oh come on, once we get started, I doubt I'll be able to shut you up." Bing said

"We'll see. An *interview* of all things. Did Adrian have any crib notes?"

"It's going to be fine. Relax. Take a nap. But no more wine. You and Anton look like you've been doing more than just moving furniture," she concluded, rolling her eyes.

LATER, ON the far side of Soual, we turned onto a narrow dirt road leading to the farm. And what a farm it was. Cows everywhere. At least a hundred, along with all kinds of automatic milking equipment in two huge barns, plus two other buildings housing heavy equipment, tractors and such. And the whole operation was run by one family, the Rigales and their teenage daughter. We later learned the girl, René, was in agricultural college and planned to take it all over herself someday.

Madame Rigale turned out to be a wonderful surprise. She spoke so clearly, probably the product of talking to cows most of the time. She was easy to understand. So we had a *real* conversation. In French! She walked us through the house with an inventory sheet in one hand, checking off two sofas, ten chairs, pots, pans, knives, forks, spoons, on and on, establishing for both parties that everything was there when we checked in. It was a great vocabulary lesson. Bing did the acceptance signing. My job was to write out the two checks. Of course everything was in triplicate—one copy for us, another for Mme Rigale, and the last for the rental agency to have on hand when the government taxman came. Everything in its place, including us.

The house was luxurious. Beautiful kitchen. Grand dining room. A salon. A large living room. Three airy bedrooms. Two baths. Television. Clocks. Radios. Central heating. A terrace overlooking endless fields full of cows and crops. We were on a hillock shared with another dairy. There were woods and streams in the valley accommodating an amazing rabbit population bouncing and diving into holes everywhere. A hillock heaven.

As the cloud-draped sun settled on the horizon, the chilling damp air crystalized to ground fog. Farm noises grew louder around us. Cows called for their evening milking. Geese went into a tizzy over an approaching cat. Two big hawks circled overhead, their calls going out to others of their clan that it would be rabbit for dinner. Owls passed the word; while doves cooed caution. Finally the farm bell rang for M. Rigale. Dinner was ready, the day was done.

It was like being on a stage as the sun closed into a ball of red, dipping behind the Pyrenees . . . a sight made breathtaking the way the mountain peaks added spikes of silver from their ice and snow slicing into the flaming horizon. So beautiful. Calming. For the first time since our return, we felt a reassuring warmth wrap us in its arms.

TWENTY-TWO

PROGRESS AND A SURPRISE

FOLLOWING OUR eviction, and without Jean-Jacques available for running translations, we were on our own more than ever. Nevertheless, people began to rally around us. Most days Laurant would pat me on the back and offer a cheery, "*Monsieur Ken, bon courage.*" And I'd progressed enough with the language to manage a rude return that usually gave him a good laugh. (By the way, as I repeat our conversations with our French friends from here on, understand that what I present are approximations and assumptions of what was said and meant. As Bing often recognized and tried to point out, my responses in many fast-moving conversations had little if anything to do with what was actually being said. Oh well, *vive la différence.*)

Though Laurant had an American-style sense of humor, not everyone else did. Certainly not Christophe, the electrician who was now putting in good time with us after having gone on an unannounced vacation to Spain, leaving wire placement to Bing and me in his absence. He was very *particular*, dedicatedly anal. Everything had to be done his way, though his way might be totally the wrong way. And when that was proven to be the case, he would save face by simply reversing his previous position as if he never believed otherwise. (He probably would have made an excellent politician in our native land.)

An example of this was when Bing asked that the wire covers, which would run up a surface, be coordinated with the color of that surface. Brown up wood, white up plaster. The issue first came about on the third floor when Christophe told her that it was impossible to do things that way. Brown wire covers did not exist. Bing threw a doubting *vraiment?* at him, but he stood his ground. Really? Really. M. Placo, who'd overheard the exchange, rolled his eyes and fired something at Christophe, who returned a salvo of his own. The issue ended in a draw, as best we could follow it. That afternoon, however, we drove to Monsieur Bricolage and raised the question with Blendine, Madame Bricolage. Without the slightest hesitation she shepherded us to the electrical section, and there they were. Colored wire covers, white, brown, even blue. Bravo Blendine! We bought an armful of browns.

On our return it was 5 PM, quitting time, as we climbed over the rubble heaped in Château Poubelle's first floor. Christophe was packing his tools to leave as we reached the top floor. The big smile on Bing's face made it clear how much she was enjoying handing him her bundle of brown wire covers. I don't know if he looked at them or at Bing with more surprise. (I could almost hear the gears of his mind whirring—*These Americans, they just won't take no for an answer.*) Nevertheless, he carefully studied the covers, gave the situation a mid-level shrug and a wave of the hand, seeming to indicate that the *fact* of their existence was at best some kind of *fiction*. Maybe the supply catalogue he used didn't show them, so they did not exist. For many Frenchmen, what a manual says or a blueprint states trumps reality every time. (I found this to be the case as a test pilot with Dassault when I reported a locking brake problem in the design of one of their executive jets. My discovery came via operating the aircraft. When I reported it, everyone went to and poured over the blueprints. After days of such research, the design engineers assured me the problem did not exist. I countered by taking them all onto the aircraft and demonstrating reality in a very dramatic fashion. After scaring the daylights out of them, they concluded the paperwork was at fault, not the test pilot. I think it was a first.)

In the same vein, Christophe was struggling with seeing a reality and wondering how exactly to *deny* it. So he left for home without a word, but with a furrowed brow.

Surprisingly, the next morning we discovered that sometime during the night he must have returned and switched all the covers to what Bing had wanted. But he never mentioned doing it. Weeks later when he was working on the first floor and ran out of brown covers, did he go to M. Bricolage and get some more? No way. He'd always used white, unless he was given brown by the crazy American woman, so, while we weren't around, that's how he finished the job. I think it was a matter of inertia, a mindset that had roots two thousand years deep in the very soul of Black Mountain.

IN THE long run, humor opened a lot of village doors for us, and working on the house in the center of things actually made us a part of the town's ebb and flow, treating us to a lot we would otherwise have missed.

Across from Château Poubelle, a few houses up rue Basque, lived an old man named Maurice and his one-eyed dog, Cabriole (Somersault). Cabriole had been a circus performer until a shooting-gallery ricochet took out his left eye. Maurice happened to be there when the pup went down, practically at his feet. Scooping the little fellow up, he'd raced to the first aid wagon. Fortunately the dog was unconscious, making it easier for the doctor to extract the pellet, but not without the loss of sight in that eye.

Maurice went to the circus owner and offered to take the dog home, nurse him, and return him to perform once the eye healed. The *propriétaire* was appreciative but said the dog wouldn't be of use to him one-eyed. Maurice could keep him if he wished.

What a fortunate thing that had been for Maurice and for Black Mountain. Each morning it was a treat to see the short, stout old man pacing slowly down rue Basque with his cane, Cabriole cavorting behind. The dog was small, short-haired, white with large black spots here and there—the most conspicuous of those a ring circling his good right eye.

Cabriole was amazing. One minute he'd be just behind Maurice, but walking upright on his hind legs. Then he'd bound on all fours, popping into the air in a full back flip! It was the most extraordinary thing to see. And it made Maurice a celebrity with the kids. They would gather around clapping, laughing, and calling for more.

The first time Maurice and I met, I was headed up toward the fountain when all of a sudden a small white missile flew out his window, landing in front of me. That's how Cabriole would leave the house to do his business; easier than his master having to get up to open and close his door all the time. Soon after, Maurice came through his doorway, practically bumping me too.

Short, wide, squarely built, with a deeply lined face on a slightly oversized head, Maurice was an interesting example of the rustic retired Frenchman. Dressed in blue, his hair was gray with white piping, and rather than wear the traditional beret, Maurice opted for a CAT (Caterpillar) farm equipment ball cap. Our first meeting set the tone for those that followed.

"*Bonjour Monsieur*," I said. The younger man initiates and offers the older the title, *Monsieur*.

"*Bonjour*," he returned with a wary eye.

"*Bonjour, Monsieur Chien*," I added for the dog.

Maurice brightened, offering the pup's name with, "*Il s'appelle Cabriole*."

So I patted the pooch's head and asked, "*Cabriole, ça va?*" (How's it going?) Most mornings that followed, running into me, Maurice would touch my arm for emphasis as he leaned close to pass on the latest gossip. Unfortunately his French was so guttural, I understood very little. Wanting to be polite, however, I'd offer a meaningless word or two whenever he'd pause. Sometimes it would be a Maurice Chevalier "Ooh," with a bit of growl at the end. *C'est vrai* (it's true) was good too because I could make it a statement or a question dependent on Maurice's state of agitation. *Oui* was obvious, but *alors* (well) wasn't bad either. I've always done a good *uummm*, in any language, but with Maurice I'd usually tie it to shaking my head and pouching my lips. (A very believable French couplet if I do say so myself.)

Sometimes we'd "talk" this way for minutes. Since Maurice was quite short, I'd be hunched over listening to him. Cabriole usually sat, looking up attentively with his one sparkly eye, first at Maurice, then to me. After a couple of months of this, Maurice became convinced I spoke excellent French and passed that around town.

From time to time chatting with Maurice and Cabriole, I noticed a well-dressed, handsome young gentleman observing us from farther up rue Basque. Bing picked up on him too. One night she saw him sitting alone in his car, parked on the square by the fountain, watching her. The motor wasn't running. Nothing was going on, but there he sat. Weird.

Actually it wasn't uncommon to see men around town at all hours, day or night. There were so many holidays, festivals, and vacations, few appeared to worry about work the next day. The social system helped too. Everything seemed to be subsidized. I don't know if it was an actual job category or not, but Black Mountain did seem to have one drunk-in-residence. A pleasant fellow. By no means wealthy, never unruly, but always gently inebriated. He sat at one bar or another throughout each day and apparently still collected a stipend from the government. So we wondered about the handsome young man watching from his car late at night. Was he a subsidized late-night car sitter? It wouldn't have surprised us.

One day, approaching dinner time, I'd picked up some things at the little grocery by the fountain when that fellow got out of his car, carefully locked it, and approached me with a smile and the customary "*Ça va.*"

I *ça va*'d back, but he came to a stop directly in front of me and held up his hand like a traffic cop.

"Do you like wine?" he asked, continuing in French.

An unexpected question, but I assured him I did. He nodded, looked up rue Basque, down rue Basque, then back at me. His eyes were very dark, his hair shiny black with a shock hanging over his forehead.

"Do you like Bordeaux wine?" he questioned, narrowing the inquiry.

I said *oui*, even naming a few of the famous châteaux I couldn't afford. He nodded, looked up and down the street again, and said, "Saturday."

I assured him I knew *Samedi* was the word for Saturday.

"*Chez moi*," (my house) he added.

"Why? For what?" I questioned.

"Wine, Bordeaux wine. We will have a bottle together."

I didn't know exactly what to say so stalled a bit by asking, "What time?" expecting he'd pick the *aperitif* hour, sometime around six or seven PM.

"Nine," he said.

"*Après midi*," I said, meaning nine at night. A little late for *aperitifs*, but not totally out of the question on a Saturday.

"No," he replied, "morning."

Somehow, sipping even the best Bordeaux with breakfast seemed a stretch. I declined, tempted to say I'd already committed to hitting a few bars with the town drunk. But I chickened out. To be sociable, I asked him, "What do you do?"

"What do you mean?" he replied.

"For work. What work do you do?"

More eyes left and right, then, with a bit of a hush, "*Je suis un agent secret.*" (I am a secret agent.)

What the hell do you say to that? Then I said, "*Bien sûr*" (of course). We both looked up and down the street.

"Are you on a job now?" I asked.

"No, I am presently unemployed," he replied, puffing a cheek and giving it a thoughtful blow. Expanding on his situation, he indicated his career had been impacted by the move from human to satellite intelligence. I shrugged agreeably, but still felt compelled to ask, "Is that what you put on your unemployment form at the town hall? *Agent secret?*"

"*Bien sûr*," he replied.

A S   O U R getting to know the folks of rue Basque progressed, and for that matter, all of Black Mountain, work on the house accelerated too.

Trakya and Anton had friends who painted house interiors. They'd heard the story of our fallen stairway wall and knew we needed help. When we'd first been looking for painters, after we fired the two young pretenders, their friends had been busy. Now they were free. Trakya brought them by to check out our job that Sunday when no one else was there. They looked to be a husband, wife, and partner team.

Carlo Fort did not paint by choice, only to put bread on the table. He was a musician, but couldn't support himself by only thumping on a set of drums. Trakya showed us a picture of him and his band while we waited for them to arrive. There was Carlo and a sax player, a guitarist, a fat guy on the trumpet, and a xylophonist, who also sang.

When the three arrived, it was clear Carlo's wife, Eve, should have been included in their publicity pictures, band or house painting. She was beautiful, in a gypsy sort of way. High cheek bones, dark eyes, creamy olive complexion, long legs, slim with a self-assured carriage that spoke of good breeding. That first meeting she wore a black mock turtle, matching slacks, and sturdy leather boots. She had her head wrapped in a black silk bandana, making me wonder if she was *Basque*. She didn't look like the wife of a French house painter, unless his name was Monet.

Carlo's partner went by the nickname *Nannou*. I have no idea why. Of course, for me to remember anything close to the name, I had to do another of my association drills. "Nannou" sounded a bit like "Nanook," as in Nanook of the North. Which made me think of snow (*la neige*). *Neige* and *Nannou* being sort of close, I called him Neige.

Neige looked like Dustin Hoffman with, sadly, very bad teeth. He was a handsome fellow, until he smiled. We saw a lot of this in France, England too. Our local dentist in Black Mountain told us that the health care system hadn't covered dentistry until recently. Too late for Neige. Sadly so, because otherwise he had a grace about him that was genuinely attractive.

As soon as they arrived, Bing took the lead, crunching them around on the first floor. She then led them upstairs and in and out of the rooms on the second and third floors. All the while, she was busy narrating the horror story of what had happened to us so far, in vastly improved French, primarily because it was a story we both had told many many times. She went on to describe what we would tackle next to reverse the sorry state of things at the moment. I wasn't getting a word in edgewise as the dynamic became more and more a gal-to-gal deal. Bing talked to Eve, while Carlo, Neige, and I just shuffled along behind.

Trakya hadn't been able to stay, but before she left, her better French helped us arrange a post-inspection conference at Claude's Café des Fleurs. She'd felt we'd be able to get across what we wanted done, so it would just be a matter of adding up the square meters to be painted and multiplying by their price per.

After the Bing-to-Eve *tour de force*, we took a table at Claude's to talk numbers. Over coffee and croissants, it surprised us both when Carlo took the lead and flatly stated they didn't want the job. What on earth? After panicked excursions into our dictionaries, Bing and I finally figured out they'd gotten the idea the whole project would be theirs. Not just the painting, but construction too. Bing's presentation of the problems we'd had, what still needed doing, supplemental to the painting, had been interpreted as a whole package for the three of them to tackle. And, since they were off-the-books types, *d'argent liquide* (cash) workers, they couldn't risk being too conspicuous around town. Making their money this way was common enough, acceptable as long as it was low-key. No one wanted to attract the tax collector's attention.

Anyway, it took us a lot of dictionary work to clarify the situation. All we wanted them to do was paint. And only the interior at that. Finally they got the picture. We smiled. They smiled. We ordered another round of *café au lait* while they calculated the price. It seemed fair. We shook hands and the deal was made.

A week later we learned just how good an artist Carlo really was. At his suggestion we took a Saturday drive to Toulouse, to the Air Bus Museum, where he had done a series of murals depicting how perspective can define depth in space. In the lobby, as well as in other rooms, he'd painted scenes that looked to be views out windows onto the surrounding countryside . . . but in fact were simple two-dimensional representations, *trompe-l'oeil*. I could have sworn I was looking out real windows, not just at walls. It was surreal. The guy was an exceptional talent with a brush, but one who only wanted to bang sticks on a drum. A kindred spirit. I was good at flying airplanes, but only wanted to put ink on paper. And as time went on, Carlo became like a younger brother to me, and an artistic confidant for Bing.

So, since breaking off with Jean-Jacques and Laila, we—actually more Bing than I—were discovering more elements, delicious elements of the village and its people. Just the thought and sight of Maurice and Cabriole coming down the street each morning, the warm volunteering support of Trakya and Anton's droll asides, Adrian's concern for us even as he carried such a heavy load of his own, all the shopkeepers, Claude's sometimes bizarre council— there was so much there to experience that it was slowly dawning that Black Mountain was becoming a true resource in our lives, not a detriment. As Bing would paint the village and its people, I might even be able to tell their stories . . . and ours.

TWENTY-THREE

FASCIST

SINCE JEAN-JACQUES and Laila had run us out of their lives, we were caught off guard Monday when Jean-Jacques stopped by rue Basque. We heard his voice downstairs asking Placo where Laurant was. When I came down from the second floor, he scooted out with only a cursory wave as he pulled the front door shut. Clearly he didn't want to talk to me any more than I wanted to talk with him.

I'd been on my way out anyway, but waited till he got further up toward the fountain where I saw he'd parked his Mercedes. I was surprised to see him walk past his car and turn into the house where Bing and I first saw the La Rousse & Fils van. That seemed odd. Jean-Jacques never mentioned having an interest in that place. We knew he and Laila had purchased at least two houses near the *école*, but they'd never said anything about buying one on rue Basque. A moment later I was even more surprised to see Laurant pull up on his scooter and walk into the same house.

Little fires of suspicion started to burn. Jean-Jacques had been the one who laid out our original work plans. He'd chosen who would be hired. Laurant had said something about Jean-Jacques putting into the *devis* that we would use our own contractors. And when delays developed, Jean-Jacques explained them away first as contractual problems with the *département*, then in front of Laurant, but in English, as weather issues. Laurant didn't know what Jean-Jacques told us. Ever. Something wasn't right. I was getting angry, but who was I going to get angry at?

NOONTIME, BING suggested we take a walk. I guessed she figured it was no day to get logy from one of Claude's huge lunches. Shrugging a pack onto her back, she steered me down the road by the corral and the two horses we occasionally befriended with apples, past the sheep in the lower field, further down the rock-walled lane to a lemon tree Bing liked to sit under. One of her quiet places.

She had a lot of stuff in the pack: two small bottles of Badoit (a mineral water), some cheese, olives, two slices of ham, a *petit pain*, apples, and chocolate. Spreading the bounty between us, napkins too, she jumped straight into what was on her mind.

"Kenny, you're worrying me. It feels like you're a bomb waiting to explode. Please, sometimes things happen we can't fix right away. But that doesn't mean they won't *ever* get fixed." She said this while cutting the first apple in half, then quarters, then into eighths, scooping out the seeds and handing me my share.

"Thanks," I said taking it, marveling at how compartmentalized she could be. Even when something developed between us, she might fire a few shots, but then would retreat into her chamber of silence. An enclosure I surely did not have the key to, which, at times, only upped the ante of my . . . what? Discomfort? Now and then agitation? Sometimes even anger.

"You're right. I do *feel* that way. But look. I had the manuscript's outline done before we left number 10, but only that. It should have been a finished product months ago. I should be sitting in a publisher's office right now, or with Vernon at DreamWorks, but instead I'm stumbling around in that dump of a house . . . making an ass of myself trying to speak a foreign language . . . and worrying about your wonderful hands getting hurt working like you do, maybe leaving you unable to paint. So yes, I *may* be a bomb ready to blow, but I think for good reason."

Laying out the cheddar and *chèvre*, Bing cut them into squares and pierced two with toothpicks from her kit. "Don't worry about me," she said, holding half the squares out to me, "I can take care of myself."

"I'll give you that, sure, but the mess we're in here is different for you. You're known. You exhibit in New York. You had a show in Barcelona last year. You're close to getting into MoMA. You can float through something like this, but I am *nobody*. I haven't even published, for God's sake. So yes, I'm frustrated as hell, and this mess isn't helping."

"I know it's hard, but I know you're going to make it. Kenny, your book could be snapped up by a publisher even unfinished. You don't know."

"Unfinished? No way," I said.

"Then finish it," she said, tearing chunks off the baguette like the locals did.

"Shit," I fired back. She lifted an eyebrow at my language. "It's not *that* easy. Writing is not like turning a faucet on and off. I can't work the house till nine or ten at night, then sit down and write brilliant stuff."

"You can write every morning and worry about the house after that."

"Dear lady," now I *was* getting hot. "That damned house has to get finished *before* anything else gets done. We only have so much time on our visas, and if we leave here without it being finished, well hell, we know what happens then. You've seen what happens when we're not here."

"Priorities," she said, much like my fourth grade teacher had.

"Balls!" I snapped and threw my Badoit bottle, bouncing it off her precious lemon tree. I was torqued. I wasn't sure why, but so what? I got up and strode like a big angry asshole down the road back toward that f'ing house . . . that chain around my neck.

BING STAYED gone for the rest of the afternoon. I stayed pissed for the rest of the afternoon. I knew she was tucked into another of her quiet places somewhere, meditating, being rational and mature. Probably sketching pastorals too. While I was storming around looking for someone to punch or something to break. All of which only made me angrier; then angrier still because I was . . . angrier still! I'd hate to think what label a psychiatrist would put on me; and contemplating that didn't help one damn bit either.

When Bing got back, the sun was just about down. Her sketchbook was full of great stuff. I congratulated her on the work and we both made a huge effort not to get all in a tangle again. Which worked until we were in the car driving back to Soual.

"Kenny, you've got to try to deal with things in ways that don't change you," she said looking over at me in the Princess Di way she had—head down, eyes up.

"How am I supposed to do that?"

"I can't tell you how, only what *I* do," she said. "During the troubles in my first marriage, I knew I had to find a way to handle things, a way that wouldn't damage the kids. I had to deal with a lot of situations that could have ripped my relationship with them apart. It took a careful balance. In time I began to see the route there was by establishing an inner peace, a calm center where I could think more clearly, and radiating stability to them. Sure, I could have been very angry. It would have been easy to lash out at my husband, who would have deserved it, but it would only have made matters worse. It would have made me just like what and who were hurting me so."

"So what did you do?"

"I got into meditation," Bing answered.

"Ah Bing, I'm not the type. I'm from Boston, not Berkeley," I said, and then wished I hadn't.

Bing bit into a last piece of apple, then turned to look out her window at a farmhouse and the fields around it. She didn't say anything for quite a while . . . making her point in her own way.

"Okay, you're probably right," I finally said, a little huff in my voice, "but there's no way I can sit all scrunched up like a monk for an hour. What would I think about? How would I keep my mouth shut? Why even try?"

"Actually it's quite simple. Rather than thinking about something, I go through a process of emptying my mind of all its everyday thoughts. First I focus on the simplest of things—the curvature of skin where my nose meets my upper lip, for instance. Once there's nothing else but that spot in my mind, I'll feel a prickling of change there," she said touching the place with her index finger.

"What *change* are you talking about?" I asked, feeling mildly stupid.

"Our bodies are constantly changing. Every second. Old cells die. New ones are born. Skin, muscle, bones are all part of the process," Bing explained. "So I try to tune in on, *concentrate* on, these changes throughout my body. It's in that concentration I practice *stillness*. Section by section, skin, muscle, nerves and bones, I concentrate on their sensations of change all contributing to the larger place of stillness . . . my heart . . . soul. Once that's established, I work to stay within it. If my mind wanders, if my focus falters, I go back to where my concentration broke off. I have to do that gently, fighting off any frustration. That serves its own purpose. It helps me deal with the frustration of everyday failures. And throughout the process I come to a better understanding of how each of us, even life itself, is a work in progress. Something never totally finished. Never totally perfect, but always renewable. Always able to begin again, letting hard times pass."

She paused for a moment, giving me the chance to ask, "But why such an exercise? What does it accomplish?"

"Peace, the state or *place* of peace . . . all my own, renewable, expandable everyday. It frees me of the harm, the clamor, the *clatter* of the world outside. Kenny, you are the pragmatist. Think about your blood pressure going down. Your heart beating more regularly, slower. All the elements of living being more coherent. And in doing that, you find yourself experiencing a true union of mind and matter, making you more *whole*, less torn apart by things outside you. Like the things here. The house. Jean-Jacques. Not getting your writing done. All those things that tear you down."

I didn't know what to say, so said nothing. Probably my first baby step toward that meditational peace Bing was trying to gift me. God bless her. I *could* learn so much from her, but I had this awful sensation that I wouldn't. There was too much *me* in me.

OUR TIME in Soual was giving us insights into life on a French farm. I'd never lived with a hundred or more cows before, of any nationality, so there was a lot to absorb. For instance, we were told some EU farmers keep their cows inside feeder barns the entire winter. The theory is that during those months there isn't enough forage outside anyway, so why have the cows wandering around in the cold using up energy that they need to produce milk? Why not feed them in a relatively warm, secure environment where less fodder is required to produce even more milk? The only fly in that ointment is the issue of poop. Though popular with flies, it still constitutes a challenge to the farmer's energy reserve to shovel, haul, dump, and store manure for spreading in the spring.

The farmers around us worked hard. Unlike their town cousins, who seem to have acres of free time. The farms themselves are upscale from the hardscrabble affairs common to our native New England. Stone barns, stone farmhouses, stone service buildings all roofed with tile or slate. Everything is *dur*, built to last and, in most cases, already has lasted five hundred to a thousand years. Wood is not considered *dur*.

Their equipment was generally new, so it needed minimal maintenance. Large tractors, small tractors, spreaders, bailers, every kind of big ticket items a Vermonter could only dream of, were snug in our Soual stone barns. None of it was left outside to rust.

The quality of food the French system produces seems unrivaled too. The tomatoes tasted sweet and juicy, not like cardboard. Every vegetable we'd buy at the Saturday morning *marché* had levels of flavor we'd only heard about, but hardly tasted until we got to Black Mountain. Our American beef is far better, but forget about getting into a cheese war with these people. Charles de Gaulle was reported to have remarked, "How can one expect to govern a country with 258 varieties of cheese?" (Though the famous cheese expert Roland Barthélemy said the good general was off a bit; the number was probably closer to 365.)

Then there is the bread, wine, duck, rabbit, and ostrich (which we found indistinguishable from filet mignon), to say nothing of the incredible oysters, mussels, shrimp, and seafood laying in the *marché* stalls just waiting for us to walk by. Oh, okay, America wins on crackers too, but with bread like the French have, who cares about crackers?

Americans roar through our days in pursuit of the all-mighty buck for the security it brings, but we miss a lot of good living in the process. One day Bing said, "Kenny, people are so civil here. The *Bonjour* as we enter a shop, or pass on the street. And the way clerks really try to help, almost as friends."

"Except at Lumière," I said, mentioning the electrical shop in Castres that seemed to find joy in giving us a hard time. A store run and dominated by, I figured, Nurse Ratched's sister.

"But that's been the only exception," she pointed out. "Maybe it's the system. People have security, so they don't worry so much. Trakya told me the other day that the summer bookings for the art workshops were way off. She said she'd probably lose two-thirds of her summer income, but then she smiled, saying she didn't care. Now she would have more time with her kids. The money loss was not an issue."

"The quality of people in the simplest jobs, the checkout clerks for example, seems much higher than at home," I added. "I think salaries are incidental since the benefits are so extravagant."

"And the slower pace," Bing said. "I don't see many Type-A's around. Besides you, of course," she said with a smile.

"Right. Probably because I'm not in the system. You either, love," I smiled back.

"It's a gentler world here," Bing concluded.

"But can it last?" I asked.

"Probably for as long as we'll be around. So let's enjoy it," she said, leaning her shoulder against my arm.

"Even in English you sound French," I said.

"Careful, I speak some German too," Bing countered, bumping me with her hip again.

OUR COMMUTE each morning took us through two small towns we hadn't known before. Usually we'd stop for bread in one or the other, grab a coffee at a *café*, or drop into one of the markets.

We got to know people in each, as we had in Black Mountain. Because we worked on the language, laughing about our screw-ups, the locals had fun playing teacher.

We were progressing. Sometimes people asked if we were Swiss, or Dutch, or French-Canadian. That meant a lot. Not that we aren't proud of being Americans, not at all; but it was heartening to have adapted enough to be thought more a part of their European world. A lot of Americans, as well as Brits, seem to locate in exclusive enclaves. They don't join the community, creating Little Americas or Little Englands in the land they profess to want to know better. We wondered why they even bothered coming.

Our days were long even without much writing or painting. Early, before Laurant's men arrived, we'd walk through the place deciding what was getting screwed up and how best to straighten something out before it was too late. The day Rouge and Michel the mason were tearing up half the master bedroom floor, lowering it to match the level of what had earlier been a little hallway, was an example of such straightening. First, watching the tiles come up, we discovered how these old southwestern French houses were built. Usually three stories, most of the houses in Black Mountain were designed as a kind of stone-encased post-and-beam. The most surprising part of the layout was how the second floors were put together. As protection against the long summers' heat (when?), as well as to lock out winter cold, the medieval builders would lay tightly abutted boards across the first floor's massive ceiling beams. With these pegged or spiked in place, they'd spread about an eight-inch layer of sand or something similar over everything, wall to wall. Next they'd lay tile over that as the floor for the second level. Great thermal and acoustical insulation, though we hated to think about how many tons of wood, sand, and tile would be over our heads while we sat in the living room.

As Rouge and Michel started to re-lay the floor, Bing said, "Kenny, they're putting the tiles down just any old way. As if they're the same size and shape."

"What do you mean?" I asked, not immediately picking up on what she was talking about. "They're all level and the same color. What's the problem?"

"The sizes and *shapes* aren't right," she said with some irritation. Then another element came into play: Bing had to talk with Rouge through me to get anything done. She'd say something directly to him or his people and their eyes would turn to me. On the other hand, Laurant would only speak to Bing. It was as if the lower down the pecking order you went, the less women had a place in things. Either that, or, as I'd wondered about before, did Laurant have a thing for Bing?

"*Monsieur Rouge, s'il vous plaît . . .*" I began, and then went off in my hackneyed French on how the two types of tile couldn't be butted against each other because their shapes were different. One set square, the other rectangular.

"But this is how we were told to do it," Rouge replied.

"Who told you?" I asked, expecting Laurant was the one pushing speed.

"Monsieur Kurtz," was the surprising answer.

I looked at Bing, she back at me. What was going on?

"Rouge, please call Laurant on his cell phone," I said. "Ask him to come here."

ONCE LAURANT was there, he said (to Bing), "I see the problem, but Monsieur Kurtz said not to waste time working the tiles. Keep everything simple."

"Laurant," she said, "that was before we agreed with *you* that this floor would be added to the *devis*. Two rooms into one; ceilings down; walls out; everything. The second floor must match the rest of the house."

"But you did not say anything about floor tiles," he replied, irritatingly anal. "For any of these changes we must go to time and material," he said. (*Devis* were contractor estimates that the contractor could not change after agreed to. If the homeowner made the change, further work became time and material, and possibly open-ended.)

Bing took the bull by the horns. Getting down on hands and knees, she took the square tiles and butted them against the rectangular ones, then said, "*Désagréable, oui? Mais* . . . if you place a row of these bricks between the two . . . *comme ça, voila!*"

As she said this she was laying a herringbone path of tiles. And it looked terrific. Laurant stared at it, then at Bing. Rouge stared at Bing. Michel stared at the dividing pattern and nodded. Bing and I smiled at each other. The floor was going to look great. And we felt great.

As PLEASANT as it was to solve problems working alongside Laurant's guys, the long days led to difficult nights. After they left, we were so involved with whatever the job of the day was that night would be upon us before we realized it. The sun doesn't set in June until near ten. With light still in the sky, we would lose track of how late it actually was.

Christophe, our erstwhile electrician, would often show up at some crazy hour too. Since he worked alone as an independent contractor, he broke all the French work rules, especially dietary. The guy was thin as a rail, and we were learning why. Unmarried, he didn't eat much more than what he could carry in a back or jacket pocket while he strung wires and soldered connections. Sometimes Bing would bring him something from the farm, but usually he was happy with his crust of bread and a chunk of cheese to gnaw on, hopefully taken out of the coat pocket.

It was great to have someone show up after hours like that, but we questioned why he wasn't around more during the day. In time we began to suspect his other jobs didn't involve crazy Americans.

Some nights, even as late as ten o'clock, we'd find ourselves locking up and feeling so tired the idea of fixing supper back at the farm seemed just too much. The only place in the village open at that hour, with any chance of food, was La Brasserie.

In the beginning we didn't know Michel, the *propriétaire*, that well. We had stopped in a few times in January when we first were in Black Mountain. We liked sitting in front of the huge walk-in fireplace. We'd warm ourselves and breathe the aroma of the pot of stew hanging from *la crémaillère*. La Brasserie was incredibly charming. It had originally been a stable and tack room serving the ancient military academy across the way. It had high ceilings with wonderful old beams bridging from one great stone wall to the other. The bar, maybe five meters long, running half the length of the huge room, greeted us as we came in.

One night late, Bing and I staggered in dog tired, covered in plaster, paint, even blood in Bing's case, after she banged her head on a joist spike on the third floor. What a sight we must have made.

Literally hat in hand, I apologized to Michel as best I could for our appearance, and asked if there was any possibility for some food at such a late hour. It was a quiet Tuesday night. A few grizzled types were at the bar. Only one table was still set. Theirs. He, his wife Jesselyne, and their two teenage boys were finally sitting down to dinner. And yet, without the slightest hesitation and a smiling *bien sûr*, he grabbed two more chairs and place settings for us to join them.

We were touched. Our rough French only destroyed the conviviality of their quiet dinner together. We felt terribly awkward, yet warmly welcomed. For the weeks while we struggled with that damn house, Michel treated us like that, family.

Interestingly enough, Michel did wonders for all Black Mountain. Thursday nights he brought classical music ensembles to the village—strings, or woodwinds, sometimes brass. There was one cellist he'd occasionally book who would pack the place. Friday and Saturday nights were for jazz. Terrific. There was a saxophonist from Paris who'd sometimes appear, strolling in casually, like the totally cool singer Yves Montand. He wouldn't bother to warm up. Just open his case as the others were playing, assemble his instrument, then jump in with a solo that would blow the locals out of the room. One time another sax player from Toulouse was sitting in. He wasn't about to step aside, so when the two of them went head to head, man, it was a night to remember. As a kid I'd played the sax, but I never got near the way these guys blew.

The drummer was the lead vocalist. He sounded like Tony Bennett and would sing his versions of dreamy American ballads. "I Left My Heart in San Francisco" sung in French by a guy who sounded like Bennett was weird but terrific.

The Hoagy Carmichael–looking piano player was an old guy with an Ahmad Jahmal touch who was an expert at cadging drinks from characters like yours truly. We got along great.

Little by little we were making a lot of friends in Black Mountain. Because we didn't yet have a house of our own, we started using La Brasserie as a place to take people for dinner. If we invited an older couple, we'd take them there on a Thursday night for the classical music. With younger people we'd go for the Friday or Saturday jazz. One night, when we asked Trakya and Anton to join us there for dinner, they said flatly, "*Non.*" Which seemed strange. What could be the problem? They were so laid back and certainly music lovers, why the "No"? When I asked what was wrong with La Brasserie, they said, "We don't go there. The owner is a Fascist."

"Michel? Michel a *Fascist*?" Bing and I were amazed.

"Yes. He is a Fascist and we will have nothing to do with him or his kind."

A few other people said the same thing. It seemed crazy, considering nobody in that nifty little village had been better to us than Michel and his family. He broke bread with us. Shared his private table. Originally he helped us contact Christophe the electrician and tried to step into La Maison Framboise garden situation too. The guy never stopped being helpful. One time Bing even noticed Michel pouring a bottle of good estate wine into our carafe rather than the *vin du pays*. Nazi my butt.

One evening when the place was practically empty and I'd gained some ground linguistically, I asked Michel to sit down for a glass with us and I said, "Some of our friends will not come here. They say, *Michel is a Fascist*. What does that mean? *Are* you a Fascist?"

He rolled his eyes. It was as if he'd been expecting this for some time. Looking away for a moment, then doing the traditional cheek-puff-and-blow-with-shrug, he said, "One presidential election, the candidates were in the region making speeches. I sent word to their people that I would open the Brasserie for them to come and speak. Debate. But the only one who came was the Conservative candidate. Because of that, I have been branded a Fascist."

"That's it? That's all?" I asked.

"Was that in the last election or when?" Bing questioned.

Michel looked at the two of us with an ironic smile and said, "Bing, that was nearly twenty years ago." Then he asked, "How long have the people lived in Black Mountain who won't come here?"

Hah! Trakya and Anton had lived here for five years, so this whole deal happened fifteen years *before* they even came to Black Mountain! Much the same story for the others too. Ridiculous.

Then, quietly, his eyes moving from mine to Bing's, he said, "Bing. Ken. How could I ever be a Fascist? I am a Jew!"

THERE AREN'T that many Jews in France anymore, but there is still considerable anti-Semitism. One time, a woman who wouldn't go to La Brasserie with us made a long speech emphasizing that what the Fascists had done to the Jews was the primary reason she could never have anything to do with Michel or anyone like him.

Our friend didn't leave it at that either, she continued waxing lyrical about the brilliance of the Jewish people, their sensitivity, their interest in the classics, and their long and endless suffering. Finally she summed up with a flat, "I love Jewish people."

"Excellent," I said and reached across the table to touch her hand, "all the more reason for joining us at the Brasserie."

"Why? I don't understand," she said.

"It's simple," I said, looking her straight in the eye, "Michel, you see, is a Jew."

The woman's mouth dropped open. Her eyes went wide. She started shaking her head. She tried to speak, but at first only managed a gasp. Then she said, "Michel a Jew? I cannot believe such a man could ever be a Jew. He is a Fascist. He cannot be both."

"Exactly the point," Bing offered.

"But I don't think many people know that he is Jewish," I added. "Perhaps it will be easier for him if it remains that way."

I don't think our friend understood us. It was as if she was in the midst of an intense internal struggle. Finally she blurted out, "There were lots of Nazis who changed from being Jews."

"Not if the SS knew about it," I countered.

"Self-hating Jews who joined the Fascists. And *they* were the worst."

"Do you honestly believe Michel is one of those?"

"He must be."

"But he told us his parents died in the camps."

"Someone who would side with those who murdered his own parents is the worst."

This was getting really weird. I tried another tack. "You have said you are a Christian who hates what the Fascists did to the Jews."

"Yes, of course," she returned.

"Okay, then, as a Christian, aren't you obliged to go to Michel and ask him about this? If he is being falsely accused, and you do nothing to find out for yourself, aren't you hurting yourself also?"

"I don't want to talk about this anymore," she said.

I started to speak. Something like this couldn't just be dropped. What about Michel, for heaven's sake? Bing put her hand on my knee and for once I did shut up, though I felt guilty doing so.

"Ken," Bing said later, "we've already alienated one set of friends over how Christians should treat people. That's enough for now. Let's just let her work this out for herself."

IT'S SAD how negative we all can be sometimes, yet how encouraging when it can be turned around for the good, as in Michel's case. Here the accused proved himself greater than his attackers. For us it was a wake-up call. The setting was small, though the issue was large. And people are just people, everywhere. Not saints. Here in Black Mountain we knew all the players, people we saw every day and liked. Yet the question raised was: How can such good people get things so wrong? The good news in this instance was that it's never too late to change. As our friend did, finally joining us for dinner and warm conversation with her new friend, Michel Bond.

TWENTY-FOUR

GREEN FIRE

THOUGH WHAT little work I was starting to get in on finishing my novel was miniscule, Château Poubelle's renovation was progressing smartly. The time when Bing and I could start living there was inching closer. Placo had done yeoman's work putting up new walls on the second floor. He'd layered in acoustical and thermal insulation behind the *placoplâtre*, reducing not only street noise, but that between the rooms as well.

Carlo and Neige, though no Eve because she was down with the grippe, had painted their way from the third floor, around the stairwell to the second, finishing the guest bedroom and our bedroom, and were then laboring in what would be the master bath after I got the tub, shower, and other fixtures in place. Since Christophe was also a plumber, he couldn't stop giving me advice. Most of which I didn't understand, while what I did, I tended to ignore. I'd plumbed three houses at home. Some of his ideas, and my way of doing things, didn't jibe.

Rouge, Placo, Bruno, and Deux, and occasionally additional cameo cast members, were now doing a lot of grunt work knocking out walls and ceilings on the first floor. But, as hard as any of these guys worked, none put in a more difficult day than Bing. She was teamed with Carlo, asked to chase down the right colors, types of paints, and run errands, in addition to steaming wallpaper off the few salvageable walls, then plastering in the necessary patches. Everyone was hugely impressed with her grit. I doubt they'd seen, or worked alongside, a woman like Bing before. Gloria Steinem would have been proud.

Then came, *finally*, some summer heat. Thunderheads sucked in strong gusts of electrically loaded air, showers fell in sheets, but after each storm the humidity disappeared. We'd go to bed with warm and beautiful sunsets, only to wake up a couple hours later grabbing for covers. Such was the strange weather of La Montagne Noire.

Bing continued to be a heck of a lot better at being "French" with our struggles than I was. Of course, she had that center of calm built around such things as Al-Anon's *God, grant me the serenity to accept the things I cannot change; the courage to change the things I can; and the wisdom to know the difference.*

O N E   D A Y we took an afternoon off, but went our separate ways. Bing threw on her backpack full of art stuff to hike up La Montagne Noire's first ridge, called Berniquaut. Her two old horse friends who enjoyed the apples she brought were still pasturing there and posing for Bing's latest sketches to fill out her *Dream Horses* series.

I slipped into my long-neglected running togs. 10K or die! No more sighs and bitching. Back to health and happiness. There was a time I ran huge distances, caught up in that culture of marathon running to prove my self-worth, keep the weight down, and still be able to drink lots of beer. Sixteen miles a day I'd run. My dear late wife once said of it, "Ken, if you run just one more mile a day, you'll become the most boring man I've ever known." Which I didn't take as a vote of confidence for my program, no matter how I looked at it. But that was then. Though I'd managed to keep up on the beer part, my running had fallen off severely. At one time 10K had hardly counted as a workout, now it was a challenge.

Being a New Englander, *country* to me meant narrow winding roads through small farms, over hills and minor mountains with tall pines marching up their slopes. It's the land of "What's around the next turn in the road less traveled?"

Vast open lands were not my heritage. I had been to the Scottish Highlands, renowned for terrain like that, but I never ran there. During those earlier honeymoon weeks in Black Mountain when I'd had more time for such things, I was struck by the almost eerie affect the vast rolling fields had on me. So, as I chugged along that afternoon, I found myself extraordinarily conscious of the *power* of the earth under and around me. The crops were diverse—sunflowers, soybeans, rye, mustard, barley, peas, beans, corn, and vast stretches of wheat nearing another harvest. I felt incredibly insignificance in this vastness. Here was the *nourriture* to feed all of France and much of Europe pushing, pushing hard up from the earth.

As a child I'd had only one nightmare, but I'd had it often. I would find myself alone on a vast squared plain. A rook on a huge chessboard. The pattern of squares surrounding me seemed overwhelming and frightening. It was an out-of-body perspective where I saw myself as totally insignificant in the midst of this orderly but vast emptiness.

Running that day, in a foreign land, in a direction away from even what little I knew of in Black Mountain, I was that frightened child again. Topping a small rise I looked down onto a sea of wheat with stalks long and fruit heavy at the top—an incredible abundance as far as I could see. And then, as if to confirm my latent fear of the expanse on which I was only a speck, *whoosh!* I was almost blown off my feet, from the left side of the little road across to the right.

From out of nowhere a one-hundred-kilometer gust of wind slapped me hard. Almost sixty-five mph! I'd heard about these phantom gusts from Adrian, but this was my first real experience of them. As I struggled for footing, I watched the blast hit the fields below. An amazing sight. The stalks lay over, nearly flat to the ground, showing the green of each stem, so different from the beige at the tip. As the wind ran, the fields of beige blew green with it, creating the effect of a fire racing wildly across the land. A fire without flame . . . a green fire riding on a wind as alive as the earth it traveled.

Then, as suddenly as the gusts had come, everything was calm again. Almost surreally so. The fields were still. The green turned back to beige and the air grew heavy.

I'd never experienced anything like this before, other than in my childhood dream. A nightmare then. What would it be now?

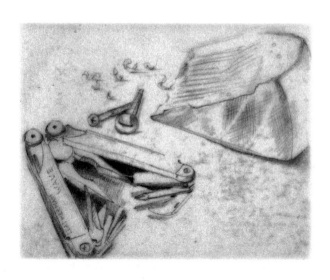

❧

TWENTY-FIVE

LEATHERMAN

L EATHERMAN IS the all-purpose pocket tool with a plethora of uses. It's long been one of my best friends whenever and wherever I've had house-fixing jobs to do. In Black Mountain it was a lifesaver. Don't take that as an ad, take it as a fact.

I don't know who first came up with the concept of a tool combining maximum portability with such functionality, but he or she was a genius as far as I am concerned. Certainly at Château Poubelle, my Leatherman was indispensable since nothing is plumb in a medieval house. Walls are not vertical. Corners are not ninety degrees. Floors, doors, moldings, all are at least slightly off. Trying to use sophisticated equipment, radial arm saws, mitering tools, T-squares, any of that good stuff, forget about it. Straight lines do not exist in ancient places. Not around Black Mountain anyway. So, as we worked to repair or re-create a handheld device small enough to get into tight places, with a variety of available tools attached, it was just what the doctor ordered.

M. Placo ate his heart out watching me cut tight fits of thick wallboard to press flush into irregular rock-faced walls. He'd never seen such a compact saw-toothed blade before. He had to use a keyhole saw—big, cumbersome, and dull. One day I took over his work with my Leatherman blade and cut his time in half. No pun intended.

Leatherman was good for everything. Picnicking one time we used it to pull a cork, cut a loaf of bread, slice and even grate our cheese. We needed it so much we started jokingly using the line, "This sounds like a job for Leatherman."

Leatherman was always on my belt. That is, until I helped Anton with a water hose problem on his truck. One day he and the Secret Agent man were looking under the raised hood at his motor as I came down rue Basque. There was a puddle of fluid at their feet, running from under the engine. I walked over to see if I could help. Standing by the opposite fender I saw the lower radiator hose had a break in it. Anton had just picked up a replacement, but hadn't made it home before overheating, and he didn't have his tools with him.

"*Quel pensez-vous, Monsieur Ken?*" Secret Agent asked, as Anton went to the cab looking for at least a screwdriver.

"Need to replace the radiator hose," I said in passable French.

"You misunderstand," he replied, puffing his cheek and rolling his eyes. "We are breaking for *aperitifs*. Do you think you would like to try some of my Bordeaux now?"

Stupidly I checked my watch before answering. It *was* five in the afternoon. So . . .

"*Pourquoi pas, mais après j'ai fixé la voiture,*" I agreed, reaching to the holster on my belt and pulling out my trusty Leatherman. Coming back to where I stood, Anton's shrug indicated he did not have even a screwdriver lying around in the cab.

"Here, let me fix it," I said, unfolding the tool's Phillips first and getting to work unscrewing the clamps. With those off, I hacked through the hose line with the saw blade, pulled the two pieces of hose off their nipples with the pliers, cleaned the rusty clamps with the file, then mounted the new hose and refastened the clamps—all with only that one device. The look on Anton's face said it all—*I lust for your Leatherman.*

After a very nice Château Rothschild on the fountain wall, in glasses brought from Secret Agent's apartment, I felt I owed Anton for all the help he'd given us moving furniture and supplying us with firewood. So I gave him my Leatherman. He didn't know what to say, though I thought I saw his Teutonic eyes starting to mist. He even grabbed me in an awkward, I guess, *edelweiss* embrace, mumbling repeated *danke, danke, dankes.*

A few days later I ran into Anton at the *boulangerie* and asked him if he'd been using his Leatherman much. He scowled a moment, looking down at his feet, then back to me, saying, "No. It was too heavy on my belt. I gave it to Claude."

I resisted giving him a kick in the pants, and settled for perhaps an over-civilized nod and the wish for him to have a pleasant day. I also resisted adding "*dummkopf*" at the end. See, I was learning from Bing's influence. *Growing,* one might say.

What now? Without my Leatherman I felt naked, incomplete. And then, amazingly enough, a flyer from a supply house in Toulouse fell into our *boîte aux lettres* that advertised a one-day sale, Saturday, and the Leatherman was listed as one of the items included. Excellent. Bing and I would be there as the doors opened.

Our trip to Toulouse did not go well. I'd thought picking up the Leatherman would be the start of a happy day. We'd follow it by a run to the huge Ikea store for kitchen things, cheap chairs and whatever else caught our eye. We would have a bite in their pleasant cafeteria, and then loop back into the city to the Musée des

Augustins, where Bing's great-great uncle's work was on display in the *Salon Rouge*. Depending on how the time went, we were thinking about dinner there, or perhaps continuing back toward Black Mountain with a stop at Raoul's *brocante* to see what new old stuff had been added to his barn since we left our furniture there.

What we'd planned to weave into a full, fun day quickly frayed. The Leatherman pictured in the brochure, the replacement for the one I gave Anton, was not what they were selling. Nothing like it. Okay, no big deal, but it was still irritating and perhaps a harbinger of problems ahead. The first of these occurred while we were crossing a busy street near the parking garage in downtown Toulouse. I saw a car coming from our left, moving too damn fast for the narrow street. Bing was just stepping off the curb, looking the other way. Instinctively my hand shot out and caught her arm, pulling her back onto the sidewalk. I'd been unintentionally rough. She'd been surprised, in turn surprising me with a fierce look as she snapped, "Don't grab me!" She pulled her arm free and marched angrily on across, still not looking left.

I hurried over behind her. "You were going to get hit . . ." I said in too loud a voice, pointing down . . . the now empty street.

"That's no excuse for pulling me like that," she shot back, eyes blazing. "You've done that before."

What was going on? I thought I'd been Mr. Goodguy, saving her from at least a broken leg, and she was mad at *me*!

"Bullshit," I unfortunately said, turning people's heads and mortifying Bing.

Once back in the car heading toward Ikea, I did a slow burn. When I tried to explain about the car, she would just shut me down with one of those "I don't want to talk about it" deals. Which only made me angrier, leading me to shout a few rude things at the window and steering wheel, while I slammed the shift lever unnecessarily hard every time I had to change gears.

All of which drove Bing into a deeper silence, further angering me, until . . . she started to weep.

Ahh . . . *damn*! I was so mad I wanted to open my door and bail out. Tears are the killers. Men shout and kick things; women shout sometimes too, but when they start to cry . . . ahhhh! It's all over. Including the shouting.

We got to Ikea, but along with everything else going wrong, I needed a bladder break. Great. It was probably the tears rolling down Bing's cheeks that psychosomatically set that off.

The entrance was crowded. There was a pair of electronic gates that reluctantly opened as people approached, actually slowing traffic. I saw a jostling bunch of teenagers approaching from behind us, which would add to the problem, slowing us more. And now that my mind was on it, I really did have to pee. So, rather than step aside for the rowdy boys, I wanted to make sure we got through the gates without delay. Not thinking, I put my arm behind Bing's back to kind of whoosh her past me, putting me between her and them. What I again thought a Sir Walter Raleigh gesture, she felt was a push, which, when added to my earlier grab, amounted to additional physical abuse.

"Do not *push*!" she snapped.

"Hurry up," I said.

"Well, don't *push me*!" she repeated. She was angry, planting her feet.

I lost it, shouting, "You're holding everybody up!" I pointed at the teenagers with the crowd building behind them. And of course everybody stared at the pair of arguing Americans blocking the way.

"You're the rude one. Rude as hell with me. I wasn't pushing. I was trying to move you along to keep you ahead of that bunch of boys. Damn it, why can't I get the benefit of the doubt in anything today? Balls!"

"You don't have to act this way. You don't have to talk that way. And you can stop pushing, grabbing, and *shoving* me around. I do not appreciate being treated like that," Bing fired back. "Go do your business."

By then my need to get to the *toilette* overrode everything else. I pushed by her, heading straight for the men's room.

We didn't buy anything. We had a lousy lunch. We skipped the museum. We skipped the *brocante*. I don't think more than five words were spoken between us the rest of the day, and for that matter, the rest of the night, much less the weekend. Of course, I was the guilty party. Shit.

MONDAY WASN'T much of a day either, though the weather was fine, perfect for working at the house, especially tearing up the cracked cement courtyard now that the huge nasty oil tank had been hauled out. While the crew blasted away with jackhammers, I was watching Placo destroy an area near the base of the wall dividing our courtyard from the neighbor's on the left, the Moroccans. After he'd cut through the five- or six-inch slab and his bit sliced deep into the rubble below, I got a glimpse of what looked like some Orangeburg pipe at the bottom of his hole. As he levered up the chunk of slab, I asked him about it. He said it was nothing, just some of the ancient system that went under the courtyards behind the houses, on down to the street in front of the *café*. He said he'd checked the charts in the *mairie* to make sure he didn't hit anything important. I was impressed, but still had my doubts. But like Bing, Placo didn't seem to be paying much attention to me either.

Then, on the opposite side of our little court, against the other neighbor's wall, Bruno (Numéro Un) discovered a debris-filled, long-forgotten well. More of the ancient past. Laurant was called to come check it out. When he arrived about an hour later, he started speaking directly to Bing about what to do next—leave things as they were and put the new slab over it or re-dig it to help take down the water level? The latter would be a twofer, adding the charm of a well to the courtyard as well as reducing the threat of dampness to the house.

As the two talked, I felt like the proverbial tits on a bull. Even when I threw in my two cents on something, Laurant would give me a minimal glance and continue directing what he had to say to Bing. That whole process, a regular conversational jerk-around, did not make me feel loved, by any means, by anyone. Add to that our miserable weekend, Bing's continued minimal dialogue with me, and now this—yes, my temperature started to rise.

Bing, it seemed, certainly had no problem chatting it up with good old Laurant. But not with me. What really stuck in my craw was that I actually could babble in French better than she could, even if she understood more of what was being said. But now, with Laurant ignoring me too, I was getting edgy, irritable, very cranky indeed.

RELATIONSHIPS, LIKE sunny days, can suddenly cloud over. Locally, changes in the weather had more to do with the wind than anything else. As I've said, stiff gusts always lurked in the Mediterranean to the east, or the Atlantic to the west, and would eventually come buffeting off the Pyrenees, like a bank shot in billiards, to swirl through the Lauragais and whirl into Black Mountain.

Bing's and my relationship seemed to be falling into a similar pattern. We hadn't been married all that long, so there was a lot neither of us knew about the other. No one said it would be easy. My kids especially. Son Brit having been the most *puissant*. He'd given a warning about rushing into our marriage that I had ignored. But was that rush any different than the rush Bing and I made moving on this house? We hadn't discussed it with anybody. We heard Jean-Jacques' proposal, counted to ten, and then went ahead. Our marriage and buying the Greenwich house, and then this house, had all been examples of the same precociousness. But so what? We'd felt we hadn't all the time in the world to dillydally. We weren't young anymore. Most of our lives were behind us. Again, so what? Rain fell. Winds blew. But the sun always came up, even after the stormiest nights.

Yet none of that made me any more comfortable lately, with Bing hardly speaking to me and now Laurant seeming to follow suit. On and on the two of them chatted about the well, the court-yard walls, and even the back building that was supposed to be *my* office one day. Where was I in the discussion? My attitude was definitely clouding over.

So, I PICKED a fight with Laurant. Off with my nose. Take that, face. It started after lunch when our morning work crew didn't show up. A scene-setter for sure.

Bing and I had been having a silent, "meditative" lunch, sitting on tile crates in the war-torn first floor while Laurant and his people were back at his depot for their more elegant *repas*. Actually, it seemed Bing and I were getting closer to talking to each other again. The well discovery had helped, along with the mysterious Orangeburg-looking pipe Placo had hit in his dig. And there was our mutual interest in the house-up-the-street issue. Was that house at the crux of why work on our place had suffered so many slow-downs? Bing had been the most suspicious of it and prodded me a couple of times to confront either Laurant or Jean-Jacques if things slowed down again.

And wouldn't you know it? After we finished lunch and two o'clock rolled around, Laurant's crew did not show up. But we saw one of his trucks roll by. So we went to our door to check it out, only to watch as the truck pulled up and unloaded in front of what we now knew must be a Kurtz house. *Confrontation time!*

We both walked out into the street, hands on hips, looking up toward the fountain.

"That's our whole crew," Bing said. "Every one of them is up there putting up scaffolding. What *is* going on?"

I didn't say anything, just pulled out our cell phone and punched in Laurant's number. It rang immediately. He answered. I told him Bing and I wanted to talk to him *tout de suite*. We knew where he was and we were on our way.

As we got to the fountain, Laurant came out of the Kurtz house and crossed to where we stood. We caught a glimpse of M. Maçon on his hands and knees putting some tile in place.

There was a lot of clatter as Bruno and Placo and Placo Deux and Numéro Deux were busy pulling the scaffolding pipes and fixtures off the truck onto the cobbled sidewalk. Inside and out, our whole crew was working for Kurtz, not us. I was one very angry American.

It was difficult to work within my vocabulary and still express how totally enraged I was. Bing was silent, but her expression said she was damn angry too. I really let Laurant have it.

"*Pourquoi* Laurant?" I demanded, nodding toward his busy people.

"Contract."

"With whom?"

"Monsieur Kurtz."

"How long?"

"From the beginning."

"Why?"

"He was first."

"His house was always number one, yes?"

"Yes."

"Our delays were because of this house."

"Yes."

"Not the town? Not the weather?"

"Not much."

"You never told us."

"No."

"Why?"

"Monsieur Kurtz."

"I thought you were our friend."

"I am."

"You screwed us."

"I had Kurtzes' contract first."

Up to that point Bing had been with me, right with me, but then I lost control.

"You son of a bitch!" I shouted at Laurant in English.

"Ken," Bing put a hand on my sleeve. I shrugged it off . . . like she'd shrugged me off in Toulouse.

"*Qu'est-ce que c'est* son of bitch?" he asked, looking to Bing, which only dug into me that much deeper.

"It is a *fils de chien*. You are a dog. Nothing but a miserable dog!" I shouted.

"I am not a dog."

"What are you then?"

"Your friend."

"Bullshit. *Vous êtes un morceau de merde*. A piece of shit."

"Ken . . ." Bing tried to intercede.

Laurant looked at her and asked, "Why does he say these things?"

And as I saw the two of them start another of their f'ing *tête-a-têtes*, I came unglued.

"Damn it, you're talking to *ME*, Laurant! Not her! *I* am the one you have been cheating. You talk to me, you son of a bitch, hear me?" I shouted.

Shutters opened. The look on Bing's face echoed Laurant's. Now it was *me* . . . not Laurant, not Jean-Jacques or anyone else who was at fault. Strictly, absolutely, and unequivocally, I was the problem. Again. Balls!

I was so mad I was shaking. I stepped forward, very close to Laurant, and shouted directly in his face, "*Fous le camp, morceau de merde!"* Which I'm ashamed to translate as, "Fuck off, you piece of shit!"

Everybody in the village seemed to have caught that one. Boom, boom, boom, the shutters slammed shut. And Laurant's guys stopped what they were doing. Everyone.

Laurant's eyes and mine were locked. Our faces very close. I was in a rage, not giving a damn how grossly I'd insulted him. *Publicly* insulted him. At that point I was not about to apologize.

His eyes moved from mine to Bing. I wanted to punch him in the fucking face!

Shaking with anger, I barely managed to turn and get the hell out of there. As I went, though, out of the corner of my eye I saw Bing's hand reach out to touch Laurant on the arm. I accelerated down to our door, which I shoved open with a shoulder and then slammed behind me. Standing staring into the first-floor rubble, I wanted to break something, but everything in the whole fucking place was already broken! I grabbed my leather jacket. My wallet. Gloves. I looked around, not even knowing what I was looking for as Bing came in.

"Bing . . ."

She stopped. She stared at me, trembling.

"Bing," I repeated, trying to reach out to hold her, but she moved quickly past me.

"Don't touch me. Don't talk to me. Just leave me alone. I've got to think . . . Leave me *alone.*"

She strode up the stairs to what was one day to be our bedroom, then slammed . . . and *bolted* the only operative door we had in the whole damn house.

Everything was still. I turned back to the front door and looked out, down the street to where Laurant's truck had been. It was gone. The crew was gone. Even the start on the scaffolding was gone. The whole village seemed to have gone into freeze-frame, and I was the asshole who had put it there.

I SHOVED my gloves into the jacket pockets. I took the car keys out of my jeans and threw them into the *boîte à lettre* that protruded through the wall by the door. My wallet was in my back pocket. I looked around for my Leatherman, and realized I'd given the damn thing to Anton, who'd given it to Claude. I was going to replace it Saturday in Toulouse. Saturday in Toulouse, when I got *myself* replaced . . . in Bing's life.

I stepped out the door back into the bright afternoon light. It was coming up on three o'clock. Still nothing was moving. Rue Basque was very quiet. I closed the door behind me and for a moment just stood there. I was on the edge of vertigo. Suddenly, I was totally alone. It was as if I'd walked to the edge of the earth. One more step and I'd be in free fall. What was I going to do? Then I saw a bus round the corner by the Maison du Parc, the historical society. The bus looked huge, like a giant beetle with enormous rectangular eyes. Two faces, like irises, were peering out from its front seats. In another minute it would stop at the telephone booth in front of Claude's. I started to run. I wasn't sure why, other than it was coming toward me, not away like everything else.

The driver saw me sprinting toward the stop. He slowed, pulled up, and waited. A few strides away the slab-like door moved out, slid forward, then came to a hissing stop. My eyes counted the stairs, four. I started up. The driver was wearing a gray woven sweater matching the color of his eyes. His glasses were large and rectangular like the bus's front windows. This orderliness was soothing. I handed him a twenty-franc note to take me to the end of the fucking line. Wherever that was. I didn't care. I just had to get out of Black Mountain.

The door hissed behind me, sucking itself back into its closed fit. I walked past the lone rider to a seat in the back. Once we got under way, he and the driver started talking. When the bus stopped, the conversation stopped. Their voices and the diesel motor were a chorus that soothed me.

It was an hour of stops and starts before I thought of getting off. By then we were in Castres, with the river and waterfall running through its center. I loved the view from the bridge we crossed. Gondolas, docks, stone houses rising five stories on both sides of the river. I felt my eyes brimming with tears it looked so beautiful.

Across the bridge the road widened where another joined it. As the bus stopped at the light beyond the intersection, I decided to get off. At first I had no idea why I got off there, but standing at a crosswalk as the bus pulled away I saw a huge red, white, and blue sign over the long storefront I faced. In great italicized capitals it read—THE AMERICAN DREAM.

Without thinking, I stepped into the street. There was a shriek of brakes, a horn, headlight flashes, and a black BMW zigzagged past me. The driver's angry eyes over a pointing cigarette glared at me. It was too late to jump back to the curb, even too late to give the driver the finger, though I knew I was the one at fault . . . as I had been all day, all week for that matter.

Next to The American Dream was an *auto-école*, a driving school. That seemed appropriate. As an American it was my dream that someday these schools would actually teach Frenchmen how to drive. Right now they seemed only to pass along bad habits— driving too fast, jamming up against your ass-end, passing on curves and up hills, or simply driving drunk. Of course this mental discourse was from an angry, lowlife, jaywalking, *mal élevé* (badly raised) *idiot* (fool).

The American Dream sold Harley-Davidson motorcycles. Though I'd driven past the place before, I hadn't been inside. I went through the front door. Inside the walls were white plaster bordered with red and blue trim. Painted on the showroom wall opposite the office was a huge blowing American flag. Used Hogs everywhere—two old knuckle heads, a pan head, the rest Evolutions. Most modified. There was a Fat Boy with a rear wheel that

looked like it came off a Boeing 747. Several machines had bene-
fited from engine work, over-sized everything. One with a blower,
another with a set of the hairy-looking side-mounted aviation
carburetors which ice up when the temperature hits forty degrees
Fahrenheit or below; but who cared? Looked great, ran like shit.
The story of my life.

Leaning on its kickstand by the office door was a late-'90s Elec-
tra Glide Classic. Black with trim lines of red and gold, branch
heads, and an S&S Super carburetor. White walls too. It really
was an American dream. My anger melted slightly at the sight of
it. All I had to deal with now was the gorilla of guilt separating me
and that bike.

Talking motorcycles, my French is pretty good. Jean-Luc, the
proprietor, told me the Glide had just come in on trade for the
newer model with fuel injection and counter-balanced driveshaft.
It had been prepped and was ready to go. I told him I had a Classic
back in the States just like it. I showed him the picture I carried in
my wallet, along with another of the modified Low Rider I'd sold
the previous summer. We talked heads, fuel injection (he was
against it), carbs, cams, counter-balanced shafts, all the good stuff.
Then I told him I was rebuilding a medieval house in Black Mountain. I needed some time on the road . . . to get my head straight.
He gave me a look like he knew what I was talking about.

I produced my international license with its checkmark for
motorcycles. And my USAA insurance card, as if that meant anything. He seemed to think it did. For the hell of it I showed him
my pilot's license too, and surprisingly he showed me his. We'd
both been *pilots de chasse* (fighter pilots). He was impressed that
I had gone on to fly commercially. This led to a deal, a price that
was right. He took American Express, so, without another thought,
I bought the sucker. I also picked up a full-faced helmet, heavy
leather chaps to go with my jacket, and a heated vest. The bike
was already wired for one. The grips were heated too, as a backup

to my light gloves. It could get damn cold in the Pyrenees. And what if I decided to ride south to Spain or on to Portugal?

The radio and cassette were in working order. The trunks, side and top, were clean and had liners. I bought a heavy black Harley sweater and a bandana scarf with LIVE TO RIDE on one side, RIDE TO LIVE on the other, in French. Jean-Luc let me use his shop tags and papers. Threw in a roadmap too. We shook hands, and then I rolled the glistening black beauty out into the alley to start my journey to . . . I didn't give a damn where. Flipping on the radio, the pop singer Claude François came booming from the speakers back at me. Man, I loved that guy, especially now, as he started making me feel about as happy as one miserable son-of-a-bitch could feel. I was on the road again. On a machine I loved. I felt things coming together. Everything . . . but my marriage and the rest of my life.

TWENTY-SIX

ON THE "DREAM"

R IDING THE great Harley out of the alley really was like
a dream. The pulse and rumble of that engine, its throb and
throaty roar as I accelerated into traffic, gave me a feeling of balance, equilibrium, a sense of *self* in a world suddenly gone terribly wrong. Though I knew much of what had gone bad was of my
own doing; at least now, with a clutch in one hand, throttle in the
other, left foot working the shifter, the right by the rear brake, my
misery index was on the decline. Vertigo gone. All motion straight
ahead, riding high on this uniquely American beast. Every turn of
the wheel was part of my escape. I knew I was being selfish, but I
needed the moment. Like Bing needed her silence and meditation.
Damn it, I nodded to myself as I checked my right rearview

mirror, this was *my* meditation. Sauce for the goose and all that. It was me-too time.

Where was I going? I didn't know nor care. But wherever it was, I was going on the saddle of this wonderful retro, low-tech, shiny black Hog. So what if my French was bad? So what if I'd alienated my wife, our contractor, and probably the whole village of Black Mountain? At least I was on the road again and feeling the first nibble of a deliciously evil . . . *freedom*. An American cowboy riding into the sunset, squinting off down the road to who knew where? Leaving the bad times behind.

I wasn't paying much attention to direction, and the traffic lane I was in eased me south. Of course a *merde*-colored Puegeot nearly took me out, despite my signal flashing well before I started the turn. For a second I felt another flash of hot-metal anger seer through me. Damned if I didn't want to chase the idiot down, drag him out of his car at the next light, and kick his sorry butt! Man, I really was full of road-rage.

I restrained myself. French jails, Pierre had made abundantly clear, were not nice places to reside, especially for foreigners. So, without injury or handcuffs, I found myself on the road to Mazamet. Bing and I had been there before. I saw no real reason to go there again, but for the exhilarating ups, downs, lefts, and rights of the road leading there. Plus there was a sign showing Carcassonne to be fifty kilometers beyond. I needed Carcassonne. I needed its stone walls, battlements, drawbridge, moat, and mews. I needed to disappear into its stone belly, into its narrow ancient streets just to hide for the night. To lick my wounds and begin the process of figuring out how I was going to make what had gone wrong, better or worse.

The ride was calming—the joy of a rumbling Harley rolling through small villages, watching heads turn and seeing children waving at the man in leather on the big black bike. It felt good being noticed, perhaps even envied. Far better than being reviled.

A sign to my left pointed to Hautpoul. Bing and I had been there, too, a sad renegade redoubt crushed by Simon de Montfort in the thirteenth century, as so many villages in Cathar country had been. Which gave me an idea for where I would go. What I would see. Maybe even what I would think about for however long I would ride.

Late in the afternoon I found an *auberge* on the western shore of the Aude River, just before the grand bridge crossing into Carcassonne's old city. There was a snug alcove under the inn's terrace to park the bike. I took a room with the castle view for the night. Then I called Bing.

The cell phone was programmed for seven rings before the message service took over. At six, Bing answered.

"It's me," I said.

Silence. She said nothing.

"I'm in Carcassonne. I took a room for the night. Here's the telephone number," which I read to her from the phone pad by the bed.

No response.

"I love you Bing."

She hung up.

IT WAS a tough night. I'd walked from the *auberge* across the bridge, through the old city, and up to the castle. I found a table outside at the Comte Roger restaurant, my leather jacket and sweater making the difference against the cold evening. Probably the temperature led me to the *cassoulet* on the menu. I also ordered a bottle of the local red grown just outside the castle walls. I'd thought the heavy food, the wine, the ride, and the brisk night would lead to a good sleep. I was wrong. I was miserable. Lying in bed later, all I could think about was the son of a bitch I'd been. To Bing and to Laurant.

The next morning I decided to respect Bing's silence with a day or more of my own as I headed southwest, into the mountains. I still had no idea how long I would be on the road, but that would be more up to Bing than to me.

As I said, on the ride from Castres, the sign for Haupoul had made me want to see more of Cathar country. At the moment, ruined old castles somehow seemed appropriate. The weather was still chilly, but the almost blinding sun rising in the east said the day would soon warm.

I decided to ride the small roads, the first toward a place named Palaja. As I rolled along the ever-narrowing pavement, I thought of how many pilots, especially fighter types, like bikes. Controlling them is similar to flying the high-performance jets. Banking left, banking right, leaning with the body as opposed to lying in aileron with a stick. Twist the throttle and go, much the same as slamming the throttle outboard to kick in a jet's afterburner. Accelerating over the top of a rise and catching a moment of zero-G, common to bikes and planes alike, is rare on four wheels. I hadn't missed flying when my career was over because I had motorcycles. I'd had my own plane once, but found it boring. Like Bunny Berigan singing "I Can't Get Started": *Being high in the sky was my idea of having nothing to do.*" You just hung there. But down close, on the road on a machine, the world whips by. In the air, even the speed of sound is just a number on a dial or a digital readout. Sixty on a narrow French road with trees, stone walls, cliffs and ledges rushing by is raw speed and all the thrills attached.

It wasn't long until my trace of a road bumped into the next *département*, which took me over a twelfth-century bridge across the Orbieu River into Lagrasse, a medieval village of the Corbières region. I stopped for coffee there and I learned from a brochure that Charlemagne had founded the local abbey, from which he launched campaigns against the Saracens to the south. Centuries later that abbey, under the Benedictines, sided with Simon

Montfort and the Crusade against the area's nobles who had been protecting the Cathars.

The caffeine picked me up. I cranked the hog back into life and enjoyed the luxury of a slow roll down the village's ancient rock-slabbed Roman streets, still with center troughs for waste-water to run to the river. The town of Lagrasse was the real thing: a proper gateway to Cathar country.

Having run into Charlemagne's name in Lagrasse, I was eager to press on to another of his incredible redoubts, Peyrepertuse Castle, further southwest toward the Pyrenees. The roads to it were a challenge, defined by the amazing cut of the Torgan Gorge with its huge foreheads of granite hanging down from the cliffs above, some even sheering to the river below. In places, tunnels were cut through these, or the right-of-way curled around them, creating so narrow a slip, one car would have to wait for the oncoming car to pass before proceeding. It was a blessing being on a bike in places like this.

Peyrepertuse, I learned, meant "pierced rock." Accordingly, the castle on top of that near-vertical ridge looked like a needle pushed up through the earth's rough canvas. Along the way, at Cucugnan, I stopped for a break and some food. After parking and locking the black beast where the summit path began, I hiked up to the ruins to picnic in the high castle keep. I had cheese, an apple, a baguette, and Badoit. The same fare Bing would have packed, but I was alone.

The height and then the sheer drops on all sides were awesome. No one else was there. I felt at first deliciously . . . then terribly alone. Being so high in the sky, on what seemed the head of a giant pin, only intensified it. The far Pyrenees looked only the reach of my hand away. Breathtaking. For that matter, all of this region of France is breathtaking.

The sky began to darken as it can suddenly do in the mountains. I'd have to get back to the bike before the probably icy rains began.

By one o'clock I was rolling again. My spirits picked up with the joy of riding the great twists, sweeps, and corkscrew valley plunges the road led me along as I made my way to the next high mountain pass at Puilaurens. The rain had held off, so I risked another break, sipping espresso in a *café* at the foot of the mountain. Continuing to worry about the weather, I decided not to hike up this one and pulled out my Michelin map to plan the rest of the afternoon. To head in the direction of Pic du Canigou, the nine-thousand-foot peak that guarded the eastern end of the Pyrenees, would take me through Céret, the art town Bing and I had intended to spend a weekend in once the house was done. I decided to move the calendar ahead and stay there on my own that night.

As the sky continued to darken, I motored on through tiny towns I'd never heard of and would probably never see again. Thuir, Llupia. Terrats, Fourques, Mons, Llauro. By the village of L'Ermitage de St. Férréol I was growing weary, and the rains did come. Tight, narrow, twisting roads are a challenge on a machine in the best of weather. Sand, gravel-strewn turns, oncoming idiots (or their landsmen who don't bother to stop at blind intersections), all could lead to any number of thrills, if not actual spills. Lay on a heavy rain as I had here, and the pucker factor goes off the chart.

Motorcycles do not have windshield wipers. This Harley had a high windscreen that blurred badly as the rain splattered into it. I hadn't thought to wax or Rainex it, so there were times I couldn't see a damn thing. All I could think of, blinded like that, were those precipitous drops to the valleys below which edged the road. I really needed to stop for the night before I killed myself.

A sign said CÉRET 10 KM. Hallelujah. As if God heard my elation, He reduced the torrent to a sprinkle, a drizzle, down to fog, and finally to clearing skies. Then the late-day sun dropped below the cloud layer as it prepared to bed down behind Pic du Canigou.

Gorgeous cherry trees lined the road's last five kilometers. It all was so beautiful I fantasized I might be rolling into the Garden of Eden.

I was on the Avenue d'Espagne, which led into the old city through a fortified gateway and the Place de la République. Overhead, above the plaza and the buildings around it, was an umbrella of the *platanes,* their leaves just starting to open. Despite that thin cover, it was dry underneath. Noise was muffled too, which created an odd sensation, like rolling onto a soundstage. I was *outdoors,* but felt *indoors.*

Across the plaza I found Les Feuillants, which proved to be an extraordinary inn. Its surrounding walls defined a covered garden, already set with tables for dinner. Inside was a charming bar looking onto a formal dining room. Thick oriental carpets suffered my wet, bad-biker boots as I strode to the reservation desk. Though my leathers were soaked and noisy, almost wheezing as I passed the concierge's station, he just smiled and nodded me toward the waiting clerk.

My room overlooked the garden. It was large and luxurious. Stripping off my soaked riding gear, I got the shower running hot and poured a glass of port from the rack on the shelf. I ached that Bing wasn't there. What a wonderful place to share with her. What a day to have had her with me. What a hell of a mess I'd gotten myself into . . .

As INCREDIBLY lonely as I was choosing to be, my appetite had not suffered. I ate too much fish, too much duck, creamed spinach, bread, cheese, desert; I drank too much wine. All in all, I was like an animal on the loose. I seemed to know no restraint without Bing by my side. So I ordered a snifter of Armagnac.

Sipping the last, I turned a sleepy eye back into the nearly empty dining room. Oops. Entering behind the *maitre d'hotel* was a lone young woman. She was tall, x-ray slim, but blessed with breasts her sheer blouse implied she wanted to share. Oh my goodness. The possibilities of the situation shocked me back to my airline days. As an international 747 captain, I'd been a target for flight attendants looking for a man. On one trip to Rome, after settling into my hotel room, the phone rang. The sultry voice on the line was that of a stunner who'd served the first-class cabin on the trip over. Now she wanted some service of her own. She told me we should room together for the next two days. I asked why? She said to go to my window, look across to hers, and I would know. When I did, she was standing across the courtyard from me. She certainly had been beautiful in her uniform, but without it, wearing nothing but a smile, she was dazzling. I returned her smile, waved, then closed my blinds and went to bed. Alone. First wife Bobbye had made a one-woman man of me. So, in this encounter I decided it was too late to teach this old dog new tricks.

I couldn't sleep. My head was full of questions. Number one on the list—had my son been right about my not waiting long enough before marrying? Was this situation with Laurant and Bing the first heads-up that she and I might not be totally suited for each other? Had I, in fact, been so adrift without Bobbye that I'd reflexively grabbed for Bing like she was a lifesaver?

Bing's highborn New England lineage could well be inhospitable to the likes of a rule-breaking fighter pilot born of rebellious Scots. Wouldn't an extended courtship have best decided that?

I'd grown up the last of four boys. We were a rowdy bunch, rolling and wrestling, shouting, kicking, and punching; but within minutes of such roughhouse, we'd lock arms as brothers, especially if threatened by outsiders.

Bing, on the other hand, was the last of four *properly raised* young ladies. Her professorial father and genteel mother probably had zero experience with the world of rough and tumble. Besides, girls had their own means of dealing with things—whispers, silent broodings, sometimes nasty ways of getting even. For boys, recovery was quick. Girls, however, seemed to need time, lots of time . . . which might lead guys like me to hit the road.

As the church bells rang 3 AM, the emptiness of my room was like a nightmare. I'd hardly ever been alone. I'd grown up in a house bursting with life. College, the Marine Corps, marriage, and flying around the world with teams of flight crews had never left me isolated like this. As magnificent as this French village was, without Bing beside me, it was empty.

Why couldn't I control my temper? Why did I have to self-destruct? What the hell could I do to get myself out of this mess?

G R O G G Y   A N D   a trifle hung over, I was late getting under way the next morning. Céret was just too beautiful to short change. The hotel had a breakfast service waiting for me inside the walled garden. Bright sunshine sprinkled through the trees. Church bells continued to ring each hour, accompanied by doves cooing lovingly to each other from tree tops to chimney pots. Which only made me feel even sorrier for myself. So, in defense, I ate too many croissants and *petits pains*. I drank too much coffee too, ignoring the price I would pay later, having to stop for multiple *rustica* by the side of the road.

My leathers were dry and tighter. I packed my few possessions into the bike's top case, and then strolled to the Musée d'Art Moderne to enjoy the Picasso, Chagall, Matisse, Gris, and Maillol offerings. It stung that Bing wasn't there to savor them with me.

A couple of hours later I was back on the road, headed deeper into Cathar country via Puilaurens, then westward toward the breathtaking Montségur en route to Foix and its incredible count's castle, Château de Foix. A lot of riding. A lot to see. Days, if not weeks to do it in. Who knew what would follow?

Then it happened.

By the time I reached A-9, the major highway through the area, my coffee-laden bladder said it was time to pull in. A large *l'aire* lay ahead: a big one with a restaurant, gas station, campsite, shops, the whole deal. I figured to find a *Herald Tribune* to catch up with too. After finishing my coffee-related chores, comfortable with the paper to read later with lunch, I was again off and running.

As fate would have it, there was a Volvo in front of me on the feeder back out onto A-9. Volvos could be dangerous to a biker's health and well-being. The fact is, motorcyclists are totally defensive drivers. Accordingly, each car type has a signature known to everybody on two wheels. It goes like this—BMWs are driven by people who really believe that *Ultimate Driving Machine* stuff. So they drive too fast, change lanes too abruptly, and generally act like horses' butts. At home, Cadillacs tend to ride in the left lane, no matter what and no matter how slowly, particularly in the South. But the Volvo drivers take the cake. Often they seem to have no clue about driving. They have bought a Volvo simply because they were told it is "safe." All well and good, except they extrapolate that to mean that not only will they survive any crash they are in, but whoever they hit will not be hurt either! Safe means *safe*, totally. Right? So motorcyclists give as much berth as they can to Volvos, anywhere in the world.

So with this Volvo wagon leading me out of the feeder I immediately went into alert mode. The A-9 we were joining had three lanes plus the long feeder, a good half mile of four lanes to work with. It shouldn't have presented a problem for anybody.

As I closed on the Volvo, I checked my rearview mirror, even cocked my head to the left for a better view of what was coming. I was pleasantly surprised to see a group of motorcycles moving up from behind. They weren't roaring, just enjoying the scenery from the slow lane. Twelve or so machines, with several two-up. I felt good about joining a bunch of like-minded spirits. I thought I might lay in with them a bit and get a feel for how European riders work as a group. Would they be a formation or a gaggle? I decided to find out.

My first mistake was focusing as much as I did on the bikers. I should have thought more about what idiocy the Volvo driver might have up his sleeve. As things worked out, it wasn't more than thirty seconds before I found out.

Rather than use the long stretch of feeder to blend into the highway's three lanes, the Volvo elected to lunge to the left—directly in front of me and the approaching group of bikes! My instinct was to swerve left, too, but the first of the motorcyclists was already near my shoulder. And several high-speed cars were overtaking them further to the left. I was boxed in, but if the idiot would just accelerate, everything would be salvageable. So what did he do? Exactly as no one in his right mind would ever do, he jammed on his brakes! *Anything* but that would have saved me. So, with that boxy piece of crap swerving to a stop smack in front of me, I was trapped. I couldn't jog left around him or I'd plow into the other bikes.

I grabbed a handful of front brake and slammed my right boot down on the rear peddle. I hoped nobody was behind *me*, though it wasn't going to make much difference in another second. When my front wheel started to dish out on a touch of sand, I knew I was going to hit the Volvo. Down I went in a slide of sparks, smoke, and shouted obscenities. Now it was a case of how much protection I'd get with my wheels, frame, cases, and good Harley steel.

The last things I remember were bright red brake lights, a left blinker suddenly swapping to right . . . then two impacts. The first must have been my helmeted head whacking against the bumper or fender, then a terrible shot to my shoulder and ribs . . . then blackness.

TWENTY-SEVEN

A LONG LONELY ROAD
FOR BING, TOO

WHEN KEN called me that night from Carcassonne, he'd said, "I love you Bing." I hung up. The instant I did it I realized I had no idea *why* I had. A reflex. The pain of doing what I did, and what he did, hit me. I let out the most awful wail, a cascade of tears, a flood I could not control. I hurt. I hurt so badly it felt like I'd been *assaulted* on the one hand, *abandoned* on the other.

A character in a Larry McMurtry book Ken once showed me said, "Fate is such an accidental thing . . ." In its own way this whole French experience had been an accidental thing. For that matter, much of my life had been. My first marriage, when I was very young and had allowed myself to be swept off my feet, started with unexpected adventure: driving a Land Rover from

Paris to Calcutta on a photo project for *National Geographic*. Though my children were not accidents, disappointment was. And divorce. Oh yes, I'd had my share of life's accidental things, good and bad. Ken's coming to my sister's Halloween party was one of the good things.

Strangely enough, in our past lives, married to others, we had lived just a few miles apart. Despite all the places, parties, and events we'd had in common, we'd never met. My years of loneliness and Ken's loss of Bobbye put us both on the same painful road that eventually brought us together.

Before Ken drove his Jimmy Truck to my farm on New Year's eve two winters ago, I'd expected, and had accepted, that the single life would be mine the rest of my days. Then he was at my door and in my heart. That moonlit night, gazing across the fields beyond the far tree stands to the Long Island Sound's glistening waters, Ken had said, "I can't live with this emptiness, Bing. It hurts like an arrow through my heart." I knew what he meant. And I accepted when he asked to marry me.

Now I am the one hurting and empty, devastated by the way Ken attacked Laurant—shouting, *cursing*, with the whole village hearing it—at that moment he was someone I'd never known before. I was mortified and suddenly filled with doubt. Had I made another huge mistake of the heart?

It's true Laurant hadn't been honest with us. I was angry about that, of course. But Jean-Jacques had been the one manipulating all of us. Our language skills, or lack of them, blocked us from realizing what he was doing. I doubt Laurant knew what Jean-Jacques was telling us in English either. Yes, I wanted to let Laurant know we were disappointed in him, but not like Ken had, shouting obscenities and waving his fists in his face. How could someone I loved for his sensitivity act so insensitively?

Actually, this whole mess probably started days earlier, in Toulouse, with Ken's pushing me, pulling me, shouting at me. Where had this side of him come from? He'd always shown an ironic sense of humor to take the edge off things. Now, all of a sudden, he was lashing out everywhere and at everyone. I don't know if he even remembers it, but over breakfast that morning before we'd driven to Toulouse, I'd innocently told him the new coffee he'd bought soured his breath. You'd think I'd attacked his manhood or something! Then the pushing and shoving crossing a street, and much the same going into Ikea. And all this with Laurant! I am hurt and even a little frightened. I wonder if our love is nothing more than a house of cards, already falling down. When I hung up the phone it hit me. I felt so empty. All I could do was cry, cry my heart out.

That evening I'd found the book, the one with the *accidental* passage. On its next page I was struck by what (accidentally?) jumped out at me: "*So sure of himself on the surface, yet so riddled with doubt like everyone else. And I wondered: when would it hit him? When would he realize that this is all such a deeply flawed business? That we never get it right? Most of us proceed forward with good intentions. We try our best. Yet so often we fail ourselves and others. What else can we do but try again? It's the only option open to us . . .*"

Good heavens. It was all there, practically slapping me in the face with its simplicity. It was as if the two of us were living in a world a size too large for us. I'd been so focused on *me*, on my being slighted, insulted, treated less than how I thought I should be . . . and not getting past it. Ken had acted terribly. He had a legion of reasons, not the least being his frustration with not finishing his book. He's so close, I don't understand why he can't just sit down and *do* it, the house be darned. If he had taken my advice and done just that, I doubt any of this would have happened. But how would I convince him of that? How could I even talk with him now, wherever he was?

HE HAD not called since I'd hung up the night before. I didn't really want to talk with him even yet, but I kept the cell phone handy. I was anxious, but still needed down time. Time to be alone. To think. To meditate myself back into balance.

I stayed at the *gîte* house all the next day, out with the cows, walking the fields. I couldn't bear to face Laurant and his people. Especially alone, which made me feel somewhat the coward, thinking I'd leave it to Ken to deal with Laurant when he got back. *If* he came back.

Carcassonne. I wondered how he'd gotten there. Rented a car? I doubted he picked up a ride, *un autostop* as the French called hitchhiking. Perhaps he'd bused or taken a train.

By the second day without a call I was beginning to wonder if Ken had been right about trying to talk things out, not letting them fester as they were doing now. At least I assumed that was what he'd meant. But it had been too soon for me. I'd needed time. Distance. I'm not so spontaneous. I can't just slap my hands, shake my head, and start all over again.

THREE DAYS and still no word. No calls. No contact from any-body. Now I was getting worried. Where was he? This silence was so unlike him. I didn't know what to do. Who to call? I was in a foreign country, speaking the language poorly, with no idea of what I would say. "I don't know where my husband is." Women are looked at differently in France than at home. They seem to be more defined by the men they are seen with, married to, or in some cases *kept* by. Even if I could properly explain my concern, I'd probably appear the fool. *Your man is tired of you. He needed to taste some forbidden fruit. That's the way men are. What's your problem? You have the car. In time he'll come back for that, if for nothing else. That's how men are.*

Finally, I called Adrian. He was at the boat. But before I could tell him my situation and my worries, he told me he had some good-bad news about his daughter Aimee. She had been misdiagnosed at the hospital, he said. She was not neurotic, she was schizophrenic. As depressing as that news might normally be, he was pleased. Now she would have proper medication to deal with her problems. Of course he was upset over her having lost valuable treatment time, but at least she was finally on the right track.

Then I told him Ken was off somewhere but I didn't know where. I hadn't heard from him for days. We'd had a . . . a situation, a difficult time, and he'd disappeared. He'd called once from Carcassonne, but we hadn't talked then or since.

"Actually, Adrian, I'd hung up on him," I said.

"Maybe he deserved it," Adrian said kindly.

"I thought so then, but now I'm not so sure. I must have hurt him. Terribly perhaps, since he has not called for days. It's so unlike him. I am worried something has happened, but I don't know how to find out. He didn't have the car. I have it. I do have a telephone number at the place he stayed the first night. But I don't know what they can tell me other than he's not there."

"Bing," Adrian said. "Give me that number. I will call them and see what they can tell me. To register in a hotel, if you arrive in a car, it's required to put the tag number on the sign-in sheet. If he rented a car, they will have the number. Then we can go from there. I'll get back to you. Don't worry. He is not suicidal like my family. We'll find him quickly enough."

I felt relieved. Adrian knew what to do, all of which now made me feel . . . French—a woman dependant on a man in a man's world. I didn't like that feeling at all.

"HI, KENNY . . ." *was how Bobbye would greet my telephone calls from wherever in the world I was while she was in the hospital that last year. She was always upbeat, reflecting confidence. She always lifted my spirits. Later I learned, from those who were with her when I called, that it had taken tremendous will-power to put that sparkle into her voice. I'd had no idea how she'd shielded me from what she had no shield against herself.*

"Hi Kenny" was the first thing I "heard" as I struggled to rise out of the black hole I'd fallen into. Where was it coming from? Whose voice was it?

Bobbye was in a coma for a long time. She came out of it for about a month before the darkness recalled her . . . forever. During that month she was with us, she said the coma wasn't painful, other than the pain of knowing everything that was going on around her without being able to participate. She could hear our conversations, feel our touch, but she couldn't touch us in return. It was like being outside one of the windows of our family room on a winter's night, she said, seeing what was going on inside; hearing the voices and understanding what was being said, but unable to come in from the cold.

She knew there was a fire in the fireplace, but she couldn't move to join in its warmth, the warmth of the love she felt radiating from us in front of it. One of the last things she said to me was that she would always be a little angel on our shoulders, one we could not touch, but one we could be sure was always there. Maybe I'd heard her angel's voice.

My dark time was different. I hurt like hell. And it was hard to breathe. I couldn't define where all the pain was coming from any more than I could say where the voices I was hearing were coming from. I didn't know if I was alive or dead. I suspected alive, probably because I'd heard of so many near-death experiences where there was a vast white light. I was in darkness. I couldn't open my eyes, much less move my body . . . not arms, legs, anything. My head felt terribly heavy, so heavy I couldn't raise it, turn it, do anything but let it lay there and muddle through a few scattered thoughts before things would go black again. And I felt no little angel where I hoped I might, even if it was her voice speaking to me.

Bobbye had died at two in the morning on the last day of spring. I think today was that same day here, wherever here was.

Her passing was all the more poignant because summer was her season. She was a sun-filled flower person. She planted, nurtured, and loved growing things, along with the sun that fed them. Daughter Lexi, son Brit, and I were her family bouquet, she our sun. Bobbye had been the lily of my life. It was sad her last day hadn't been summer's first. And now the anniversary of that date was the day my own world went black.

On the bed, in a cold, antiseptic hospital room, I'd held her tightly in my arms. At the foot of the bed Brit embraced her feet as he prayed. Lexi had Bobbye's Bible open by the side of the bed, reading Psalm after Psalm as if to incant away the dark shroud pulling over us.

"Lord, who may dwell in your sanctuary?" she read, tears splashing onto the page. "Who may live on your holy hill?" She stopped. The silence caught my attention. I ached for her. It had been a terrible struggle to keep reading, but she knew her mother loved listening to the Psalms. There wasn't anything else she could offer now.

"She . . ." There was a long pause as Lexi pulled herself together, then managed to finish the answering stanza with, "She whose walk is blameless . . ." Her voice cracked.

I was holding Bobbye tight. Was it too tight? Was I trying to keep her from going, or trying to help her go?

As if in response, Lexi read, "Be merciful to me, O Lord, for I am in distress; my eyes grow weak with sorrow, my soul and my body with grief . . ." How many Psalms did she read those hours before the end? Brit put a crumb of unleavened bread to his mother's lips, then a touch of the cup. Throughout that year of hospitals, pain, and sadness, he'd been the one to make sure she had the Lord's Supper she treasured so much.

Then Bobbye's breathing stopped. The room was totally still . . . until one last long sigh.

Lexi closed the Bible. I got up to get the nurse, who would call for a doctor. I saw Brit start to straighten the bed. His sister joined him. They tucked the covers as they knew their mother liked them to be.

I was outside the door in the hallway. Alone. For a moment I'd forgotten how I'd gotten there. I saw the nurse's station and walked woodenly to it.

When the one you have loved so deeply for so long leaves, irrevocably leaves . . . that first instant you know you are now alone is devastating. Quickly a dull ache sets in. Only time reveals the constant companion it will become.

"BING, ADRIAN here," he said, not an hour after we'd first talked. "Ken had been on a motorcycle. I was able to get the *carte grise*, the tag number, from the hotel as I thought I might. I have a friend in the *gendarmes* checking if there are any reports relating to it. If there have been any problems, we'll know shortly."

I didn't speak. I was holding my breath. I'd been willing to ride with Kenny on his Harley-Davidson in Connecticut, but after seeing how crazy the French drivers can be, I told him he would ride without me here. Which made for a tense evening or two, but we'd been so busy it didn't become an issue.

"Are you still there, Bing?" Adrian asked with concern.

"Oh, forgive me, Adrian," I blurted out, "I am sorry. Ken on a motorcycle has me worried. I'd told him I wouldn't ride with him here because so many of the drivers seem either crazy, drunk, or both. I hope I wasn't clairvoyant. Now I really am worried."

"We'll know more once the tag is checked. If he did go down, the owner or shop or whatever will have been contacted. Try not to worry. I will get back to you the soonest."

LATER, AFTER *all that could be arranged was arranged, Brit went to his car and I found myself walking across some grass toward mine. After a bit of a stumble, I stopped and found myself looking up, almost startled by the incredible mosaic of stars and galaxies above, and suddenly remembering when Bobbye and I were first married, how many summer nights we'd lie in a field on our backs looking for Betelgeuse, Orion, Vega, the North Star, or Mars. We hadn't had the money for more than maybe a movie a month, so the huge sky overhead had been our private theater. This night, the only sound was a breath of wind through the leaves. I felt crushingly alone.*

Earlier Lexi had read, "When I consider your heavens the work of your fingers, the moon and the stars, which you have set in place, what is man that you are mindful of him . . ." I wished I could have remembered those words as I stood looking up. But only actors on stages or in movies seem able to do such things. The rest of us just live as best we can, wishing we could do better.

Such thoughts of death started me thinking about life, my life before entering this strange cocoon I was wrapped in. There had been a time I stood by an empty field just before sunrise. Over it lay a ground fog. Suddenly a shimmering rectangle of light rose from the fog and hovered just above the field. I couldn't move, could hardly breathe, watching whatever it was. My attention went to the center within the rectangle and I saw . . . all I can say of what I saw was . . . eternity. Clear and in focus, eternity.

I started toward the apparition. Could I step through it? Could I get to the "other side"? Then where would I be?

And again, from my black cocoon, the shimmering rectangle returned. If I moved toward it, could I move through it? Or would it again just contract and compress? Was it life or death? Would I live or die?

" B I N G ,   T H E American Dream motorcycle shop in Castres was contacted by the Autoroute Authority. One of their Harley-Davidsons had been involved in an accident on A-9, south of Perpignan. They were waiting for the release of an address on the foreign rider. They had his international license, but it had no local address. They were waiting for the hospital in Perpignan to allow their investigators to talk with the person. They had the last name as Adams. I know you've said we French often take the MC of Ken's last name as initials," Adrian said. He paused.

"Adrian, I've got to get to that hospital as quickly as possible." Grabbing my purse and looking frantically around the room for the car keys and whatever else I would need, I said, "Where—" but Adrian cut me off.

"Bing, I suggest you get in the car right now and drive to me here at Port Lauragais. It's on the way to Perpignan. While you are on the road I will get through to the hospital for more information. I have your cell phone number. As soon as I have anything I will call you."

"I am on my way," I choked out, adding, "thank you, thank you Adrian." I hung up, threw my cell into my purse and ran to the door.

W H E N   I   W A S *able to open my eyes I was freezing cold. Shaking uncontrollably. Some man in white was hugging me. God? No, a man! Maybe I was dead but in a gay hell. Oh, Lord.*

I had a pile of blankets over me. Above and high around me were bags and tubes and oscilloscopes with marching waves of light, beeping monitors. All the accoutrements of intensive care. I must be in a hospital. But why was I so damn cold and shivering with this man hugging me? I felt like a hockey player down on the ice with a referee sprawled over me. What was going on? Then shivering, shuddering . . . I was in the black place again.

IT WAS amazing how quickly Adrian got us through the emergency room red tape and into the orthopedic surgeon's office. When I'd picked him up at the boat I was surprised to see him in a sport coat and slacks rather than his usual jeans and sweater. Then I realized the ribbons sewn onto the jacket lapel indicated he'd been awarded the Legion of Honor and Croix de Guerre, which obviously helped us get so far so fast.

The doctor spoke English. "Madame," he began, "your husband has suffered many injuries due to a motorcycle accident on A-9. Most importantly, however, is for you to know he will survive. His life is no longer in danger. He has been through a rigorous surgical procedure, however. When admitted, we found he had three fractured ribs and a double compound fracture of his upper left arm and a concussion. As best we have been able to determine from some other motorcyclists who followed the ambulance here, a car swerved in front of him, knocking him down and partially under that vehicle, then, for some unknown reason, the driver stopped, reversed direction and drove over your husband's upper body, causing the damage I described."

The doctor, whose name plaque on his smock read M. Diddier, went on to say that he'd had to set the ribs to avoid puncture of the lungs, as well as connect the left elbow, the major bone segment, and the shoulder with a stainless steel rod. The process of rebuilding the upper arm with the rod implanted would make for a much easier recovery.

"Fortunately Madame, the breaks where clean and had not cut much muscle or nerve tissue. Nevertheless, because of their clean nature, the only way to ensure a strong mend was the use of the rod. It can remain in the arm without a problem, though Monsieur Adams will be more sensitive to cold in that area."

Ken was to be out of intensive care the next day. He was being sedated and seemed comfortable for the moment. According to the attending nurse, a man, the O.R. had been so cold that, to fight bacteria, he'd had to do his best with wrapping heated blankets around Ken to fight off the chill before they put him under for a night's rest.

The nurse, Monsieur Chappel, found me a comfortable sofa chair to wedge into Ken's small area. I gave Adrian the car keys to go back to the boat for the night. I was staying close to my sweet Kenny this time. No more walk outs. No more hang ups. This time the two of us were going to see this through together.

MORNING CAME, and with it a voice, a sweet woman's voice whispering in my ear, "My sweet Kenny, I hold thee in the light."

My muddled brain hung on to that, turned and tumbled it, then recognized it as one of Bing's Quaker phrases. That told me she was near and it was her light, not the other bright white light I'd dreaded, which was greeting me. Thank you Lord.

Slowly, through my fluttering lids, I began to make out a form . . . and for the first time in a very long time, I could see Bing's face peering down at me, Adrian behind her.

"How is the bike?" were the first words my dry raspy throat could muster.

They looked at each other, then back to me. Their expressions told me they were encouraged I could talk, and that under the circumstances, the outrageousness of my question indicated I was pretty much back to normal.

I was pleased too. I remembered the bike and laying it down, though nothing after that. Then I found I could move my head and was also able to raise my right arm to reach over and touch the wrapping of my left. It didn't feel like plaster. And my left hand was still there. Puffy and painful, but *there*. I could wiggle my toes and even move my legs a bit before sharp pains cut into my chest. I was not dead and perhaps not in terribly bad shape, all things considered. Whatever those things to consider might be.

"Actually, the Harley is not that bad," Adrian said, a dedicated

H-D rider himself. "I spoke with the fellow at the shop in Castres. He said it was mostly cosmetic damage, no frame problems. He'd sent a *camion* to pick it up. Apparently the bike fared better than you did. Of course, it wasn't backed over by a car. We had a chance to speak with two riders who were with you when you went down. They stopped by yesterday to see how you were doing. They are eager to file charges against the idiot who cut you off."

I took all this in more as an observer than participant. I imagined, gratefully, that I was full of pharmaceuticals. Then my eyes found Bing's. Though my vision was still blurry, I could make out the tears tumbling down her cheeks—which made me feel very, very bad. I had left her angry and hurt and now I'd added these tears. All in all I was one royal shit.

IT IS AMAZING how time served in a hospital seems to alleviate the worst situations, conflicts, and misunderstandings. Especially when the prime perpetrator arrives by ambulance, passes through O.R., intensive care, and finally lands in a semi-private room wrapped in heavy bandages with pieces of shiny metal holding a limb or two together. Of course, I don't recommend the process for resolving all our disputes, but in this self-inflicted mess, I must say things couldn't have moved along more smoothly. Bing kept hugging me. Laurant showed up with flowers and a bottle of red Gaillac to reestablish our working relationship, but I'd been asleep. We would have to talk later. Even Jean-Jacques sent a card, as did Nigel Cork from London. Amazingly, like a phoenix, I seemed to be rising from the ashes of my iniquity and alighting on a pedestal of forgiveness.

The second day after I came out of ICU, the roommate of my semi-private was discharged. After his bed was stripped and remade, Bing arrived and we had the room to ourselves. Finally we had our talk. As she pulled a chair close to the side of my bed and leaned over to kiss me, I held out my good hand with all its attached tubes and laid it on her arm.

"Oh Bing, darling," I started, my voice still little more than a croak, "I am so sorry. I hurt you. I hurt Laurant. I made a fool of myself in front of the whole village . . ."

"Shush, hush," She comforted, taking my swollen left hand in hers. "It's important that you rest and not trouble yourself with such things. We've gotten through it . . . you're alive and we are together . . . as we will always be."

"Bing . . ." I could feel a lump growing in my throat, "I am so sorry I exploded. You . . ."

"Please, Kenny. Hush. I understand," she said, squeezing my hand. "I am sorry I have to go to my quiet place when something goes wrong. Try to understand. It's not a silent condemnation of you, it's just my way. I have to sort things from within before I can reach out . . ."

I struggled to explain, "Darling . . . that day I thought you were as angry with Laurant as I was. I thought we were standing together . . . and then you seemed to back away. It was as if you'd taken his side . . . when I thought I was fighting for you. For us."

The heart monitor on the wall started making noises as the numbers below it paraded faster and faster across the screen. Glancing up, Bing's expression showed concern.

"Kenny," she whispered, "this is the last time we're going to talk about this. We're leaving it here, in this hospital, like a germ. And in the future, when we think any more about it, we'll give thanks that, as awful as our argument was, it's been a blessing. You were nearly killed. Nothing is worth losing you over. So if ever another situation threatens to blow up like this one did, we are both going to step back and think about how much we mean to each other. You can be like a lion and maybe I'm a deer. That's our reality. So we'll deal with that. As long as you don't roar, I promise I won't run off and hide. We can do it, because we are going to do it together . . ."

I don't know how much more Bing said. I was so full of the happy stuff pumping into my veins I began to fuzz up, finally drifting off. It was hours before I came back. She was still there. Reaching out to take my hand again, smiling and gently kissing me on the lips.

IN A WEEK my ribs were manageable. My left arm started getting some exercise not long after that, though it had to stay tightly wrapped and in a sling most of the time. I was released a week after my eyes blinked open. Though it was clear I wouldn't be banging nails or laying tile anytime soon, I would at least be mobile and able to keep an eye on things, along with continuing to mend a lot of personal fences, and now be free to finish *When Eagles Fall*.

BING AND I spent my first two days out of hospital on Adrian's barge at Port Lauragais. Since he had to reverse it around at the quay for some scraping and painting, we got a brief voyage out into the canal, then back to his mooring. The brisk air, the engine's throb, just the gentle movement was a treat.

The third day Bing carted me back to the farm in Soual. Though the hundreds of rabbits hopping about seemed joyful at my return, Madame Rigale was saddened to tell us we'd have to move for two weeks at least. The guests expected to cancel had not. We, or more accurately Bing, would have to load the car with our bags and assorted stuff and find another place to hang our hats. Back to the Gypsy life . . . with our first stop being the Abbey Hotel where we'd stashed Nigel Cork and Leathan Bobb weeks before, back in Black Mountain.

TWENTY-EIGHT

COMING TOGETHER

During this transitional period, Laurant had his people back working on the house. We were past the three-month mark, nipping into summer, and still waiting for the turn of that magic key.

When Bing checked me out of the hospital, we paid the bills in full. This had an unanticipated side effect on the application for our *cartes de séjours* (extended stay visas). By doing this, we established to the French healthcare system that we would not be a drain and would pay our own way, so the paperwork accelerated through the bureaucracy and we got clearance to stay six months in-country, a whole year if we weren't concerned about paying French taxes. Hah.

Though the frustration of not getting my novel finished was

always there, at least we weren't up against any legal barriers as before. And now, banged up as I was, despite lingering headaches and the ongoing ingestion of painkillers, writing would probably be the only really productive thing I'd be capable of for several weeks. Perhaps I was seeing the glass half-full for a change.

Before we left the *gîte* farm for the Abbey Hotel, Bing brought me up to date on some harrowing events that had taken place in my absence at Château Poubelle.

"Kenny, remember the broken orange pipe you saw under the slab in the courtyard? Where Placo was digging?" she asked, sitting next to me where I was stretched out on one of the couches.

"I do, but I hardly dare ask what came of it," I said.

Before getting on with her story, Bing started popping seedless grapes into my mouth and announced, "You need more fruit in your diet."

"Whatever," I managed as I crunched a mouthful of the sweet beauties.

"Well, last week they poured the new slab and after it set, started laying tile. Everything seemed fine until I went upstairs onto the balcony for a view of how it all would look from above." Chomping on a few grapes herself, she paused to make sure I was still munching. Satisfied, she returned to her story. "I happened to look over the wall to the neighbor's courtyard. It was amazing. The Moroccan lady and her pregnant daughter were standing knee-deep in water, with that rollout washing machine of theirs plugged in and running. They were about six inches of water away from electrocution."

"What do you mean?"

"Their whole courtyard was a foot deep. Another six inches and the washer's electric motor would be under. Plugged-in, they would be electrocuted."

"What did you do?"

"I started yelling and pointing and trying to remember vocabulary for electrical shock situations. They had to get out of there, but I couldn't make them understand. I guess when you come from the desert the mindset is that water is totally wonderful. Anyway, I ran down to the living room where Placo was working and dragged him upstairs so he could see what was happening. He caught on immediately and yelled at the women to pull the plug and get out of there. Which they did."

"So what turned out to be the problem?" I asked, trying to visualize the whole scene.

"After Placo broke the orange pipe, then filled it with cement for the slab, he'd sealed their courtyard's drain. When the ladies do their wash, the machine just empties each cycle's water onto their tiles, then into that drain. They do a lot of wash, plus friends' diapers, in tubs with their hose running. Gray water from the kitchen feeds into the drain too. And it had rained for a couple days. I guess the water rose gradually and they didn't pay any attention."

"Good for you saving lives, but how's our tile?"

"Back to normal," she said. "But Placo felt terrible. He had to jackhammer out a three-foot section next to the wall, dig down to the old pipe, and put in a new piece.

"Everything works fine now. Once he retiles the spot you'll never know there'd been a problem. Of course the Moroccans are grateful. They brought me *méchoui*, one of their lamb dishes. I took it to La Brasserie for Michel, Jesselyne, and the boys to share. I'm sorry you weren't around to enjoy it with us."

"Hey, darling, nothing beats hospital food, even in France."

Bing reported good news on the painting front too.

"Carlo and Neige have finished the second floor. By the way, Eve is up in Paris and might have a modeling job for the summer. Anyway, every color suggestion I made they got right the first time. We used shades of peach in our bedroom—the farther from the windows, the lighter the color. With the exposed beams over-head, Kenny, it is gorgeous. I even added a *ciel de lit,* a halo of lace hanging from the ceiling over the head of our bed."

"What bed?" I asked, trying to recall if we'd stashed one out at Raoul's *brocante.*

"I went to one of the brass shops in Durfort. The owner, Jean-Paul, is a race car driver, and his father had been a pilot with the Free French. He wants to meet you as soon as you're out and about. Anyway, he was emptying his storeroom of old stuff and he had a beautiful, blue-antiqued, wrought-iron queen-size I couldn't resist. So," she smiled, "it's now under the *ciel de lit.*

"And Kenny, the guest room, the *chambre d'amis,*" she bub-bled, getting on a roll, "Carlo and I did that in soft autumnals—citrus, orange, and lemon. In the dim evening light you'd think you were in a nineteenth-century Parisian hotel, a guest of Tou-louse Lautrec.

"And the big bathroom, Carlo painted that in a marshmallow white. Then he ran two French blue stripes around three walls at the level of your sink. The fourth wall, opposite the fireplace, he sponge-pressed with lavender on white. He is a real talent."

Though I had gotten the sink in place before my disaster, I had not installed the corner tub or the shower stall next to the toilet, catty-corner to the sink. With my arm the mess it was, I'd have to get Christophe or somebody to finish those jobs. Such was life, something I guess I was starting to accept with a little more maturity.

SOON I felt strong enough to start moving around under my own steam. The ribs seemed healed, my headaches were pretty much gone, and I was off most of the goofball pain killers. Bing would still have to do the driving, but I was anxious to get to the house to see with my own eyes all she'd been describing. And . . . I was going to have to get together with Laurant to straighten out the mess I'd made of our relationship. I felt so damn guilty for the awful things I'd shouted at him, in front of the whole town no less.

The next morning, about eight o'clock, Bing pulled our rental car to a stop on rue Basque, in front of number 9, dropping me there while she parked just beyond the fountain. I stood in the street watching her, stabilizing myself with one of our tall walking sticks. Every now and then I'd been getting a case of the whirlies. I didn't want my return to rue Basque to be a flop on my face.

The front door was closed, locked, and covered in dust. Nobody around. I didn't feel like going inside just yet, so I started a slow walk toward the fountain where Bing was standing, letting me feel my way back into the flow of Black Mountain. A sensitive touch on her part.

Then Cabriole came flying out of Maurice's window! He landed on all fours in front of me, then flipped onto his rear legs and danced a circle of paw-waving "hello's." I was surprised and really delighted. He seemed so glad to see me, I was truly moved. Then Maurice came out his door, looked hard at my condition, arm in a sling, weight loss, pretty frail I imagine, and he started telling me how he'd been in much the same condition after an engagement with the Nazis on La Montagne Noire in 1944. Amazingly, I understood most of what he said.

As I reached the square, Caroline came out of the *patisserie* with her arms full of bagged *pains* to put in her delivery truck. Seeing me chugging along toward the fountain, her big blues opened wide, a huge smile filled her face, and she turned to call for François to come out of the shop to add his welcome to my return. And, across the way, M. Villedieux, proprietor of the mini-grocery where we'd first gotten our gas tanks, cocked his head in my direction and gave me a wave too. Then some of the old folks up in their windows at the Maison de Retraite smiled down at me and called, "*Bonjour*," adding, "*Est-ce que vous êtes en forme?*" (Are you in good shape?)

Wow, I felt like Andre Agassi after winning the US Open, bowing and waving to the four points of the stadium. "*Merci, merci, merci beaucoup,*" I called to all so warmly greeting and, it seemed, forgiving me. Then, from behind, I heard, "*Tu n'a pas un merci ou bonjour pour moi, mon ami?*"

I knew the voice, but for him to be using the familiar tense was a big surprise. Before I turned, I looked at Bing standing in front of me with a huge smile on her face.

"*Laurant, mon Dieu . . .*" I said, honestly taken aback.

"*Pas ton Dieu, ton ami,*" (Not your God, your friend) he smiled as he walked toward me, his arms wide.

I hobbled two steps his way and, amazingly enough, he laid his hands gently on my shoulders and touched each cheek to mine in the most familial way one man can greet another in France.

THE THREE of us had some time together on one of the benches by the fountain. At least until a troupe of others joined us, turning our reunion into a small party. Caroline and François brought croissants and *pains au raisins*. Maurice had told folks at the *café* I was back, so Claude and Sophie strode up with pitchers of hot coffee, warm milk, and cups, "*compléments du Parti Communiste*" (complements of the Communist Party), they assured me with a laugh.

Several more people appeared, among them Mme Crespi from across the street and M. Propre, Mr. Clean as I'd named him, the *balayeur*, or street-sweeper. He was on his morning rounds, but was happy to stop for a *café au lait*. Mme Fontaine, ninety plus years old, whom we soon got to know better as La Reine de la Montagne Noire, the Queen of Black Mountain, strode up with her huge dog Medussa in tow, or was it the other way around? And quite unexpectedly, L'Agent Secret slipped from behind the wheel of his black sedan parked on the far side of the square, again equipped with a bottle of Bordeaux in one hand, two glasses in the other. I guess if a secret agent wasn't good for some early morning claret, then who was?

When things finally settled down, Bing helped Claude clean up the bits of debris the *rendez-vous* had produced, then she and Sophie managed to drag the slightly tipsy Secret Agent back toward the *café*, giving Laurant and me a chance to be alone.

"Ah Laurant, I am so sorry for what I said. The way I acted. I—"

"Please, please, please. In this country, my friend, we understand anger. We all get *agité de temps en temps*, but we also know how to let those feelings pass, as time passes. Each morning brings a new day. We say *au revoir* to yesterday, *bonne journée* to what lies ahead. Please, forget the past as I have forgotten it."

"But I said some horrible things, in front of the whole village. I—"

"*C'est vrai* you spoke with *d'énergie*. And I will add, your accent was quite good. Perhaps a little more Midi-Pyrénées than Tarn, but you are doing well," he said, patting my back. "Remember, for we French, it is not what you say, but *how* you say it."

"Laurant, you are kind, and very forgiving, but there is still something that troubles me and was probably a large part of my explosion. When Bing and I are working on the house with you, you speak only to her. It is as if I am not present. You did that the day I got so angry. I was already upset with what Jean-Jacques had been doing to us; your speaking only to Bing was the *coup de grâce*."

Laurant gave me a quizzical look, cocked his head, then puffed his cheek and let the air hiss out.

"So . . . now I see. Look, my friend, and I really mean *mon cher ami*, our custom here is to speak to the woman of the house when discussing matters of the house, even when the husband is present. The home is the domain of the lady, the wife. . ."

"But everyone else speaks to me, not Bing."

"Because they are the workers. *Je suis patron*. We speak at different levels. All of this is part of, what you call, old Europe. The old world. You are from the new. There are many differences which can be confusing. So, that is all that happened here. A mis-understanding. Nothing more and certainly nothing relating to the ladies. Look, I am a Frenchman, but that does not mean I will try to take *every* man's woman. Perhaps a select few, but certainly not your Bing. Trust me," he finished with what had to be a mis-chievous smile.

"So, come, let us go back to the house. I have some questions about the well in the courtyard. How you wish it constructed. And, while Bing is with us, I promise to be nice to you too."

I laughed out loud, at his humor as well as with relief for the weight he had lifted off my conscience. I had been forgiven by Laurant, my *friend* Laurant . . . one hell of a decent man.

WITH A room rented at the Abbey for the foreseeable future, I guiltily succumbed to a nap each afternoon after a morning of writing and before hobbling down to Château Poubelle for the day's last look-see. And because of these solitary walks, I got to know still more about the village's rhythms, its ebbs and flows. My sorry physical state, and seeing Bing taking charge of so many things, seemed to win the town's sympathy. And, being the only off-season Americans around, we had first been known as Les Americans; but now just Bing and Monsieur Ken. (My gray hair won me the *Monsieur* designation. Since Bing looks much younger, she escaped *Madame*.)

One villager I ran into a lot was Phillippe Beaugeste. He had probably been the most understandable person we met during our first stay in Black Mountain. His face was plastic and he used his hands, shoulders, and entire body so effectively we could usu-ally figure out what he was trying to tell us. (For all that, I thought it only appropriate his name was *Beaugeste*.)

He and his wife were incredibly hospitable, inviting us for

aperitifs and in time, Sunday lunches, even multi-course dinners. At one of these Bing asked them, "Why do you have us to your home so often? Our French is improving, but we make so many mistakes and are so slow. It must be terrible for you."

Madame Beaugeste laughed, saying (as best we could understand it), "Not at all. We enjoy hearing the way you say things. Very entertaining. For us you are like television . . ."

So, Bing and I had become Black Mountain's private sitcom.

As a small payback for people's concern, especially Claude's, Bing got the idea to spruce up the big flower boxes out front of his *café*. Since he was Black Mountain's leading Trotskyite, and the Communists had held a five-person rally by the fountain on May Day, it seemed appropriate to brighten his place in commemoration of the event. We bought two dozen sets of impatiens from Point Vert, a big nursery nearby, and before sunrise one morning we planted them in the big boxes. By mid-morning, with the sun beaming down, people were walking by and nodding their approval of the colorful blossoms brightening the *café's* outdoor terrace.

Bing and I didn't say anything about them when we sat down for the *plat du jour*. But, after the meal, as we paid our bill, I couldn't resist commenting to Claude about the new plantings.

"*Bien sûr, mes amis,*" he said, "that is one of the blessings of our socialist system. The government plants pretty flowers for everyone to enjoy. It is too bad you do not have the same in the United States."

"*Pas grave, mon camarade,*" I said, shaking my head, "perhaps someday we will be so fortunate."

After Claude walked away, Bing put her hand on my good arm and asked, "Are we now socialist government workers? Wow. Maybe they'll pay your medical bills."

We shared a good laugh and promised never to tell Claude who planted the flowers. The five-person May Day rally had been bad enough. What if he discovered *capitalists* were responsible for *les jolis fleurs*?

MY RECUPERATIVE walks also introduced me to the beasts of Black Mountain. Michel at La Brasserie was the village's number one rescuer of castoffs. The first of the strays he'd taken in years earlier was named Lundi, Monday. This mutt had at best a jumbled bloodline, making him look like a stumpy-legged, bob-tailed Rhodesian Ridgeback. He'd been terribly mistreated in his youth and consequently had a growlingly miserable personality in his old age. He would bark and snap at most anyone who came near. Perfect for sitting around in a restaurant? Right.

Mardi, Tuesday, was a huge female Great Dane who'd been left as a pup in a box by the door. Lundi ignored her. She ignored him. Mercredi, yes Wednesday, was a goose. The rest of Michel's week was made up of cats, but for Dimanche (Sunday), an iguana who sat in front of a hot lamp by the bar and ate flies as entertainment for the human bar flies who also frequented the place.

My old friend Cabriole would occasionally wander into La Brasserie to harass Lundi, but the main threat to Lundi's tranquility was Monsieur Coq's giant cat, Maximus. To me that monster looked a cross between a Lynx and a Pyrenees mountain bear. He must have been fifty pounds. Even horse-like Mardi gave him wide birth. Only one animal in the village seemed to have the guts to go head-to-head with Maximus, and her name was Medusa. Madame Fontaine's big Bouvier.

We first chatted with Madame Fontaine when Medusa, paying no attention to my infirmities, bumped me aside as she galloped down rue Basque in hot pursuit of Maximus. But most extraordinary in this was the elderly lady attached to Medusa, comfortably jogging behind without noticeable concern for the brouhaha developing ahead—*la reine*, Mme Fontaine, the queen.

Stopping by me, with Bing coming out our front door, the

grande dame reigned in her beast with one of those clutched fishing-reel type leashes, cranking the mountainous hound back to where it offered a wet-tongued hello to us both. During the process, Madame Fontaine took hold of my good arm to stabilize the wobble Medusa had set me into, and with twinkling eyes announced, "*Demain J'aurai quatre-vingt-dix ans.*"

"You will be ninety years old tomorrow? Impossible," I said, Bing nodding her own surprise. "Madam, you cannot be a day more than fifty," I offered with a smile and bow.

"You are very kind, *mon chevalier,*" she returned, long eyelashes gently lowered, "but in fact it is true . . . and ninety years are quite enough for one life."

The way Madame Fontaine said that unnerved us a bit. What would tomorrow hold? Suicide? I glanced at Bing, whose eyes darted back to Madame with equal concern.

"Therefore, "she said, placing a soothing hand on my good arm, "the day after tomorrow I shall . . . commence my next life!"

All three of us burst out laughing, and Madame Fontaine invited us back to her house for some tea and *un petit bisquit, peut-être.* We accepted.

Medusa seemed delighted to have new friends to jump up on, which I feared might re-break my aching ribs. Madame quickly noted my discomfort and scolded Medusa. (Bing and I agreed it was terribly deflating to be in the presence of animals that understood French better than we did.)

Walking along the narrow sidewalk behind Bing and Mme Fontaine, I was surprised at how youthful her carriage was. So many older people are saggy or shapeless with pipestem legs, and shuffle along with an almost defeated air. This was hardly the case with Madame. She had calves, even a pert *derrière* she sashayed along with like a woman half her age. And she dressed well—a nicely cut wool dress with a short-sleeved sweater, black Mary Jane shoes, and a white scarf. She looked great. Later she said she considered her body like her shop, something to be kept present-able and *propre*.

Entering the little mews leading to the Fontaine house (with the number 1 on the door), we felt we were stepping back hundreds, if not a thousand years in time. The narrow way was cobbled, but only a meter or so wider than a Mini Cooper. Her house was of stone, across from a walled garden. At the end the lane the cobbles turned right, curling around the Abbey Tower itself, which we later learned shared an interior wall with Madame's shop and a bedroom above. This was the tower rebuilt by Charlemagne's father, Pepin, after the Visigoths laid ruin to it in the sixth century.

Madame Fontaine gave us the grand tour. Though in the very center of the village, her own walled garden made it seem we were off in the country. Flowers, vines, trees, a tiny fish pond and a large cage full of chirping birds complimented the setting.

Returning to her living room for tea, she gave us a peek into the charming shop she opened afternoons and weekends. Here she showed us her own oil and pastel paintings, as well as the *poupées* (dolls) she created. On the shelves were displays of her writings, novels, and poetry. Knowing that I wrote, she produced her current diary for me to review. She said she wrote in it every-day and from it drew inspiration for her fiction.

I glanced across at Bing. The expression on her face must have mirrored my own. Here we were grousing about being saddled with redoing the house and how little time that left us for paint and pen, when this near-ancient woman was producing a multitude of works every day, with only a smile and a *c'est la vie* shrug at the rigors she faced.

"Madame Fontaine," Bing began, looking around in honest wonder, "how do you do all this? You produce so many things. You are amazing."

"Oh dear girl, I do so little, but I intend to do more soon.

Shortly I will be starting classes for the area's budding talent between the ages of nine and sixteen. The problem today is that young painters have no discipline in the fundamentals of brush, stroke, color, and composition. I am especially pleased this new project will commence in the first days of my *new life*."

A F T E R   O U R tea, walking back down rue Basque toward Château Poubelle, dusk was closing in. I felt a little whipped by my busted-up body, and at the same time invigorated by what we'd just been exposed to. As frustrated as Bing and I were with all the crap that had come down, Madame Fontaine had been an inspiration. If she could do all she did at age ninety, then certainly we could too. Of course, that had always been Bing's attitude; I was the late arrival onboard.

I decided that after leaving Bing at the house, I'd get back to our room at the Abbey and work on the manuscript. My fictional terrorists were just about to send a sunrise rocket into the crown of the Statue of Liberty, opening their Day of Jihad. New York City buildings would fall, engulfing the streets in flames. "Infidels" would die, while Allah would rise up supreme on a sea of the unbelievers' blood.

Before we reached the front door, something solid as a rock slapped me hard off the side of my head! What the hell?

TWENTY-NINE

THE FERAL FAMILY HERE AND MADAME FONTAINE THERE

I HAD dropped to a knee. What happened? I was totally confused.

Bing's momentum carried her a few steps further down the sidewalk, but the *whop* stopped her. She turned and stared at me wide-eyed. I'd gone into a defensive crouch, partly from the impact, the rest from reflex . . . a flicker of the Marine still alive in my bones. I looked up to my right, and there, in an open second-floor window across rue Basque, stood a grinning teenager just letting fly with another hardball—white, round, fast, and whistling straight for my head.

American boys grow up catching and throwing balls and, like riding a bicycle, we don't forget how to do it. So, I pivoted instinctively, raised my right hand, and caught the thing coming at me. I was so pumped I wasn't feeling any pain, at least for the moment. Getting back on my feet, I strode forward, and fired whatever it was in my hand as hard as I could straight back through the window. *WHACK!* A precious moment. I'd caught the nasty boy smack on the forehead! It sounded like a baseball bat hitting the ball. He dropped like a sack of cement, out of sight below the windowsill. I'd won the kewpie doll! And a lot of hurt along with it.

I crumpled against our doorjamb. Bing jumped to my side, reaching under my good arm to keep me from going down. My ribs were killing me, but between leaning against the front of our house and Bing's support, I was able to ratchet myself up to a standing position.

"What . . . ?" I questioned staring down at the ball-size glob in the gutter.

She bent and picked it up. It was a wad of old plaster tightly wrapped with masking tape. It was hard. I was surprised the thing hadn't fractured my skull. I didn't care what I had done to the kid's fat head.

Then, up by the fountain, the headlights of a black sedan flashed several times. What was going on? I felt like the central character in a B-movie. The car's door opened and out came the Secret Agent. Ah hah. Was I ever happy to see that crazy character's face.

"*Monsieur, Madame, bonsoir,*" he said, reaching into his jacket pocket and withdrawing a small leather day-planner. Slipping its clasp, he withdrew a pen. "I saw everything. Have you a statement you wish to make?"

Bing held up the missile for the Secret Agent to see and said, "A boy threw this from the window up there and hit Ken on the head."

M. Agent uncapped his pen and jotted something onto a notepad in the planner. As he did so he muttered, "*Gitan.*"

"The boy is a Gypsy?" I asked. "How do you know that?"

Without a pause in his writing, he said, "I know many things."

"Hmm," I returned, not totally convinced. Finally straightened up, I said, "I never saw anyone but the old man with the closed eye living there."

"The old man had been in the Maquis. He died. While you were away. I closed the house. These people asked to rent it. *Le notaire* handled it. They have a year's lease. Of course, once they are in, it is difficult to get them out."

"Interesting," said Bing. "Is that how things are here? Renters have special rights?"

"I believe your language speaks of birds in bushes or hands. Whatever . . ." he said with a shrug.

"We call it *squatters' rights*," I said, feeling a sharp pain across my chest. Shit . . . ribs or heart? I didn't need either.

"Keep me informed. I will stay on the case. Good evening, *Madame. Monsieur*," he said. Replacing his pen, re-clasping the day-planner, and sliding it back into his jacket pocket. He nodded to us and moved around the corner past Claude's *café*.

BEFORE MY accident, we had been working with a French teacher named Edwige. She was a youngish friend of Madame Fontaine's who had prodded us to meet the Grande Dame, if for no other reason than to absorb a lot of the local lore, of which she was known to be the main curator.

Edwige was kind enough to come to the Abbey for our lessons during my recuperation. Today we told her of our adventures with the hard-throwing teenager. Then I asked about the old fellow who used to live in that apartment, the man whom I had smoked out back when I got the bad fireplaces burning at number 10.

"Ken, there is a fascinating story involving that man, and Mme Fontaine too," she said. "I will arrange dinner with her so she can tell you the whole tale herself. I will translate whatever is too difficult for you."

Two nights later we were all gathered around Héllé Fontaine's table to hear her story of the Maquis, her role in the Resistance, and how she had run into the man who had lived across the street lo those many years since the war.

"First, let me explain a few things about what we did here," she began. "The word *maquis* means scrub brush. When Hitler started taking our young men into his army, most elected to run away into the forest, to hide in the brush. And so the name, Maquis. La Montagne Noire around us here is wild. It also happened to be under the air routes the French and American bomber groups flew from North Africa to Germany and back. Over the course of the war, many of these aircraft were shot down. Their pilots would bailout and hopefully be picked up by the Maquis. They'd be hidden in villages like ours until transport was available over the Pyrenees to Spain and on to Portugal for pickup. I hid many under a stone slab in my entry foyer here."

At that point in her narrative and at the end of her fish course, Héllé trooped us out of the dining room, through the salon, to the front door so we could see how the slab she mentioned would move, then lift and open to the compartment below. Extraordinary.

"Now," she began again while gathering up the first course dishes. "In 1943, the SS marched into Black Mountain. The Vichy collaborators were failing to enforce Nazi policies, especially relating to deportation of Jews and hunting down the Resistance.

"Well, early one morning I was advised a Free French pilot had been shot down a few days earlier and was hiding in Arfons, on the mountain, but would be coming to my door momentarily, in just minutes. He and our people had evaded the Germans, but before entering Black Mountain, I later learned, they made a mistake. As the sun came up, rather than stay inside the forest, they'd dashed through Durfort and were seen."

Moving behind us around the table, Héllé poured one of her dependable Côtes du Rhônes to compliment the next course of *côtelette d'agneau*. It was amazing to watch this very old woman handle such a meal service alone. She would start with at least three plates stacked at each place setting. Course after course would be ready on her kitchen table, waiting to be served or to be heated prior to serving. She would enter the dining room with a tray, from which she would slide each portion onto the top plates. As that course was finished, she'd gather those dishes, take them into the kitchen, and repeat the process. Her wines would be uncorked and breathing when we arrived, and she would serve these and water throughout the meal. She did it all so neatly, and with the kitchen so close, she never interrupted her discussions.

Sitting back down and fluffing her napkin into her lap, she continued. "The report the Germans received was only of a sighting in Durfort, not that the group had continued in this direction. So, first the Durfort homes were ransacked looking for Maquis. Though the Nazis didn't find the pilot, they did find a short-wave radio. Accordingly, the family in whose house it was were made examples. The entire village was forced to watch as they were lined up against the *mairie* wall and a squad with machine-pistols cut them down. The grandfather, mother, and father. The young daughter was spared but forced to watch, held tightly in the arms of the mayor's wife. To this day the bullet scars are on that wall."

Héllé brushed a few loose strands of gray from her forehead, sighed, then sipped from her glass of red wine.

"We could hear the shots from here. We had heard them a lot that year and knew perfectly well what they meant. Our villages were practically adjoining. Then a staff car and two motorcycles pulled up in front of our door at the very instant the aviator slipped into the house through the garden. What to do? It was too late to get him under the slab. I was already hurrying across it as the rifle butts banged against the door. Oh, how that *thump,*

thump, thump, sounded like the drum of a funeral procession . . . and the beat of my heart.

"My father grabbed the pilot's arm and started him up the stairs. My mother stood on the first step as if to block the way. I was sure in moments we would all be shot dead.

"I opened the door. A young SS officer was standing there next to a sergeant with the rifle. Behind them were a car and two motorcycles whose riders had *schmeissers* at the ready. The officer had a swagger stick and black leather gloves in his left hand. He held his right out to me as he said, '*Guten morgen, fräulein. Wirden-wir eintreten!*'"

"I speak German. Nodding, I stepped aside for them to enter, but I did not take his hand. Terrified as I was, I felt I was on stage, just playing a role. I asked the lieutenant if he and his men would like some milk, since it was so early, or perhaps beer? Anything to gain time. The soldiers' expressions said "*Ja,*" but the Lieutenant said, "*Nein danke.*"

"My stomach was in a knot. The pilot wasn't where he should have been, under the floor. There was no place to hide upstairs. *Thump, thump, thump,* continued my heart.

"After they inspected the main floor, they started up to the *premier* and *deuxième étages.* Somehow my parents were calm. I wished I were so brave.

"Every room was given precise Teutonic attention. They looked under beds, behind curtains, in armoires, everywhere in the master bedroom, including its closet, where they slid the clothes left and right on the steel pipe while paying close attention to a small wall door in the back. Kicking it in, they found its space empty. They thumped on floors, banged on walls. If a man was anywhere in that house, they would find him.

"He had to be in the attic, I thought, huddled helplessly under the eaves. We all felt the tension as we mounted those last stairs. I heard the lieutenant mutter "*Aus liebe zu Gott*" under his breath. I think he was starting to think what his *Oberstleutnant* would do to me when they found the fugitive.

"My parents stayed on the landing as I continued up behind the Germans into the attic. I knew my parents desperately wanted to take each other's hands, if only to hug and pray . . . but they knew if they did, it could lead to their death. As I reached the last step the soldiers were already thumping about, pushing things aside, banging and crashing against whatever was there. I knew in a moment there would be a scream and a shot.

"As I entered the *grenier*, the lieutenant called to me, '*Vas ist das?*' He must have found the man! I thought I would faint. But no, all I saw was him pointing at the dust-covered grand piano that had been there for years . . . which had a sheaf of documents under its cords that I had planned to sew into my skirts to take to Paris for the *Maquis* that evening.

"Continuing to point toward it, he asked, 'Do you play?'

"I hesitated, risking a quick look around for the pilot. Nothing. 'No, I don't. But the attic mice do, and they have been playing so often and so hard, some of the keys have stopped sounding notes. What good is such a piano, other than for mice to play?'

"The lieutenant looked questioningly at me, pulled away the cover, and hit a low register key. It sounded. He hit several more, until he heard a dull *thunk*. Then a few more until notes sounded properly again. Of course I was terrified he would open the top and look inside. But he only smiled and said I was right. The piano *was* only fit for mice. He turned and indicated that I should lead the way back down the stairs. He'd found nothing in our attic. I was amazed, but breathing again. No documents found. No pilot found. How could that be?"

Topping our glasses, Héllé went on to say that when they'd trouped back to the front door, the lieutenant snapped to ridged attention, his sergeant following suit, they clicked their heels, and nodded formally. The lieutenant thanked the Fontaines for allowing his inspection and offered his regret for upsetting their morning. He added how pleased he was that they were not the kind to harbor enemies of the Third Reich. He touched his gloves and stick to his cap, then turned smartly to his car. The sergeant followed and took the forward seat next to the driver, who started the engine. The cyclists tucked their machine pistols on their slings behind them and kicked their motors to life. With engines roaring and gravel pinging down the lane behind them, they were quickly away, headed toward the town hall.

"I could hardly breathe," she continued. "We were totally confused. Where in the name of God could the pilot be? Like smoke, he seemed to have disappeared into thin air. We dashed from room to room, but nothing . . . until, in the master bedroom (the only one with a closet), we heard a whispered, 'Are they gone?'

"I couldn't tell where it was coming from. I went into the closet. I felt something, a *presence*. I looked up and, *mon Dieu*, there he was! Pressed against the ceiling, above the steel pipe that held the clothes. The pilot had suspended himself horizontally, feet against one wall, with his heels hooked over its crown molding, his forearms against the other. How was it possible he'd kept himself so rigid for so long? Later he said God had given him a strength he'd never realized he had. At the end of the war he decided to stay where he'd found God. And yes, Ken, he was the neighbor you smoked out of his house that cold night last winter," she concluded with a roll of her eyes and gentle smile.

But there was more to Héllé's story. She'd still had her mission to Paris to complete. That night, as the last train from Toulouse was pulling out, a dark caped figure jumped aboard the end car, unnoticed by the increased Nazi security. Sitting with great composure in an otherwise empty second-class compartment, her cape wrapped like a blanket around her, Héllé said she could feel the pressure of the envelope she'd sewed into her skirt heavy against her thigh. She'd been thinking of her children, who had been with neighbors overnight when the Germans came that morning. They were still there. Would people ask questions about that? Though she had been strong through so much, sitting alone like this made her feel vulnerable. The compartment door opened, giving her a start. Instinctively she smiled at the conductor as she handed him her identity card and the ticket she'd bought a day earlier. She added a letter that appeared to be on official hospital stationary advising that her mother was near death in the central *retrait* (retirement) facility in Paris. Mama had asked that she be with her at the end. The French conductor hardly glanced at the documents before handing them over his shoulder to the man in the trench coat behind him. It was several minutes before they were handed back.

Throughout the process Héllé said she tried desperately not to move for fear the envelope in her skirt would make a crackling sound. Her stillness paid off. She got safely to Paris, executed the *rendezvous* as briefed, and then got back to Black Mountain before afternoon of the next day. No one was the wiser.

Amazingly, she had foiled the Germans twice in one day, a high point in her career as a Maquis operative. An extraordinary woman to say the least. One who was beginning her second life, or perhaps her third, when that of a spy for a Free France was counted in the mix.

Later, as we walked home, I asked Edwige more about the old man. She explained that the pressures, the terror of those days escaping the Nazis, along with injuries he'd suffered in the parachute jump, had led to a stroke later. But, she reassured us, it was probably that very trauma that saved his life in the end, which she explained as Héllé had told it to her before.

The German contingent stayed on in Black Mountain, increasing their numbers and making it all the more difficult for the village to function as a way-station in the *Maquis* escape network. For the pilot, the stroke had put him into a wheelchair. He was pushed around town as an invalid, but an invalid with a shortwave radio built into base of that chair, from which he continued to serve as the Maquis' message master for the region.

I HEARD an interesting addition to this a day or two later when I was going back to our room for my nap. Héllé was walking Medusa. She intercepted me and was as talkative as ever. I asked her how it had been fighting the Nazis at home while so many in Paris were collaborating.

"Ken, you must understand," she said, laying a hand on my arm in emphasis, "Paris is not a part of France. That has been true for more than a thousand years. Paris is for *les Parisiens*, who have only distain for the rest of France. We are on our own. Always have been. Remember, Paris capitulated to the Germans in five days. We of Black Mountain, all the region, fought the bastards for five years. With America's help. Which we have not forgotten, though Paris and its politicians have. For them, history goes back no further than yesterday's sunset."

THIRTY

NOT THE SOUND OF MUSIC

HAVING A room at the Abbey Hotel kept us in the village more than we would have been otherwise. More and more people were getting to know us, and we them.

The hotel watched Bing's canvases stacking up around our room and asked to display ten of them in prominent locations throughout the building. This led to her being invited into the Art Association, which had its own small gallery down rue de la République from the butcher's shop. What could I say? Bing was a heck of a successful compartmentalizer. Despite all our upsets and setbacks, she'd trooped on with her painting, working around the edges, and earned these tributes to her mettle. So, growing more comfortable in the village, we decided not to go back to the dairy farm in Soual when it became available.

Also, being around this much, we got a feel for the special place family has in the life of small-town France. In general, we found working parents don't commute. If there is a job locally, no matter how little it pays, they tend to take it rather than drive a distance for something paying more. As I've said before, since they have lifelong security, money is not as important to them as it is to us in America.

Then there is the two-hour midday break, which brings parents and kids together in their own homes for lunch. The half-school days each Wednesday and Saturday also added to that quality time. And yet, despite all the French families have going for them, bad influences still lurk, especially on the outskirts of larger cities and towns. In one word—McDonald's.

Don't get me wrong. When my bladder is full, I know McDonald's has great bathrooms. Coffee too. That is true in France, and probably all over the world. So, on driving trips, that's where we stop when we need to. And that's where we saw French family values most seriously undermined.

In general, their kids in restaurants are superb—quiet, respectful, as adult as any young person can be. At McDonald's, however, with the loud noisy video games, jarring colors, clattering music, rides, rough-and-tumble play areas, and all that American stuff, the French kids seem to become just as noisy, frenetic, and less respectful of the adults as we see ours being at home. All of which set me thinking.

"Bing, do you think the kid who hit me on the head eats at McDonald's a lot?"

"We could check with l'Agent Secret," she answered with a wink.

"Good idea," I said. "I'm feeling well enough to walk down to Claude's for a glass of red. The Agent might be there. Want to come?"

"I'm ready," she said, and we were on our way.

Before getting past the fountain, however, catty-corner to the *patisserie*, we saw our man's black VW sedan . . . with him inside. Alone. What a strange dude. Stopping by the driver's-side window, I tapped on the glass. He slowly turned his head and looked up, much as a self-assured cat would.

"*Oui?*" he asked.

"*J'aimerais un verre de vin. Bing aussi. Et vous?*"

After only the slightest eye action, he replied, "*Le même.*"

Claude seemed surprised we walked in with the Secret Agent. Though my calling him l'Agent Secret had caught on around town, and seemed to have made him more of a public curiosity, we never saw people spending much time with him. I'd never even seen him with a group playing *boule* or just hanging out at Claude's or La Brasserie. Perhaps some of it was his air of always being on the job. I guess few people wanted to get in the way of that.

"What can you tell us about the boy who hit me on the head?" I asked l'Agent Secret as Claude put three glasses and a carafe of red on our table.

L'Agent pulled his day-planner out of his pocket, eyes sweeping the room. After checking the facts, he started speaking in a Detective Joe Friday monotone, like he was reporting his findings to the chief or something.

"Name, Camille. Lives with sister. Father dead, mother in prison. Sister has nine-year-old son. No husband. She does not enjoy having her brother around. Can't control him. Camille's ambition—courier . . . of pharmaceuticals. Expects to have a *moto* soon. Believes mobility will give him his start. Expects to be caught, but sees prison time as career enhancing. Camille influences another boy who hopes to be his partner in the future."

"What a mess. How did you get him to tell you all this?" Bing asked, her brow wrinkling.

"I told him I had connections."

"What kind of connections?" I asked.

"Inside and out."

"Of what?"

"Prison," he said, his eyes holding ours in a flat stare.

"*Really?* Good heavens. What did he say to that?" Bing asked.

L'Agent thumbed through a few pages of notes, ran his finger down till he found what he was looking for. Eyes left, right; then he said, "*Cool.*" Interview over.

As the Secret Agent set off around the corner, Bing let out a sigh. "Oh Kenny, do you think there's anything we can do to help?"

I was wondering the same thing. "Pierre works in prison reform. Maybe we could get him involved. *Before* the boy gets in trouble, in this case." I was quiet for a moment, then added, "All this is so different from everything else here."

"I wonder if there aren't a lot of things going on we've been naïve about," she said thoughtfully.

"Rose-colored glasses?" I asked.

"Innocents abroad," she concluded.

AS THE THREE months mounted to four on our "turn-key" purchase, most of the street-level work was nearing completion. In the courtyard, under Bing's direction, Rouge had built a semi-circular well against the wall that separated us from Jacques the mason and his family next door, on the other side from our Moroccan neighbors. It was a beautiful piece of work of slim, cast-off Toulousian brick. Rouge laid it perfectly, and then capstoned the top with tile left over from our bedroom floor. At Point Vert we'd found an arched fountain face, which Rouge cemented into the courtyard wall over the well. Christophe ran a water pipe and *robinet* (faucet) to it, hidden in the wall's new facement. Then he connected that to the line he'd already laid to my *cabinet de toilette*, an important addition to the old rabbit hutch that was being transformed into my office.

Though Placo and Bruno redid the walls and ceiling of the office, I'd intended to put in the plumbing myself there, as I had in the other bathrooms. Of course our wacko Volvo driver put an end to that. I must say, however, my injuries had their advantages. My manuscript was finished. After a final edit, hopefully within a week, I would FedEx it to Vernon in Los Angeles. He would give it another read and a tweak, and pass it on to his contacts at DreamWorks. They would have my New York jihad thriller by the end of July, early August 2001 at the latest. Who knew what would happen after that.

In a day or two Michel, Laurant's mason, would be laying the new tile floor stretching from the back wall of my office, joining what he and Placo had already put down in the courtyard, then on beyond to cover what had been the nasty kitchen, now our *petit salon*. French doors would go in at both ends of the courtyard, giving my office and the *petit salon* an open sunny view, tying everything together into one sweet package.

While this was going on, and Bing was at the hotel helping to hang her work, I found myself watching, only *watching* in frustration, Laurant's team unload the tile. I felt especially bad because the big flatbed truck blocked rue Basque, requiring all available hands to open the street as quickly as possible, and I couldn't help. That's when I saw Camille come out of his door. This was the first time we'd been face to face at ground level since my beaning. We were the same height. Young versus old. His demeanor was *maussade*, sullen. I hoped I looked less so, but interestingly we did share something—touching our hands to where we'd been hit; my temple, his forehead, we were both black and blue.

"*Ça va?*" I nodded.

"*Ça va*," he returned.

"Why did you throw that thing at me?"

"To see if I could hit you. Why did you throw one back at me?"

"To teach you a lesson."

He blew that off as typical adult talk. "What's the truck doing?"

"Delivering tiles for our house," I said, stating the obvious. "Will you help unload them?"

"No, but I might like to be a mason someday," he replied, continuing in the *maussade* (sullen) mode.

"M. Thoreau next door is an independent mason. I can introduce you to him and to M. de Gaillac, *le padron*, if you like."

"No."

"Why not?"

"I have other plans."

"What type?"

"Deliveries. Tomorrow I will have a *moto*."

"You are very young for such work."

"I will get older. You did."

"Thank you. But what of school?"

"I don't need school for deliveries."

"The government says you do."

"For only one more year."

"Then what?"

"I will be free."

"Free for what?"

"Life."

"Where?"

"Wherever."

"Be careful."

"Goodbye."

Somehow I didn't feel Camille's future was that bright, nor was our relationship on an upward track. After our conversation with L'Agent Secret, I felt sorry for him, his sister, the younger siblings, but I doubted I'd be able to penetrate the kid's mindset. Perhaps Jacques, the mason next door, who had a friend in the *gendarmes,* or the Secret Agent could talk some sense into him. On second thought, expecting the Secret Agent to do anything of the kind was, at best, a stretch. If Pierre and Marie-Claude came back for another visit, they would be the ones to start with.

OUR CELL phone rang. It was an old Pan Am friend calling to say he and his wife were on their way to France. Oh shit.

"Bing, what are we going to do? The house is still all screwed up. I'm only fifty percent myself. The kitchen isn't in. No first-floor tile down till tomorrow."

"Kenny, you know Rich and Ann, they'll hardly notice. They're family," she smiled, taking my good hand in hers.

"Yeah, right," I said, doing a little *maussade* number of my own.

Over subsequent calls, we learned Rich and Ann were planning on a month's stay in Provence, then visiting us on their way back to San Francisco. A bit irrationally, I had added Provence to my long list of irritations. For me, it was like Starbucks. One of those places *everybody* goes to. Gag.

"Provence sucks," I said.

"Thank you for sharing that with me, Kenny," Bing said, shaking her head.

"I mean, since Peter Mayle, nobody goes to France anymore, just to Paris or Provence. I doubt anybody even speaks French there; to say nothing of the conditions—off-season rain and windstorms transitioning to high-season traffic jams and wall-to-wall foreigners all sweating heavily."

"Don't bring that up with Rich and Ann. We'll just show them Black Mountain. They'll get warm and fuzzy for it like we did," she said sensibly enough.

OUR DEAR friends rolled in after lunch two days later, in a brand new Bimmer that hardly fit down rue Basque. Big car, big people. Richard had been a football player in college and Ann was a good five foot twelve herself. Black Mountain was meeting *biggie-sized* America, in the flesh.

Fortunately Christophe had been available to install the toilet and shower in the upstairs bathroom. With that operational, we decided to put the two of them in the only bedroom equipped with a bed so far: ours. We would continue staying at the hotel. Laurant's guys had put the tile down from my office through the *petit salon,* and it'd had a day to set. We could entertain there, though the French doors wouldn't be in until the next week. A night or two of open-air *aperitifs* would be okay.

After Rich and Ann had been shown around, their baggage hauled upstairs and faces freshened, we assembled in the *petit salon.* We sat on whicker furniture we'd just bought that morning in a nearby grocery store, of all places. We'd first seen the stuff in the medieval pizza shop, and the proprietor/juggler told us where to find it. The equivalent of $200 bought us two sofas, two coffee tables, and four chairs. What a deal.

When Ann set her big purse on the floor, out popped their tiny white pooch named Jump Up, who immediately hopped directly onto one of the tables, almost toppling an open bottle of Côte de Tarn. Then it made for the plate of Camembert and *petites baguettes.* Rich quickly scooped her up as Ann filled us in on her history.

"You know me, Kenny, sometimes I forget things," she began, taking a glass of the red Tarn I offered everyone. "One time I flew into Paris from Berlin and didn't realize Jump Up was even in my purse. She sleeps so much and is so tiny. She's a Tibetan breed, originally bred to be living body-warmers for mountain monks. The dogs' body temperature is 104 degrees, and they sleep sixteen hours a day. They have an underbite so they can't nip if they get rolled on. The monks have big inside pockets sewn into their robes to slide these little heater-dogs into," she concluded, reaching to take Jump Up from Rich.

Ann took the dog into what would someday be our kitchen. She had a bottle of water she poured from into a dish for Jump Up; then she returned to the *petit salon*. After we'd sipped a bit of Côte de Tarn, Rich asked for a taste of the local *pastis*. I went back to the future kitchen where a few cartons of bottles were stacked, along with a box of glasses. I poured an inch or so of *pastis* into each glass and, spotting the water bottle Ann had left, topped the drinks from it.

The French love their *pastis*. Every country in Europe has its own version of the licorice drink—*ouzo* in Greece, for instance—though Americans don't seem too enamored with it. We enjoyed this sip, however, at least until Ann gave a little speech on how important it is for dogs to have their own water, with their own scent, and how she always carried Jump Up's special recycled water in her private bottle.

AT LA Brasserie, Michel, Jesselyne, and François, the hard-partying Basque *serveur*, were delighted to meet our American friends. It was Friday, jazz night, so the guys in the band were happy to see us too. We had a roaring time. Rich slipped into a smiling euphoria while Ann kept breaking up with laughter as she and Bing acted like schoolgirls violating curfew. I got a major itch to dance, probably attributable to the medicinal quantities of wine consumed to assist the mending of my wounded arm. (It did seem to help.) Off went the sling as I danced with Bing and Ann, and with Jesselyne, and even some snappy-looking college girl from Toulouse, to say nothing of making a couple of turns with a reluctant Michel Bond himself. We all got a lot of applause and, by the end of the evening, I must say what little of my arm I could feel, felt great.

In the wee hours, well past midnight, walking the cobbled mews back to Château Poubelle to drop off our friends, we were all arm in arm. I, for one, felt like a feather floating through a mist of fulfilling dreams. Bing and I had stepped out of all we'd known for a lifetime . . . and stepped into this faraway world of walled gardens, stone castles, and storybook people. Ahead a sudden breeze churned up the thin ground fog, sending it tumbling off the glistening cobblestones, rolling it up to halo the street lamps in orange and lemon. The sound of our footfalls echoed gently ahead of us into the night.

Then . . . up rue Basque, around the fountain, and toward the Abbey Hotel came the high-pitch screech and *blap, blap, blap* of one, then two, and finally a third wretchedly loud and nasty *mini-moto*! Camille's dream of ownership had come true . . . shattering mine.

THE NEXT morning was grim. At six-thirty, three, maybe four hours after we closed La Brasserie, Bing banged me on the back.

"Kenny, Kenny. Wake up. Raoul will be at the house at seven. You've got to be there when he comes," she said, getting herself up and heading to the potty.

I wanted to die. My skull was pounding. My arm was throbbing. My tongue and throat were like sand. And my teeth hurt. So much for moderation. "Screw Raoul," I thought, pulling a pillow over my head. But then I heard the toilet flush and, like a true Pavlovian, it was my turn for the bathroom.

Bounding out of the bed, I nearly bowled Bing over dashing for the john. Oh man. I just made it, but didn't have the luxury of really enjoying the moment. I suddenly got an attack of hiccoughs which, employed as I was at that moment, were causing some logistical problems. I was sensing this would not be a good day.

Quickly getting dressed, almost putting two socks on one foot, I dashed down the hotel's ancient stone steps, out the door, across the cobbled courtyard, and down the top end of rue Basque toward the house.

I got to number 9 just as Raoul raised his fist to whack on the door. His big truck had one side of the street blocked. Two huge armoires did the rest. Damn, I had forgotten how big those beauties were.

I croaked a *Bonjour.* Raoul turned and smiled. *"Une longue nuit?"*

"Bien sûr, et ma tête elle est cassée."

"Carrying these armoires up the stairs will clear your head. Let's get started, I only have a few minutes," Raoul said.

How to get them up was the issue. Then Rich appeared. He had been more moderate than I, so he looked a lot fresher. And, though we'd both been Marine pilots, he'd been in transports. Those guys were much more organized than grab-ass fighter jocks. So, figuring out how to get such big pieces up our tiny winding stairway was exactly the kind of thing a guy like Rich loves to sink his teeth into.

Handling the first armoire was not that difficult. We removed its top section, doors, drawers, and bottom stand, then Rich, Raoul, and his short but powerful helper, a woman, got it up to the master bedroom without serious trouble. I helped with the rest of the stuff.

The second piece, much bigger than the first, was something else. Since Raoul had other deliveries to make, he didn't waste time pursuing the options on this baby and left it to us. Clearly there was no way the thing would make it up our tight stairway anyway. As Raoul headed back to his truck, he pointed to the second-floor windows and said using them would be the only way we'd be able to do it.

Though I was funked, Rich was still in top form. He strode authoritatively to the end of the street and stopped in front of Claude's *café*. Why hadn't I thought of that? Yes. To hell with the armoire, let's have a beer.

Rich waved to me. I waved back. Odd. He waved harder, so I walked down to see what his problem was. Ah hah. In front of Claude's, which wasn't open yet, were several tall stacks of plastic chairs. Rich picked up a unit of five and humped them around the corner onto the sidewalk next to the mighty armoire. I followed suit, praying my left arm wouldn't come off. Then Bing arrived and looked questioningly at me. I shrugged. She shrugged and went inside to see how Ann and Jump Up were fairing.

Rich and I kept moving chairs until we had stacks like steps reaching to the second-floor window. Going inside and upstairs, Rich took the windows off their hinges, enlarging the opening to its maximum dimension. Then we got some rope and wrapped it around the armoire. We tossed one end up to Bing and Ann, who'd positioned themselves in the window as guides and rope pullers. Rich tipped the armoire onto the sloping stack of chairs and stabilized. The ladies pulled from the window as the two of us (mostly Rich) pushed from below. Amazingly enough, bit by bit, it went up. Of course I was sure I'd torque my ribs again, or bend the rod in my arm, but nothing of the sort happened. Finally the armoire nudged up to the windowsill. I twisted around to get the weight of it onto my back, while Rich ran into the house and up to where Bing and Ann held the rope. Then the three of them pulled it inside. We'd done it! Or, more accurately, Rich had, assisted by two beautiful women and one busted up *trou de balle*.

THE NEXT night, while we slept soundly at the Abbey Hotel, our guests were kept up to all hours by the noise from Camille and his buddy's *motos*. Two more nights of that put me at his door, steaming.

"Camille, I love motorcycles. I ride Harley-Davidsons in America and have one being repaired in Castres. So I know bikes, but I know *bruit* (noise) too. Harleys have a strong sound that is satisfying. Your *moto*, and those of your friends, are too loud and their sound is *odieux* (obnoxious). I will make you an offer. I will buy you and your friends new mufflers for all your machines, if you promise to put them on."

"*Monsieur, ma moto est parfaite comme ça.*" (My bike is perfect as is.) Great.

For the time being, with a good French shrug, I gave up and took our guests for a few days of touring, far away from Camille and his noisy boys. We saw all kinds of great places—Albi, Carcassonne, Mirapoir, Cordes-sur-Ciel, Gaillac, Toulouse, Bessier. Finally we took them to the Canal du Midi at Port Lauragais, for dinner on Adrian's barge. This was a special surprise Bing and I had arranged for Rich and Ann before leaving Black Mountain—they would celebrate their anniversary on the *Isatis*.

The evening started with *aperitifs* on the foredeck, then another of Adrian's grand spreads complete with his Lauragais lecture in the salon below. Then Bing and I made our departure, leaving our dear friends onboard to celebrate in the same suite we'd started our long-delayed honeymoon. Their anniversary would be their last day with us, so we'd arranged with Adrian to put together another of those wonderful overnight experiences for which he was growing famous.

Happily, Rich and Ann were thrilled. We felt very good about it, especially when they decided to stay on the *péniche* for another night. Black Mountain had been a special treat for them, just as it was for us. Take that, Provence!

WITH RICH and Ann safely on their way back to San Francisco, Bing and I finally moved into number 9 rue Basque. Unfinished as it was, and despite the five months overrun on the original "turn-key" date, we really were moving in. What the hell.

Camille, nevertheless, was still a problem. On our return from Port Lauragais, we discovered he'd added a gigantic boom box to his collection of noise makers. The *moto* issue had not been resolved and now this. BOOM! Boom! BOOM! Boom! Even with his windows closed the thudding and pounding reverberated up and down the street. Our windows shook from it. When the electric guitars cut in with their step-on-a-cat's-tail screech, I prayed our replaced windows wouldn't shatter. Oh, if only I'd had a gun . . .

As we knew, Camille was *mal élevé*. And like most things wild, he was growing larger and stronger. The problem was that because of this totally undisciplined boy, our delicious little French hideaway was turning sour. What could we do?

The next morning I ran into our neighbor, Jacques Thoreau. "Do you hear all that noise from across the street, morning, noon, and night?"

"*Certainement*," he said, shaking his head.

Jacques had two young daughters and a son. He and his wife Crystal were not happy about Camille being just across the street.

"What can we do?" Actually I felt a bit uncomfortable complaining about noisy people in the street after what I had pulled off myself, *vis-à-vis* my behavior toward Bing and Laurant by the fountain before my bike wreck.

"In France, process and procedure are everything," he said.

"What about success or failure?"

"Not as important," he stated, surprising me. "First a petition. Alleged offenses. Parties involved. Proposed resolution. Signatures. On to the mayor. Investigation. Conclusions. Warning. Document to file. Evidence for possible application in the future."

I was impressed. "How long would all this take?"

"No more than two years," he stated, rolling his eyes.

"So we'll have to listen to that *bruit* for two more years?" I asked, not happy.

"Unless I use my . . ." he paused to confirm no one was close by, "contacts. My friend in the *gendarmes*."

"Wow. That would be terrific."

"He is a lieutenant. With some authority. He knows how to take action, make things happen."

"I see," though I didn't. But I pressed on, "So, if normal procedures can take two years, how long will your contact's methods take?"

Looking back at me, zero expression on his face, he said, "Two days."

"Excellent," I said, "I'll let you know when to start."

"*D'accord.*"

THAT AFTERNOON I dropped by the *café* to get Claude's take on what Thoreau said about filing a petition.

"Monsieur Ken," he said, "that is not the right way in a small village. A petition is too harsh. It is important for you to speak directly with the person involved. It is polite. The other way is too much like . . . *Fascism.*"

That cracked me up. I kept forgetting Claude was the resident Trotskyite who could spot Fascism in anything and everything coming out of the mayor's office. I told him I had already confronted Camille but would talk to him again. I didn't say anything about the gendarme.

Later that evening, yet again we were jolted by the *posse* of *motos* blasting up rue Basque, juking and jiving the throttles as they clustered in front of Camille's. This didn't do my piece of mind any good. My ribs still hurt when I wasn't careful how I twisted or turned, and my left arm ached when it was damp, so having a lot of noise blasting through our open windows at bedtime was not what I needed at all.

Then . . . BOOM, BOOM, THUD, THUDDER, BOOM, and the electric guitar *screech* cranking up again! Oh God, what a racket. The whole street was vibrating, windows shaking. BOOM, BOOM, THUD, THUD, BOOM, screech, *screech*, *SCREECH*!

I was pissed. I pulled on my slippers and slacks and stormed downstairs. As I opened our door into the street, an outside door across the way opened too. A youngish blonde woman started out. When I saw the blonde hair and young face, I jumped to the conclusion it was Camille's sister-slash-surrogate mother.

"*Bruit, partout bruit! Pourquoi tout le bruit?*" (Noise, everywhere noise! Why so much noise?) I shouted at her.

Then, standing behind her, I saw Sylvie and Michel, the owners of the grocery. Oh crap. This wasn't Camille's semi-mom, this was the vegetable lady in the market. No wonder she looked so shocked. How to explain? *Merde.* All I could come up with was "*Bonsoir,*" as I cocked my head toward Camille's thundering room. Then, like a total coward, I pulled our door closed.

I felt terrible all night. I had been so ugly to very nice people, without getting a word out to the kid who was most deserving of my disdain.

T H E   N E X T morning I shuffled into the grocery, stood like a naughty child in front of Sylvie at the cash register, and recited my prepared apology. Her sweet smile was enough to tell me she understood. Just to make sure, I walked down the side aisle to the fruit and veggie section and bought a big shiny red apple, which I marched back to her counter with and pressed into her hand. She laughed and laughed and called out to Michel about "*ces Americans fous.*" (These crazy Americans.)

I felt much better.

B Y   N O O N of that day the sun was bright overhead and the sky a startling blue. Claude had tables and chairs out front of the *café* with a large lunch crowd of holiday proportion.

Bing and I were walking down rue Basque in that direction, set to enjoy our own outdoor luncheon, when all of a sudden Camille threw full power to that miserable, mind-blasting box of his, this time with all his windows open. That was it. And I'm sorry to admit it, but I blew my stack all over again. I couldn't hold back; I had scores to settle with this sad little shit. So, there I was again— *the raving madman of rue Basque!*

"Camille, *Camille*! What in the name of God do you think you are doing with that horrible noise? *Tu es mal élevé, très très mal élevé!* You are destroying the tranquility of our street. You are destroying the tranquility of Black Mountain. Our neighbors are preparing a petition to the mayor about your noise and your lack of respect for every citizen of Black Mountain . . ."

I went on and on until finally the little twerp appeared at the window.

"What is the problem?" he asked, the height of innocence. Of course he had to repeat the question several times because the racket was so overpowering. Finally it occurred to him to turn the volume down.

"The problem is the noise. *You* and the noise. Everywhere you go there is noise. Your *moto*. Your cassette. Your stereo. All noise," I shouted, very noisily myself.

"*Mais monsieur*," he offered, as if talking to a total moron, "that is not noise, that is music."

"Music, little boy," I bellowed back, "is music when the volume is at a civilized level. When the volume gets to your level, it is no longer music. It is noise, racket, *bruit*, insulting to the community. It must stop! If not, the petition will be presented to the mayor and a report will be made to *les gendarmes*. For sure, young man, *les gendarmes*!"

Actually shaking, I turned to take Bing's hand, wondering if she'd storm off again in protest of my outburst. Oh Lord, damned if you do . . .

She took my hand and squeezed it tight. No more River Styx between us. And then, as we turned the corner at Claude's . . . a whoop went up from the tables on the terrace. Holy cow. I was getting a standing O and chants of *"Bravo! Bravo! Bravo!"*

Claude marched us to a table, and as we sat down, feeling embarrassed, Sophie strode up with a chilled bottle of champagne and four glasses. Apparently this time, at least, I'd been ugly and awful for a good cause.

As I lifted my glass to the whole *café*, I caught sight of our neighbor Jacques, by his car, raising his portable to his ear. He nodded my way.

THE NEXT morning, idling at the entrance to rue Basque was a huge blue humvee-like *gendarme* vehicle. It squatted there through the morning, then the afternoon, and didn't leave until sunset. The first thing Camille saw when he left his door that morning was the monster idling there, complete with a dark presence studying him from inside. When he arrived home later, the driver's-side window slid down and he was beckoned over. From our window, all we could see him doing was nodding, first slowly then faster and faster. This whole scenario must have been a product of Jacques' contacts. Wow. Most impressive indeed.

Camille got the message. The following morning he pushed the bike all the way down rue Basque to the intersection before starting it. And when he came back in the evening he cut the engine in front of Claude's, coasting quietly up to his door. No more loud buddies or horrible blasts of the boom box either. The young dragon had been slain.

On a sunny Saturday morning two weeks later, a van with trailer attached pulled up and parked across the street. Camille, his sister, his friends, and a couple of swarthy men carried their stuff out the front door. Once they loaded it all, they hit the road to places unknown.

Watching the whole bunch go, I said to Bing, "You know, maybe the situation will be a heads-up for Camille, his young sidekick too. Maybe he'll think a little more about working as a mason. Who knows, someday he might come back to talk to Laurant or Jacques next door."

"Who knows?" she said. "But I doubt it."

OVER THE week that followed, it seemed the mood on rue Basque brightened. François and Caroline at the *patisserie* congratulated us on our coup. Sylvie and Michel smiled more than usual when we were at their grocery shopping. They owned the building Camille's apartment was in, too. Bad renters are France's immovable curse. My attack had relieved them of that problem down the road. They even presented us with a bottle of fine Medoc. And Michel at La Brasserie said he admired the way we had dealt head-on with the situation.

"*Très American,*" he said. "*Vous êtes vrai cowboy.* We French would never do such a thing. We would dither and chatter, but never take action. We *talk* our problems to death or just let them die of old age. Absurd, totally absurd."

THIRTY-ONE

DIFFERENT FOLKS

W ORK AT the house went on a roll. *Finally*. With Jean-Jacques out of the picture and my fountain-side explosion a thing of the past, Laurant now seemed totally focused on turning Château Poubelle into Château Nous. (Trashcan Castle into Our Little Castle.)

Appliances rolled in, all of which had been ordered half-sized—fridge, freezer, washer, dryer, oven—specifically to fit under the counter I would build against the kitchen-side wall of the big room. Yes, *I* would build it. My arm and ribs felt ready. I was back in shape, *en forme*. Time to kick butt.

The store where we got a lot of our stuff was named Fly. An excellent outfit. The supervisor, a young fellow named Jean-Luc, made it that way. Despite the fact we'd often caused problems—changing orders at the last minute, having furniture delivered when we'd thought the house would be done but wasn't and then had to be refused—he never howled. A true gentleman.

On the other hand, there were other stores not so *aimable*. The electric fixture company Lumière, near Fly, which I mentioned earlier, was a different ballgame altogether. Though charming when we first bought some lamps and track lights there, the instant we tried to return just one purchase (proven defective), they went nasty. The following is a compilation of things they said to us without a flinch, one accusation after another—

"The light was fine when it left the store."

"You broke the light when you installed it in your home."

"Your electrician did not install the light properly and caused the malfunction."

"Your electrician wired your home improperly."

"We have never had a problem with that model light."

"That was the only one of that model we ever had."

"The light cannot be sent back for exchange because the model is terminated."

"Even if the model was still produced, the manufacturer is out of business."

"We are not responsible for faulty equipment we sell."

"You do not understand how our system works."

"You are wrong."

"You are foreigners."

I kid you not. And that attitude was company-wide. The sales person, supervisor, and manager all recited the same mantra. But it worked. They wore us down, not making good on anything. Though we never traded with them again.

THE COUNTERTOP I intended to build was to be constructed with three fifteen-inch-wide, three-inch-thick, thirty-five-foot-long planks. These would be glued and bolted together, then mounted on posts with cross-members all six inches square. At the interior end of this countertop, butting up to the wall formed by the stairway, it would turn the ninety-degree corner with a mounted stovetop. We'd continue the counter across the back wall with a sink and drain board mounted on it, shelves underneath.

Laurant directed me to a lumber mill on the outskirts of Black Mountain for the wood. He called the manager, who said he could fill the order. Laurant said he would send me right over. He described me as a linguistically challenged American who was, nevertheless, reasonably capable. Thierry was the man to see.

Entering the mill office, I explained I was there to see Thierry. The attractive receptionist nodded, then asked me something in a very rapid, clipped fashion. As sometimes happened, I had a linguistic relapse. These happen, from time to time, when your mind is going a mile a minute translating. It just runs out of steam. So, she waited for my reply, didn't get one, then buzzed Thierry. We smiled at each other. Her smile was sparkly; mine was more of the foolish, embarrassed variety.

Thierry walked in. Wow. He was probably in his late thirties, medium height, very handsome, with long sandy blond hair in a Prince Valiant cut. The husbands and fathers of Black Mountain would be wise to put a bell around this guy's neck so they would know when he was in the area and could lock up their wives and daughters. He turned out to be a great guy. He went out of his way, trooping me around the yard, showing what they had. Besides being a confirmed lady killer, I learned he also played the guitar, road mountain bikes, skied, hiked, climbed . . . oh man, suddenly it occurred to me, could *he* have been the lover boy with the hiker gal up on La Montagne Noire when we were first here?

While we were pulling planks out of a stack together, we talked about the differences in our systems. He was a totally confirmed Socialist and gently expressed his feeling that the way Americans chased money was insane. He agreed that, relatively speaking,

Americans had a lot more of it, but added that the French didn't
need so much because the system took care of their needs. I agreed, but
I came back with the point that two-hour lunches and innumerable
holidays plus six-week vacations assured that little got done in France.

His answer: "So what?"

After careful deliberation, Thierry and I chose three superb
planks and carried them to the milling machine. They were hon-
ey-colored ash that would sand to a sweet rustic finish. Laurant's
truck would collect them after lunch. So, a few minutes before
noon, we started the big rotary saw, using its extended roller feed
to slide the first plank through the whirling blade, trimming one
edge, rolling it over, and repeating the process on the other side.
But then, with the second plank halfway through its first run,
the noon whistle blew. Everything, I mean *everything*, stopped
dead. All power throughout the plant quit, and in a flash every
worker was out the door to a car or onto a bicycle. Getting home
for those two hours of food and family was paramount, totally.

I looked at Thierry. He winked back at me, holding up what I
guessed was a master key. He walked to the power panel by his
office door. Speaking over his shoulder, he explained that the
unions, with the support of the government, set the plant's central power grid to disengage at exactly twelve noon. No one,
except the plant manager, can restart the system.

The rest of the job took only a few minutes. Then we carried
the long pieces out to the loading dock for Numéro Un to pick up
after lunch. I'd carry the shorter pieces home in our car now.

Free at last, Thierry jumped in his hot red Porsche and blew
gravel out of the lot as an appropriate *au revoir*. I waved and
laughed, shaking my head. He was a heck of a nice guy with a real
handle on life, or should I say *on the art of French living*.

BEFORE THE long pieces arrived at Château Poubelle, I started
assembling the six-inch posts and cross-members the planks

would rest on. My arm felt okay. Not very strong, but serviceable. Actually, I was looking forward to this. Unlike the other work Bing and I had done on the place, this was going to be our creation from the bottom up.

While I was specing out the job ahead, Antoine and Placo Deux were completing the plasterwork on the fireplace that he and Bing had designed. This was on the opposite stone wall of the big room from where I was working. To help him get done I'd lent him my new Leatherman, recently arrived by FedEx. Unlike Anton, who gave away the Leatherman I'd given him, Placo loved that tool. He was in hog heaven with it.

Our plan, actually more Bing's than mine, for the countertop (*planche*) was to construct it at a height so that all the half-size units would fit underneath. Starting at the street end of the wall, Bing diagramed a storage area for soaps and pails, brushes and such. The next space between the support posts would hold a drier with the washer beside it. The third slot would have a half-size freezer next to a matching refrigerator. The last space would hold the oven, with the corner-mounted cooking surface above. The same theme would continue around the corner for the sink and drain board, with shelves under those.

Bing came up with the idea of covering the fronts of the appliances with half curtains that would slide on a wire mounted under the counter lip. Dominique, who was helping with cleanup, knew a seamstress who did costumes for the theatre in Toulouse. She agreed to do the stitching. When finished, we would have an easy-to-work-in kitchen, modernly equipped, but still reflecting the medieval motif.

Everything was falling nicely in place, at least until the water heater proved inadequate to handle a shower and fill a bathtub at the same time. Panic.

The entire design of the kitchen would be threatened if we had to put a conventional water heater in the system. We'd have to reconsider the nifty little powder room and wine cave we'd shoe-horned under the first floor stairway; possibly have to rip them out. The snowball effect of this one mistake could be awesome.

When we first speced the job with Nigel Cork, M. Roget at the plumbing supply place in Revel had done the calculations address-ing capacities. He'd figured we *could* get away with this small, quick-fired unit we'd mounted on the front wall above the coun-ter. But now it wasn't doing the job. Memories of our war with Lumière Electric gave me knots in my stomach.

So, heading back to Roget's the next morning, I was conflicted. In one sense we had no right to try to bring the thing back. We'd been using it for minor hot water needs for a month or more. The problem now was that it didn't do what Roget assured us it would. Could my language have been the problem? I kept thinking how Roget repeated, "*Vous commandez? Vous commandez?*" The verb "to command" always sounded more powerful than "to order." Had I pushed him into something he knew wasn't right?

I plodded into his shop. M. Roget, the eternal cigarette dan-gling from his mouth, bounced around the counter to take my hand after I'd mumbled my *Bonjour* to those assembled. Then I stumbled through my prepared explanation of the situation.

"Not enough hot water for the bathtub with the shower run-ning too."

"No, no, no."

"Yes, yes, yes."

"A moment please."

Roget sped back to a stack of manuals on the shelf below his tele-phone and came up with a dog-eared catalogue from the *chauffe-eau* manufacturer. Flipping through the pages, lighting another cigarette, he plowed along, confident the equipment he'd sold his American friends was up to the job as I'd described it. And *there*, I feared, was the escape clause—"as I'd described it." Since the plumbing part of the restoration had come early on with Nigel Cork and company, my abilities for discussing *anything* back then had been very limited. I suspected I'd innocently given Roget some very garbled intel.

Jotting down a blur of figures, then flipping to the bathtub catalogue, he ran another set, squinting hard at the lot. Then he looked up and said, "We close at five. I will be at your house before five thirty. The unit is adequate for your requirements. Something is wrong. I will find what it is."

M. Roget actually did arrive on schedule. And he surveyed, calculated, pondered, smoked, measured, marched up and down the stairs, measured some more, calculated some more, then announced, "*Mes amis,* I owe you an apology. All your problems are mine, not yours. My calculations were wrong. Originally I had not come here to inspect the installation. I did not consider the long runs of pipe on this floor and then up to the other floors. These count as capacity to be fed. The unit I sold you was adequate if the installation was more compact. It is my mistake. So I will give you full credit for the unit. I will supply you, at my cost, an *on-demand* system that mounts even more compactly, will be more efficient, and has greater capacity. I will pay the labor costs for your additional plumbing requirements. Will that be adequate?"

Holy cow! I could have kissed his ring, the top of his head, his feet, whatever. *Vive le Roget! Vive la France! (Sud-ouest.)*

The next morning we were able to get Christophe in, and together he and I took down the old unit, loaded it into his truck, and zipped back to Roget's, where he made good on his promises. Christophe installed the new heater the next day as I continued work on the *planche*. By the end of the week, our great groaning-board countertop was in place, along with shelves above, mini-appliances below, cooker at the corner, and the sink tucked along the stairway wall . . . with *beaucoup* hot water everywhere.

We had a kitchen at last! And a great room (of small dimension). And we had a house. Château Poubelle had finally become Chez Nous. (Our house.)

THIRTY-TWO

MADAME'S NIGHTS

As we discovered on our first visit to Madame Fontaine's house, Chez Fontaine is the French house we Americans all dream about. The tiny cobbled mews, the façade of stone with red, yellow, and white roses climbing toward the stately abbey tower above, it's all there. It's always breathtaking, but especially as the setting sun turns it to gold.

Edwige, with whom we traded English lessons for French, was becoming an increasingly essential friend. Having her with us at Madame Fontaine's made things much easier. She filled in the blanks we otherwise would have had in the rich long tales Madame loved to tell. Edwige would whisper clarifications when she saw our brows furrow, and file away other gems to explain to us later as well.

Assembling in the foyer one noon, Bing presented Madame Fontaine with a pen and ink still-life she'd done during our first stay in Black Mountain. Madame studied it for at least a minute. Her face lit up and her eyes sparked as she pronounced, "Bing, oh Bing, you truly are a talented artist. My compatriot for the future perhaps? I would be very pleased if we could paint together in my studio here from time to time."

"Madame Fontaine—" Bing began, but was immediately interrupted.

"Please, I want you to call me Héllé. Madame is far too formal for a friend."

"Mad . . . Héllé, thank you," Bing stammered. "I am honored, and yes, it would be wonderful to work with you. Perhaps we could go to the Canal du Midi sometime. We could visit our friend Adrian on his barge and sketch from there."

"Yes, my dear, we must." Héllé smiled, extending a hand to guide us toward her salon. "I no longer drive. I would look forward to getting out. But for now, *des aperitifs.*"

From our last meal with Héllé, we knew to expect anywhere from three to five courses. And our readings on provincial etiquette told us that despite the three or more hours at table, bathroom breaks were frowned on. It was a Louis XIV thing. One had to arrive prepared.

After Porto and Muscat, we moved to the dining room. As before, Madame Fontaine, without help, handled the whole affair effortlessly. And refused to let any of us assist. She started with a *saumon fumé.* Plates one and two removed. Then a tricolor salad with an incredible oil, garlic, vinegar, and spice dressing arrived on the return of plate two. The process continued through a *gigot* of lamb, surrounded by very thin *haricots verts* and tiny roasted potatoes. Another plate removed. Her presentation of cheeses boasted everything from Auvergne through Camembert, *chèvre,* and *brèbis*, leaving one plate to go for desert. I chose the *tarte de pomme* while Bing, Edwige, and our hostess enjoyed a rich chocolate mousse. Coffee and a selection of *digestifs* concluded the meal.

Throughout all this, Héllé held forth as a *raconteuse extraordinaire*. Only when she was busy in the kitchen did she leave the conversational duties to anyone else. And since there were three women present, the focus was not on football, rugby, or formula one racing, but on what it was like to be a young woman seventy-five years ago in rural France.

"Edwige, did you know anything of men before you married? I mean physically," Héllé asked, placing *demitasses* of black, teeth-etching coffee in front of each of us.

"Well, yes," Edwige nodded. "My parents were progressives."

"Bing?"

"My mother didn't tell me anything. My first menstruation was a huge surprise. A real shock. Fortunately I had older sisters. They gave me the information about my body I needed for health, and later, for love," Bing said, with a gentle tilt of her head and a glance toward me.

Madame Fontaine warmed to that, saying, "But I had no older sisters. All I knew of sexual relations was what I had seen with dogs on the street and horses in our pasture."

Edwige lowered her eyes and shook her head. Bing shrugged. I studied my coffee cup.

"Horses were hard to ignore. Even for a young village girl," Héllé expanded. "I found it interesting how our stallion mounted and rammed home, so to speak. Then just hung on."

She paused and looked at me as if I might have something specific to add. I was at a loss.

"The dogs had more energy and sense of theatre. They seemed most interested in doing such things when family photos were being taken, or when the priest dropped by," she added. "Mother would throw water on them. None of which helped me on my wedding night."

Why me, Lord?

Thankfully Bing said, "Really?"

Héllé's eyes moved to her. I felt relieved. The room seemed very warm.

"Really," she repeated with some emphasis as she began another of her extraordinary stories. "My father had felt Jean-Phillip would be perfect for me. He was from a family of substance. He was preparing for a career in aviation, naval aviation," she paused, momentarily glancing at me, knowing I had been an American naval aviator.

"I was not against the match. I had been raised to expect it. I was confident a man so handsome as Jean-Phillip would be easy to love. The wedding was grand. All Black Mountain present. It was as if we were a symbol of the *new* France growing from the trenches of the First World War. Germany was a threat, but Germany had always been a threat. We believed our future was bright."

Reaching for her coffee pot and refilling our tiny cups, she expanded on her special night.

"I knew love-making involved kissing. I had never kissed as Jean-Phillip wished to kiss, however." Smiling, pausing, and looking intently at me, it was a long moment before she continued.

"And when he was kissing that way, he was breathing into my ear—'*Ma cherie. Ma cherie. Oh, ma cherie.*' Why must men do that? A time or two is endearing, but over and over. It was deafening. *Mon Dieu.* Then he switched to '*Oui, oui, oui!*' and his hands were everywhere. I'd had no preparation for any of this . . . beyond watching the horses and dogs. All I could think of was my mother throwing water on them . . . so, when Jean-Phillip did his own *plunge*, I shouted, 'What are you doing? What are you doing?' while all the time I was thinking, 'Throw the water mama!' Well, that put me into hysterics! Here was Jean-Phillip puffing and gasping and wiggling so, while I was laughing so hard tears were streaming down my cheeks!

"The next thing I knew . . . everything stopped. And the look on Jean-Phillip's face was one of total shock. Quickly he'd become *a fraction* of the man he had first been. That, I confess, only put me further into hysterics. I knew so little about the male . . . *thing*, you see.

"The remainder of our honeymoon did not go well," she added pensively. "Poor Jean-Phillip. Woe was he. Which led to Chantal, I believe his first mistress, and who knows how many more."

"But you had several children," Edwige said encouragingly.

"I did, didn't I?" Madame Fontaine said. A slight smile played on her lips.

"Extraordinary," Bing concluded.

"Life can be very complicated at times," Madame Fontaine agreed. "Think of how much easier those years would have been had I cried rather than laughed? And yet we strive to shut out our tears and encourage laughter. Sometimes God gives us what we ask for . . . then where are we?"

Héllé started gathering up our cups and saucers. This time, however, she let Bing and Edwige help.

AFTER OUR goodbyes to Madame Fontaine and Edwige, Bing and I strolled back to number 9. Along the way we marveled at this incredible woman. Born early in the century, she grew up in and weathered two world wars, played a life-and-death role with the Resistance. Created works of art. Wrote, taught and lectured from Paris to Bordeaux, all over France for that matter, and still she carried on living life to the fullest, always with a twinkle in her eye.

"Did you notice the way Héllé responded to Edwige when she asked, 'But you had several children?' It was almost a question of

So your marital affairs had broken down from the start, but you still had several children?" I said, smiling as I turned toward Bing.

"And Héllé's answer, after a pause," Bing said, "was so cryptic. 'I did, didn't I.' It begs for so much more."

"Which I'm sure we will get in time."

"I hope."

"I know," I said, "which will probably make its way into my next novel. By the way, love, while you were out walking this morning, I sent *When Eagles Fall* to Vernon in L.A. FedExed it."

"Oh Kenny, that's wonderful. I am so proud of you. Congratulations," she said, hugging against my good arm.

"If it hadn't been for the wreck, I'd never would have gotten it to him before fall. Hopefully Vernon will give it to his contact, the big guy at DreamWorks, before he goes on vacation. Maybe he'll take it with him for a read while he's chilling out, or whatever Hollywood people do. Come September, when we're back home, who knows, we could get a phone call."

"And a movie contract."

"With my track record, the end of the world would come first," I said, looking down, kicking a stone and shaking my head.

"We'll see . . ."

THIRTY-THREE

LA CRÉMAILLÈRE

For some time we had been in the process of getting fixed-line telephones into rue Basque because our cell phone bills were getting out of sight. We would need three phones. The first in the main room; the second in my office in the back building; and the third, a walk-around type which would divide its time between Bing's studio on the third floor and our bedroom on the second.

Having lived outside the U.S. in the past, we both knew phone installations could be difficult. Because we totally rewired the place, we wanted the phone installers to coordinate with Christophe. Though that made sense, we discovered that what made sense to us wasn't necessarily how French Telecom ran its business.

Their regional office is about twenty kilometers away, in Castres. Our first venture there had us on edge. Office situations are linguistically challenging. Though we had prepared what we would say, it was a bit disconcerting to see from those ahead of us that we would be seated in front of an agent, one on one. When our number came up, we marched bravely to the designated desk, where a pleasantly smiling middle-aged lady rose to shake our hands.

"*Bonjour Madame*," Bing and I opened in unison.

"*Bonjour Monsieur et Madame*," she replied crisply.

"*S'il vous plaît*," I began as usual. "*Parlez-vous Anglais? Non. Alors*, then please excuse our poor French. Perhaps *you* can be *our* teacher today? We can do business and improve our French at the same time."

"*Bien sûr*," she affirmed. We were off to a good start.

Bing took over at that point, woman to woman, explaining our needs—number of phones and colors. She added the business about coordinating with our electrician too.

The nice lady understood and presented us with a brochure displaying a *solde* (sale) they were running that would give us three walk-around phones for the price of one. Any color we wanted, seven to choose from. Excellent. She signed us up. We were really surprised the process had been so easy, despite our early trepidations.

Then came the first shadows of darkness. Checking with the stockroom, the woman found the only color they had was *shocking pink*. We declined but were assured, *pas de problème*, others were due. A week or so wait was no big deal. We wrote a check, shook hands, smiled, and departed, congratulating ourselves and praising French efficiency.

The following Saturday morning, just before Rich and Ann's arrival, the installation man came to the house. We asked if he also had our phones? He said no. They would be coming in to the office in Castres, but he wasn't sure when. He promised to pass on our inquiry and we would be contacted. All well and good. Again no problem.

We didn't think again about telephones until our friends were gone. Though we received no letter from France Telecom, we did get our first bill. A week or more after that we stopped at their office but arrived just as the doors closed. Sorry. Come back tomorrow. Which we couldn't do but did the day after, only to discover they were closed because of some *new* holiday. The next time we tried, they had no afternoon hours, like the schools on Wednesdays. Roughly a month later, just as they were trying to slam the door in our faces at one minute to five, I jammed my foot in and got us inside.

The same woman was at her desk. She asked how she could help. I said we had come for our telephones. She went into her file and advised that the order had been cancelled and the phones returned to the warehouse. On top of that, since the sale was now over, any new order would be at regular prices.

She smiled. I did not smile. Bing did not smile.

"Why, Madame, were we not notified when our phones arrived?" I asked.

"Sir," she responded with a bit of an edge to her voice, "I telephoned your number many, many times. You never answered. I assumed you had returned to the United States. I had no choice but to cancel the order."

I looked at Bing. She looked at me. Sensing I didn't have a chance of penetrating this woman's logic, I lifted an eyebrow for Bing to try her luck.

"Hmm," Bing began, smiling at the nice lady. "We can explain why we did not answer when you called."

"Yes, please do. At the time it was a mystery to me."

"You see, Madame, we had no telephones, so there was no bell ringing or anything . . . to answer with . . . even if there *was* a bell," Bing explained, puffing a cheek and shrugging her shoulders.

"You should have bought a phone to get my call." The expression on her face said: *foreigners in general, but Americans in particular, can be rather dense sometimes.*

"We bought three phones . . . from you, but you did not get them to us," I said.

"Sir, I just explained *your* mistake. You should have bought a fourth phone at a shop somewhere so I could *speak* to you." Now she was getting distinctly huffy.

"Why didn't you send a letter?" Bing asked.

"The French postal system is the best in the world," I threw in. "Your office sent us our first bill and brochures via the postal service."

"That is not *my* procedure," she said flatly, closing the issue.

"*Madame, s'il vous plaît*," I began again, trying to sound as reasonable as I could, "let me propose you talk to your *patron.* Explain the problem *we caused* and ask for authority to give us three phones from stock, any color, at our original *solde* price." I raised my eyebrows, puffed my cheeks, and blew out while cocking my head as I said this. Very French, I thought.

She spoke to her supervisor, who studied us suspiciously from his desk across the room. He too furrowed his brow, puffed his cheeks, and fired off a few frustrated air puffs of his own. But yes! He did agree.

We walked out of the place with phones—one pink, one blue, and one black—hand-me-downs, but at the sale price. So with telephones, the job of inviting people to the housewarming we were planning, which the French refer to as *une crémaillère,* would be much easier.

Having read the novel *Chocolat,* I knew our *pendant de la crémaillère* had to be a grand finale to our Black Mountain beginnings.

Bing was excited. "Kenny we've got to make it special for the people of Black Mountain. As Americans, foreigners, we've got to say thank you to everybody for the support they've given us. I've been making a list. Let's invite the Rigales from the farm. Laurant de Gaillac and his family, and his whole crew. Roget and Bernard

for their plumbing help, and Christophe, all the village shop people, everyone from La Brasserie and the *café*. Everybody who
walked by and offered us their *bon courages*. That means most of
the village . . . from the street sweeper, M. Propre, to the mayor!
Why not?"

Shaking my head and smiling, all I could say was, "I love you
Bing."

W E   N E E D E D invitations. We figured we'd write the kind of invitation a pair of friendly Americans would, then just put it into French.
Right. Who could do the translation? Trakya was Turkish, no. Anton,
Austrian, no. And just then, Doe, or Dominique, the woman who
helped us clean, walked in. She was from Casablanca. Close enough.
We came up with a simple *"Come join in celebrating our finishing
the restoration of number 9 rue Basque."* It was to be Saturday, two
weeks off, starting at seven PM. People could come alone or with their
families. All we asked was that they come. Composing this on my
laptop, we ran it through our printer, cranking out a hundred copies.
We stuffed them in peoples' mail slots, posted them to the out-of-
towners, or gave them directly to whomever we saw along the way.

When I gave Claude and Sophie theirs at the *café*, Claude
immediately asked, "Who helped with the French?"

"Doe," I said.

"She is from Casablanca," he said.

"I guess," I said.

"It shows," he said.

"How?" I asked a little nervously.

"*Pas grave*," he said.

"If it is not important, why did you bring it up?" I questioned,
puffing a cheek and lifting an eyebrow.

"You should know," he replied cryptically.

"I should know what?" I pushed, shoulders going up and
hands out.

"*Encore pas grave*," he said, and started down the bar, leaving me nonplussed.

Then he stopped, turned and took the few steps back to me. There was no one else at the bar. Lowering his head and his voice a notch Claude said, "Your ... Secret Agent."

"What do you mean?" I asked, honestly confused.

"He will not be at your party," he said. "He is, as you say, otherwise engaged."

"Meaning?"

Claude smiled, "You Americans are so naive."

"What's that supposed to mean," I asked getting a little edgy.

"You should have known as we all knew about him."

"Known what?" I snapped with growing frustration.

"That your friend is ... a drug dealer."

My mouth dropped open. "You're kidding."

"You never noticed that no one spent time with him? For us it was like a contract," he went on. "As long as he dealt outside the village, live and let live. Once he did business with any of our people ... *poof*, he'd be gone."

"I can't believe it. He is very strange, but a nice enough fellow."

"He thought he could hook you. But if he had, since you are one of us now, he would have gone *poof*."

"Has something happened?"

"He got to Camille across the street, after he left town. That was too close."

"So he's ..."

"Poofed. Goes to trial next week."

"Wow ..."

"Exactly."

Whatever we'd done wrong stylistically with the written invitations was nothing compared to what I did verbally. As our French had progressed, I'd tried putting hints of the local accent into mine. Ages before, when I'd lived for a couple of years in Berlin and picked up some of that language, I'd liked using the Berliner accent. When we drove anywhere in the country, people would know we were not German, but they knew we lived in Berlin. That had been kind of neat. So I'd been working for the same results in Black Mountain.

Using my own version of Tarnese, I thought I was telling people, "It is not important if you come alone or with your family . . ." By the reaction I was getting, I thought I was dazzling everybody with my version of the local patois. In truth, however, I was mispronouncing the word alone (*seul*) and making it sound like *soûl* (drunk). So there I was, bouncing around town telling everybody it didn't make any difference if they came to our party, "*drunk*, or with their family," just as long as they came. Brilliant.

BING DISPLAYED her Christian heart by sending an invitation to Jean-Jacques and Laila Kurtz. We had not seen them for months. Our friendship essentially ended the night I asked them "What would Jesus do?" The sneaky way they had hijacked our workforce had further complicated things. But Bing felt they deserved a look at the place they'd gotten us into.

They didn't accept. Jean-Jacques wrote that they would be in London for the foreseeable future, adding a curious note. With all his linguistic skills, he devoted a whole paragraph to what he saw as my invitation's error in calling our celebration a *pendre la crémaillère*. (Roughly "the hanging of the fixture for the fireplace pot," i.e. the French version of our housewarming.) His lengthy discourse said the phrase actually meant "being hanged in the village square." Bizarre. Even our French–English dictionary agreed with us that we were talking about a *housewarming*.

Just a day or two after we received his response, their Mercedes was parked by the fountain. They surely were not in England. The last thing I wanted was to run into them. I hurried past. At our door, however, unable to resist, I looked back up the street. Jean-Jacques and Laila were standing by their car. They saw me. I gave a perfunctory nod. They did not. I quickly went inside, closing the door behind me. I stood with my back to it, dreading a knock. Unlike when we first came to Black Mountain, however, the knock never came.

As the days marched by, there were still jobs to be done, but with our length-of-stay situation, keeping within six months in France to preclude the possibility of future tax assessments, many would just have to wait. Then we began to worry that no one would come. Or the party would be a total bust, one of those deals where everyone stands and stares, itching to get away. At home, in the good old US of A, my big mouth was usually enough to turn a dud gathering into a credibly fun time. But in Black Mountain, could I pull it off? Bing said not to worry. I wasn't so sure.

I never thought I'd honestly say it, but the house looked great. The half curtains masking the appliances under the great *planche* had come out beautifully, and the counter itself had a golden glow from the linseed oil Bing rubbed into it. Plates, dishes, cups, saucers, and little special gifts were beautifully displayed on the rustic shelves we'd mounted on brackets from the posts structuring the room's ancient stonewall.

Stepping back into the center of the large room and looking at the kitchen we'd created, we were pleased. We'd taken off layer after layer of ugly wallpaper, chipped away the cracked and crumbling plaster to display the stone behind it. All through the house that had been our approach. We had the modern conveniences, but hidden. We'd made the very old and the very new work together. Our French dream had become a reality.

Others saw it too. Madame Fontaine wrote a piece in the municipal journal describing what this pair of foreigners had done. How we too loved what she and so many others loved of the

village. She went on to say that the care we had given to our restoration had been our tribute to the people of Black Mountain,
especially those who had fought for its very survival through the
Depression and then the Nazi occupation. Her piece was a wonderful surprise, further speaking to the importance of our coming
crémaillère.

B I N G,   D O E,   and Trakya scrubbed, swept, and spruced up
everything in sight. I did some finishing touches with the paint-
brush, which is always dangerous because I can never stop. A
touch here, a dab there, oh, over here too. Finally Bing hid the
brushes and ordered me to Claude's *café* to make sure his cook,
Henri, had the food side of things under control.

Our plan was to start at seven PM, relatively early by French
standards. It was a Saturday. Knowing that many in the southwest regarded clocks with disdain, we figured arrivals would go
on for easily an hour. The standard *pastis* would be laid out, along
with Lillet, Ricard, Dubonnet, Muscat, vermouth, Scotch, and the
local reds and whites Claude decided appropriate. A little later,
Henri would march in with roasts, salads, fruits, cheeses, breads,
and all the side dishes to properly load the long counter for the
first time. (Please, Lord, don't let it collapse.)

The big room at the front of the house would be the focus of
most of the activity. The shotgun layout of the rest of the first
floor would then draw people into the *petit salon*, the courtyard,
and probably all the way back to my office. The backdoor there,
opening into the little alley (*ruelle*), would be kept open for
breezes as well as for snitching bottles from Claude's *café* stash
there, if we ran short of anything.

We were not sure how many would come. The only refusals
were from the Kurtzes, and Raoul and Evita, who had to run a
truckload of furniture to Paris. After tossing and turning through
a sleepless night, then hurrying from one last-minute job to the

next, promptly at 6 PM, one hour *de bonne heure* (totally unheard of *anywhere* in France), our first guest arrived!

Good heavens. I was naked but for my bathrobe and Bing was in the shower. Who the hell could be *thump, thump, thump*ing on our front door? Then the doorbell joined the chorus. *Les Gendarmes?* I pulled on my slippers, tightened the terrycloth sash around my waist, and tumbled down the stairs to the front door. This couldn't be a guest, it had to be somebody official. Oh God, was the house billowing smoke again?

Wrestling open the door, I was totally surprised to see Monsieur Propre, *le balayeur* (the street sweeper) standing there. And from the looks of him, he had taken my advice about coming either *drunk* or with the family. No family in sight, his choice was self-evident. He was stoned.

Most of the front rooms in Black Mountain have a small step-down from the sidewalk into the house. M. Balayeur seemed to have forgotten about that and, taking his first stride inside, pitched forward into me. The two of us toppled in a boozy embrace backward onto my *derrière* flat on the floor. The door was still open. A few people passing by, I'm sure, were surprised to see my naked legs protruding from under the prostrate figure of M. Propre.

Thrashing embarrassedly to our feet, I kicked the door shut. Going to the counter, groaning with bottles, I poured a few fingers of *pastis* for both of us, adding a bit of water to mine. With such fortification in hand, M. Propre went into a long ramble, some of which I think was about bribing judges, *boules* matches, and football; Toulouse vs. Marseille. That done, he tipped down the last of his drink, handed me his glass, spun full around, and walked smartly into the back of the door.

Bing came down to check out the noise. She wasn't altogether yet, though much further along than I was in my bathrobe. Then, still thirty minutes before party time, another rap on the door. (Didn't these people realize they were *French*?)

There were the smiling faces of M. Roget and Bernard, the plumbing shop team. Wet waders, fishing poles in hand, they had brought us two decent catches as gifts. Very sweet. They could only stay a moment, but accepted *aperitifs*. Our chat went badly because our vocabularies didn't yet include much on fishing, boating, scaling, and gutting. And too, I was distracted by being nearly naked.

After they departed, while I finished my *toilette*, Bing greeted the regular arriving guests. The Beaugestes were first, Philippe and Madame (whose first name we'd never found out, nor did anyone else in town seem to know, despite all having lived there for maybe fifty years). They brought lovely flowers. Michel and Jesselyne from La Brasserie dashed in briefly. It was jazz night for them. They brought a gorgeous ceramic umbrella stand that went immediately by the front door. They hurried off promising François (*serveur*, the waiter) would be by before the night was over. I said to tell him a party on rue Basque without a Basque would be no party at all. He did show later with flowers for Bing and a Basque cross on a chain for me, which he hooked around my neck, kissing both cheeks. I was honestly touched.

Caroline and François from the *patisserie* made it after they closed, each carrying a delicious *tarte de pomme*. Madame Crespi popped in for a moment on her way to a church retreat. Our Moroccan neighbors leaned in to say they were off to a family birthday but thanked us for thinking of them. The Thoreaus did the same. Then Jean-Paul, the race car driver I'd become friends with after my accident, and his wife Kattie appeared with champagne for Bing and a model he had made of the A4D Sky Hawk fighter/attack plane I'd flown in the Marine Corps! It had all the markings, even down to the insignia of my squadron, The Black Sheep. Diddier and wife from Durfort, who have the leather shop there, arrived with flowers and more champagne. And Madame Fontaine strode through the door with Medusa in grand fashion, followed by our beloved confidant and French teacher, Edwige.

The parade of people and the gifts they bore was startling. Madame and Monsieur Rigale from the farm arrived with their beautiful college daughter. I was amazed to see M. Rigale off his tractor for the first time. We were hugely touched by the sofa pillow Mme Rigale stitched especially for Bing.

Toward eight o'clock, Sylvie and Michel from the grocery came with more flowers and candy. Trakya and Anton returned, and then Adrian from the barge quietly smiled his way through the door and whispered for a moment alone.

For the moment the courtyard was empty, so I led Adrian there, scooping up two glasses of champagne along the way. Once outside, both of us with glasses in hand, Adrian first handed me a big jar of *foie gras*, which Bing and I both love, and followed that up with a superbly accurate scale model of the very Harley-Davidson I rode in the States. After I offered many thanks for his thoughtfulness, Adrian held up his free hand and said, "Ken, I cannot stay long. There are more problems at the hospital with my . . . my ex-wife. She has regressed. She might have to be institutionalized. I . . . oh, God."

He couldn't get any more out, and, putting his untouched glass on the garden table, he pulled me over to touch each of my cheeks with his, then strode back into the house and quickly through the gathering party. I lost sight of him even before he was out the door. I felt awful. Totally inadequate as a friend, probably as inadequate as he must feel as a lost husband and powerless father.

Before I could think any more of dear Adrian's troubled world, Laurant, wife, and daughter arrived with a gigantic bottle of champagne, along with a wrapped gift they said would be presented later. Of course I screwed up, not knowing the double jeroboam was a traditional gift to the homeowner from the *restaurateur* to be uncorked at just the right moment in the festivities, to keep things properly roughhouse and unruly. I stupidly put it by the door and promptly forgot about it. (Later, when finally informed

of my insensitivity, however, I explained to all that we still had the
front façade to do, so I was holding off pulling that cork until that
job was done too. Quick thinking. Good save.)

Antoine and Mme. Placo arrived, as did Bruno (Numéro Un),
Rouge, and Michel the mason. Blendine (Madame Bricolage) and
her beautiful daughter. Jean-Luc from Fly; Carlo, the master
painter, and Eve back from Paris made it with Neige. At about the
same time, Prince Valiant of the lumberyard strode through the
door with two blonde beauties.

More people kept crowding in. Claude and Sophie and Henri
came carrying platters of wonderful food. *Pastis* flowed, wine
flowed, Anton drank all the beer he could find, finally discovering
the unlimited supply back in the *ruelle*. Yes, the party was getting
up to speed in fine style.

One hitch we had was not knowing the phrase *servez-vous*
(serve yourself). In France, it seems, people wait for the host or
hostess to take the lead offering things, unless it's made clear to
servez-vous. The American way of everyone pitching in is foreign, no pun intended. Once we'd figured this out, things went
smoothly, if you didn't count all the champagne corks bouncing
around like cannon balls.

When there was a pause in the action, Laurant and wife Beatrice came to stand with me by the fireplace Placo and Rouge built
and Bing designed. It was a sweet moment. Clinking their glasses
to get everyone's attention, they gave a short speech about how
badly they'd originally felt for us, with the language struggle, the
house struggle, the myriad problems they'd seen us tackle, to say
nothing of my nearly killing myself on the bike . . . and how we
finally had succeeded. They went on to tell of the people walking
by over the months, wishing us *bon courage*, and how I had first
called the house Château Poubelle and Casa Poubelle. But now
they wanted it to have a new name. With that they handed me
their package as Bing came to my side. We pulled off the

wrapping and found a ceramic mosaic oval with large letters spelling out—AU BON COURAGE!

Now our house had a real name, a French name to mount by the door. I got weepy as we all hugged and everyone cheered and more corks popped. Then there was a pause. Everyone was looking at me. It was my turn to make a speech.

While Bing was beside me, holding the plaque for all to see, I said how wonderful Laurant and his crew had been. I told everybody of Bruno and how he always got the lousy jobs but did them with a smile. I asked him to come up to where we were standing. I grabbed an unopened bottle of champagne and presented it to him. Bing gave him a hug and I followed suit. Everyone cheered.

Next I sang the praises of Rouge (Eric), the foreman and another of those who were there from the beginning to the end. I made some snide remark about his "University of Princeton" pullover, and when he came forward, we presented him with an authentic Princeton University sweater, promising him that once the façade of the house was done, I'd have a sweater for him from *my* university . . . YALE! Big cheers. (The French actually know of Yale, Harvard, and Princeton, among other U.S. colleges.)

Finally I asked Antoine, M. Placo, to step forward. With him and his wife in front of everybody with me, I waxed more or less eloquently on his attributes as a worker and craftsman and artist. To each mention I made of his skills and their application, however, I'd add the phrase *de temps en temps*, meaning "from time to time." So I was saying, "Antoine when you work . . . from time to time. And when you apply your amazing skills . . . from time to time, and show your compatriots how the job is done . . . from time to time . . ." I wouldn't let it quit. Laurant got a huge kick out of the whole shtick. And when I rolled it to a flowery conclusion, everyone applauded and stamped their feet and hooted in unison, "*De temps en temps! De temps en temps!*"

But it wasn't over. Holding up my hand for quiet, I got serious.

I spoke of how Antoine could make something like the fireplace we were standing in front of, and the *placo* butting against it and against the irregular wood of the beams, and the ceiling . . . make it all blend so beautifully, the walls and floors and their wonderful fits, flush and fine (*propre*), and how he did this all with the crudest of tools. How he made the work precise, professional, beautiful.

"So," I concluded, "after a lifetime of creating beauty with *beastly tools* to work with . . ." I reached into my back pocket and pulled out the most prized tool of all. A brand new Leatherman!

I handed it to him and we hugged. When I felt the shake of his shoulders I knew he'd literally burst into tears. I patted him again, then looked over at Laurant, who had tears trickling down his cheeks too.

THEN, WITH fifty or more people jammed into the main room, up the stairway, at the doorway, and peeking in through the opened windows from rue Basque, with still more sitting on the long counter like birds on a branch, everything fell silent. Now I had to come up with *something*, something to make the evening memorable.

I caught Bing's eye. She'd slid over beside Laurant and Beatrice. Moving to the CD player on a shelf by the stairs, she slipped a disc into it and clicked the lid shut. As she turned up the volume, I held out my hand in her direction calling—"Bing . . . *DANSON!*" (Let's dance!)

"*Bien sûr!*" She called back, laughing. And *YES!* At that instant, Claude François' campy '70s voice boomed through the house! My absolute favorite. His adolescent oldies hit everybody's nostalgia nerve, spot on. Bing and I moved toward each other and people pressed back as best they could, giving us a small space in the center of the room. We fell into each other's arms and whirled and twirled like kids at the prom. *Everybody* started dancing. Inside and outside. The farmer, the painter, the mason, the plasterer, the hod carrier, the grocers, the *hotelier*, neighbors, everybody—including, as he pushed his way through the door and into the room . . . Monsieur Chevalier, the mayor!

Roars of laughter, clapping . . . and happy people dancing continued long into what seemed an endless night. Yes, it was the party we had prayed it would be. *Merci Dieu*!

THE LAST guests to leave were Laurant and Beatrice with daughter Astrid (who had been asleep most of the night upstairs), our new dearest friends. Laurant had taught me a lot. A lot about maturity, trust, and in a larger sense, love. He'd kept the even keel despite my adolescent behavior, understanding how especially difficult all this had been for Bing and me.

We thanked them again for the plaque and the new name they'd given our house. We promised we'd mount it by the door in the morning, to stand guard until we returned next year. In two days we would be driving to Brittany to spend time with Pierre and Marie-Claude before continuing on to Paris for our return flight to America.

As tired as we all were, I could see in everyone's eyes the warm glow each was feeling. It was like reaching the end of a long, painful struggle, a war, an illness, childbirth perhaps, and finding you had succeeded, won, lived, or given birth to something new, exciting, and wonderful.

There had been a lot of pain along the way. Misunderstandings. Doubts. Anger. Struggle. But successes too, including new friendships in a new country, and the beginnings of being able to use another language. It was exciting and confirming. Suddenly both Bing and I knew exactly what Madame Fontaine had been talking about when she said she now was starting *her next life*. And so too would we. And it would be here in Black Mountain . . . La Montagne Noire.

As SERGE and Beatrice and young Astrid walked hand in hand down the empty narrow street, Bing moved close beside me and wrapped my arm around her waist. We watched the three disappearing into the deepening night. Then, as they were only dim outlines ahead, we heard them call back to us, *"Bon courage!"*